Oklahoma's Carlisle Indian School Immortals

Native American Sports Heroes Series
Volume 1

Oklahoma's Carlisle Indian School Immortals

Tom Benjey

Carlisle, Pennsylvania
© 2009, 2010 by Tom Benjey
Published by Tuxedo Press
Carlisle, PA 17015
Tuxedo-Press.com

All rights reserved. No part of this publication may be reproduced, stored in a retrieval system, or transmitted, in any form or by any means, electronic, mechanical, photocopying, recording, or otherwise without the permission of Tuxedo Press.

17 16 15 14 13 12 11 10 5 4 3 2

ISBN 978-0-9774486-8-5 hardback
ISBN 978-1-936161-20-1 softcover

Cover illustration by Lone Star Dietz for Carlisle Industrial School ephemera, 1910
Frontispiece drawings by Bob Carroll, Professional Football Researchers Association
Layout by Keevin Graham, Graham Design

The Library of Congress has catalogued the hardback edition as follows:

Benjey, Tom.

  Oklahoma's Carlisle Indian school immortals / Tom Benjey.
    p. cm. -- (Native American sports heroes ; v.1)
  Includes bibliographical references and index.
  ISBN 978-0-9774486-8-5 (alk. paper)
  1. United States Indian School (Carlisle, Pa.)--Football. 2. Indian athletes--Pennsylvania--Carlisle--Biography. 3. Football players--Pennsylvania--Carlisle--Biography. I. Title.
  GV958.U33B463 2009
  796.3320922--dc22
  [B]

2009004544

To the descendants of
Carlisle Indian School students whose
lives have been enhanced by their ancestors having
overcome poverty, bigotry and ignorance

Table of Contents

Introduction 1
1 Carlisle's Football Trail of Glory 5
2 Carlisle Indians Turn Pro 27
3 All-Indian Teams 41
4 Glenn Scobey "Pop" Warner 47
5 Michael Balenti 57
6 Frank Cayou 69
7 Al Exendine 83
8 John B. Flinchum 93
9 Emil and Pete Hauser 95
10 Oscar Hunt 104
11 Victor Murat Kelley 111
12 Stacy Matlock 119
13 George May 125
14 William Newashe 127
15 Stancil Powell 137
16 Henry Roberts 143
17 Isaac Seneca 151
18 Jim Thorpe 157
19 Captains 173
Appendices 181
Selected Bibliography 183
Index 187

Introduction

The on-field accomplishments of the Carlisle Indian School football team have been written about several times and were remarkable. But what these men achieved off-field after leaving Carlisle is equally impressive. Over a quarter century before Indians were granted citizenship and the right to vote, three-quarters of a century before the 1965 Civil Rights Bill, and almost a century before affirmative action laws were introduced, Carlisle Indian School football teams competed toe-to-toe with the best in the land and more than held their own. Some today may consider the Carlisle School to be affirmative action in its purest form because enrollment was limited to students of at least one-quarter Indian blood with tuition, room, board, clothing and health care being paid by the government. Others view Carlisle quite differently. They think Richard Henry Pratt's assimilation policy of maintaining constant contact with the dominant society stripped students of their heritage and alienated them from their families and tribes. Regardless of one's opinion of Pratt, an extraordinary number of the Carlisle football players overcame obstacles placed in their way by prejudice common at that time and accomplished much in life after leaving the school. This book is the story of their triumphs and failures. Unfortunately, only those whose activities were recorded at the time in newspapers or were saved in archives can be written about. There are surely many others whose lives are worthy of inclusion but for whom documentation has not been found.

John S. Steckbeck's 1951 seminal *Fabulous Redmen: the Carlisle Indians and their famous football teams* provided a year-by-year history of the legendary Carlisle Indian Industrial School (CIIS) football program, a variety of statistics about the team, and blurbs about coaches and individual players. Much has been written about mega-star Jim Thorpe and Coach of All Ages Pop Warner. The author recently completed the biography of Lone Star Dietz. These three were not the only Carlisle football stars by any means. They're not even the only Carlisle Indians in the College Football Hall of Fame. Besides Thorpe, five other players were inducted years ago, and Lone Star Dietz is on the ballot for induction as a coach. At least twelve others received All-America mention. Warner is in the Hall in good part due to the work he did coaching the Indians and developing formations that mitigated their weaknesses and exploited their strengths.

Some – many as it turns out – Carlisle players continued their football careers after leaving the school, some as coaches, some as players and some both as players and coaches. So many of them went into coaching that they helped make the Warner system the dominant offensive scheme during the first half of the 20th century. Some were present at the birth of professional football, while others made the NFL popular when it was in its infancy.

Carlisle Indian School footballers played important roles in the development of the sport from the late 1890s through the 20th century up to WWII. Some lived public lives outside of sports and made their mark in other fields after departing from Carlisle. Unfortunately, few people alive today are aware of the Indians' contributions and their names have been largely forgotten. This book attempts to correct that situation. Those who led private lives after leaving Carlisle left behind little documentation of the accomplishments, which makes them difficult to cover. The information that can be found on them is interjected at appropriate places. Because there is no obvious thread among these individuals other than they played football at Carlisle, the book takes the form of a set of mini-biographies.

The first chapter of the book is a brief history of the Carlisle program, from beginning to end. It is intended that this chapter will provide the reader a framework from which to relate the individuals to the team and the phase of the program. The second chapter is a brief history of professional football in America, the early part of which overlaps closely with Carlisle's lifespan. This chapter is necessary because independent or professional football provided opportunities for Carlisle players after their schooling was completed. Indians also played major roles in developing the new game. Two of them, Jim Thorpe and Joe Guyon, are enshrined in the Professional Football Hall of Fame in Canton, Ohio. The third chapter briefly discusses some all-Indian teams on which Carlisle alums played after leaving the school. The fourth chapter covers Glenn S. "Pop" Warner, the coach for the glory days of the football program and a factor in these men's lives. Because Warner is referenced so frequently, it is clearer for the reader unfamiliar with him for his chapter to precede the players' chapters rather than follow them.

The remaining chapters, other than the final one, cover Carlisle players to varying levels of detail, dependent largely on the amount of information that can be found about the person. Their stories are arranged in alphabetical order with brothers sharing chapters. Little further needs to be written about Jim Thorpe or Pop Warner, but some readers may not be familiar with their histories. Therefore, a chapter is dedicated to each to provide a background for the unfamiliar. It is my hope that a previously undiscovered nugget or two about each of them finds its way into the narrative. The amount of space devoted to the others is not intended to be a measure of the significance of their contributions. The amount of information available about them today is the limiting factor. Professional football received little press in its early days, leaving behind fewer accounts of games and meetings than we'd like. Some players and coaches received little press due to their personalities, and others toiled in out-of-the-way places. The last chapter discusses the importance of team captains in the early days of football and recounts a story of courage on the part of several Carlisle captains. The author hopes that people familiar with persons included in this book will share enough tidbits previously unknown about those players to make a second edition necessary. Little is included about the girls who attended Carlisle beyond those who married players, not because their stories aren't interesting but because that would require an entire book of its own.

Col. Pratt raised the issue of how football players perform in later life at the 1902 football banquet in his talk titled, "By their fruits you shall know them." Pratt talked about how he came to discuss this topic and then talked about the methodology he used in his "study:"

> "I went to the old football pictures, called on the memories of oldest inhabitants and used my own, and succeeded in getting together the names of sixty who have played on our first teams and have gone out from the school. I have put down here and made a mark opposite each one from my memory and the memories of those who know most about it, and from the best information we have I find some very singular results.
>
> ...
>
> "Of the list of sixty who played on the first teams (I may not have them all) I have written opposite the names of forty-nine the letters 'O. K.' You know what that means.
>
> "There are only five of the sixty named that we need be ashamed of. There are four about whom I have been unable to get any information. That leaves two. We have been playing football more than twelve years and have sent out from the school at least sixty, as I have said, who played on our first teams, and only two of the sixty have passed away, and that shows that football is a healthy business."

This was the first known attempt to determine how or if football players succeeded after leaving school, but it wouldn't be the last. On at least two other occasions, in 1907 and 1910, and likely others, Superintendents Mercer and Friedman sent questionnaires to former athletes to gather data on their lives after Carlisle. Many of the quotes in this book that the athletes themselves wrote about Carlisle come from those questionnaires that can be found in former student files. It is likely that the superintendents were selective in determining to whom to send questionnaires, more selective in determining which results to keep in the files and even more selective in choosing responses to print in school publications. So, the results may well have been biased to make the school look good, but the responses that survive were freely given and accurately reflect the thinking of the person writing them.

While researching this book, the author examined a number of census forms and made some observations. Prior to and during their time at Carlisle, students were generally listed on special forms used specifically for populations likely to contain Indians. A section of the form listed the tribes of the person and the person's parents. It also included the fraction of white blood the student was thought to have. The data on these forms was often incorrect because the child did not know the correct information or because the census taker made assumptions and errors. After leaving Carlisle, those who assimilated into the larger society were often classified as white in future censuses, probably because census takers didn't bother to ask. Indians in the population may have been undercounted as a result.

Period illustrations, particularly cartoons, will be included where appropriate to show how the Carlisle team was treated, even by big city newspapers. Today many of these caricatures with oversized noses and other exaggerations would be considered racist. Others make fun of the patricians the Indians so often defeated.

Sit back and enjoy reading about the exploits of Frank Cayou, Bill Gardner, Pete Calac, Joe Guyon, Frank Mt. Pleasant, Gus Welch, the Pierce brothers, Al Exendine and all the rest. You will surely become acquainted with some interesting individuals you may have never heard of before. Surely some interesting people will be missed.

>
> Min-ni-wa-ka!
> Ka-wa-wi!
> Woop her up!
> Woop her up!
> Who are we?
> Carlisle!
> Carlisle!!
> Carlisle!!!

1

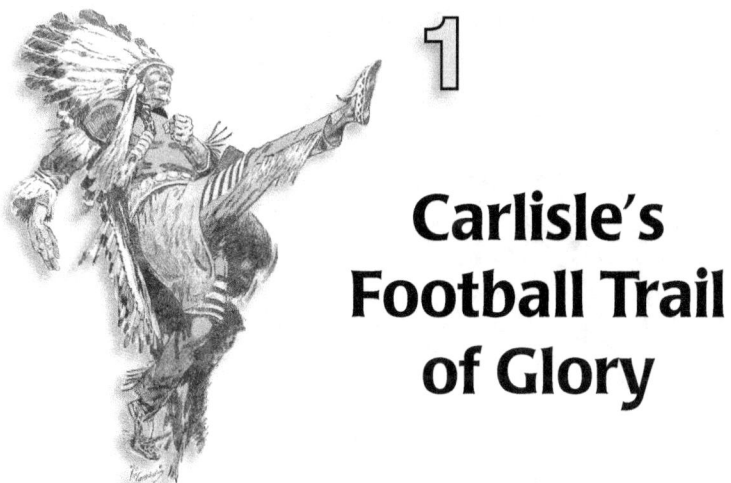

Carlisle's Football Trail of Glory

In 1875, Lt. Richard Henry Pratt, after many years of leading Buffalo Soldiers in battle against Kiowa, Cheyenne and Arapaho warriors, was assigned the task of transporting 72 Indian prisoners to St. Augustine, Florida for three years of captivity at Ft. Marion. During the imprisonment, with the influence of Quaker reformers, Pratt evolved the belief that the only hope for Indians to survive in the modern world was to assimilate into the majority culture, much as European immigrants were assimilating. His view was in sharp contrast to that of those who believed that extermination was the only viable option. Gen. Philip Sheridan denied having said, "The only good Indians I ever saw were dead." If he believed it, he was far from alone as that was a very common belief held at the time.

Their confinement over, Lt. Pratt convinced 17 of his former prisoners to pursue further education at Hampton Institute (now Hampton University). The Hampton, Virginia school had been founded a decade earlier by Gen. Samuel Chapman Armstrong as a boarding school to educate recently freed slaves by training "the head, the hand, and the heart." Educating African-Americans and American Indians in the same facility, although segregated from each other, was controversial to some in those times of racial segregation as many thought that blacks and Indians were not educable. However, the experiment was successful enough that Hampton Institute continued its Indian division until 1923.

Richard Pratt, son of a singing Methodist, summarized his philosophy as, "Kill the Indian, save the man." He formulated a model similar to that being used at Hampton and successfully lobbied the government to set up a school just for Indians at an unused Army post. On October 6, 1879, Lt. Pratt, considered by some to be "an honest lunatic," and the first contingent of students, largely sons of Lakota chiefs (boys had little economic value when confined to reservations because they could no longer hunt buffalo or make war, but families could still receive a bride price for girls), arrived at the Carlisle Indian Industrial School located in Carlisle Barracks, adjacent to Carlisle, Pennsylvania. America's second oldest military facility – the one that

Richard Henry Pratt, Susan & Mary Anna Longstreth, Spotted Tail, Rebecca Haines; *U. S. Army Military History Institute*

housed the Hessian troops captured at Trenton by Gen. George Washington after crossing the Delaware – was not being used and thus made available for the Indian boarding school.

Students divided their days between academic studies and vocational training. They dressed in military uniforms and lived regimented lives. Free-time activities included music, athletics and literary or debating societies. Although Carlisle Indian Industrial School was essentially a trade school coupled to elementary and high school academics, Pratt envisioned some of his students advancing to college and professional schools. Extracurricular activities, particularly the literary and debating societies, helped prepare higher level students for further academic work as well as to think more critically and to communicate more clearly, skills that would serve future leaders well. Although Pratt desired that his former students assimilate into the dominant culture, many returned to their tribes and used the skills learned at Carlisle to become effective tribal leaders.

By the early 1900s, the girls and boys each had two societies from which to select: the Susan Longstreth Literary Society, the Mercer Literary Society, the Standard Literary Society and the Invincible Debating Society, respectively. Susan Longstreth, a Quaker educator who operated a school in Philadelphia for young ladies for 50 years, was a long-time supporter of Pratt's experiment. Major Mercer was the superintendent of the school after Pratt departed. These societies were much more than what their names imply as some of them formed bands, played sports, held dances and put on plays. They also had their own colors and elected officers as did the Freshman,

1894 Carlisle Indians; *Cumberland County Historical Society, Carlisle, PA*

Sophomore, Junior and Senior classes. Besides the usual officers, all of these groups elected a Critic, whose function may not be obvious to modern readers. The author found a definition in the *1918 Quittapahilla*, Lebanon Valley College's yearbook: "Over each meeting presides the Critic and he, by mode of criticism, points out the strength and weakness of the respective numbers with special reference to errors in style, English grammar, elocution, logic, literary structure and the speakers' manner on the floor." While some of the details may vary between schools and organizations, the description will hold in the main.

Rather than return to their reservations during school breaks, students received practical experience in their off-campus "outing" periods to further expose them to the dominant culture. In order to "kill the Indian," Pratt kept his charges away from their families and tribes three, four or five years at a time, depending on their period of enrollment. In 1883, explaining his philosophy, he wrote, "In Indian civilization I am a Baptist, because I believe in immersing the Indians in our civilization and when we get them under holding them there until they are thoroughly soaked."

Part of Carlisle's curriculum included off-campus work and/or study with white families in the East. The government saved money by not having to house and feed the children during the outings. Students had the opportunity to earn money of their own and were forced to save a significant portion of it. As the school's superintendent, Pratt constantly battled Congress for funding and did not fare very well. He was not shy about publicly criticizing the government's stinginess and other shortcomings, particularly those in the Bureau of Indian Affairs. The outing period was essential to keep costs within budget. However, some other funding sources would emerge.

One day in 1893, Superintendent Pratt was sitting in his office attending to administrative trivia when he heard a knock. He opened the door to see forty of the school's finest athletes standing outside with something on their minds. Pratt invited them into his office and the school's best orator stepped forward. The boy presented his case so eloquently that, although so personally opposed to football that he had banned its play because serious injuries had occurred in some games played in 1890, Pratt agreed to reinstate inter-school contests. However, he had two conditions:

1. You must never slug. Because if you slug another player, the people who are watching the game will say that you are just savages.
2. In two, three or four years, the Carlisle football team will whip the biggest team in the country.

Thus, inter-collegiate football was born in Carlisle. Actually the Carlisle Indian Industrial School was never a college, but its opponents included the most famous institutions of higher learning. Soon, the school newspaper would report on "football hair" sprouting on campus each September.

In keeping with Pratt's admonition, the Carlisle team scheduled Yale and Penn, two of the "Big Four," (Harvard, Yale, Princeton and Penn) in just their second full season of play and still posted a 4-4-0 record! The next year, 1896, Carlisle played and lost to all of the "Big Four" in successive weeks, but they won the rest of their games for their first of many winning seasons. The Harvard and Yale games were close enough that the Indians could have at least tied either of them. The father of American football, Walter Camp,

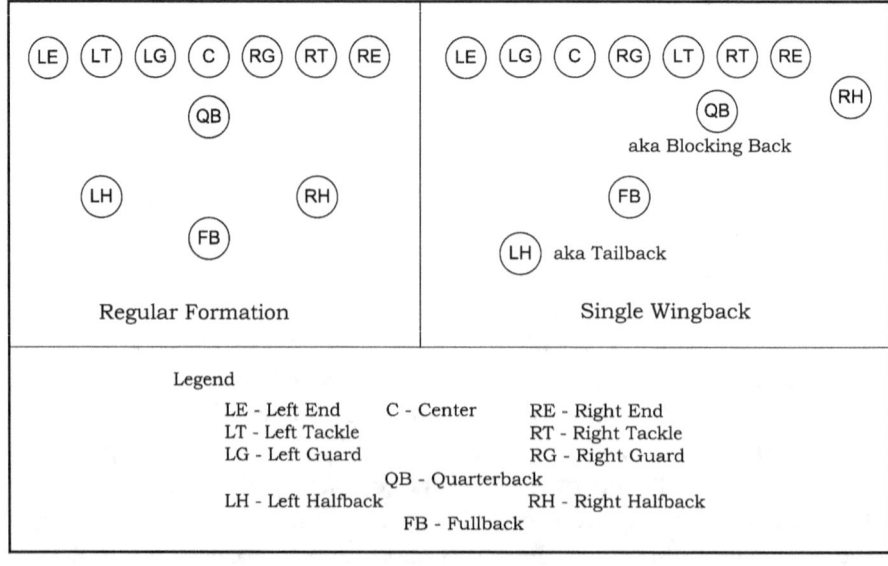

said, "The team must have put up a capital game with Harvard, and their work this season certainly shows that they are in the first class." Frank Cayou scored the first points scored against Yale that season when he raced 75 yards for a touchdown. Several writers considered the calling back of Jake Jamison's touchdown in the same game to be a major officiating blunder that cost the Indians a tie with the Eli. *The New York Sun* was favorably impressed by their play against Yale: "Never was a team seen on the football field who fought harder, fairer and with so little unnecessary rough play." *The Sun* also thought the game should have been a tie were it not for an official's blunder. The *Rochester Advertiser* echoed that sentiment in a caustic tone: "Now, if we have a right to rob the Indian anywhere we certainly have a right to cheat him out of football games." Not only did the team survive the suicidal schedule, but they also convinced the experts that they were first rate.

Newspapers alternated between romanticizing the Indians, praising them for their stoicism or clean play, and belittling them, claiming that they could not rebound from adversity while ignoring the evidence to the contrary. Headline writers and cartoonists were often not very charitable. Indians were often said to ambush their opponents or massacre unwary teams. Players were often depicted as sneaky, skulking marauders or as caricatures with large noses and buck teeth. Scalping knives and tomahawks were often shown as being at the ready.

At the end of the 1896 season, Carlisle started what became near-traditions: Thanksgiving and post-season games. The Indians defeated Brown University 24-12 on Thanksgiving Day, and a post-season game against Wisconsin in Chicago was added. The Indians defeated the Champions of the West 18-8 indoors under the lights in the Chicago Coliseum. This was the Indians' first trip out of the East. Many more would follow.

The November issue of the Carlisle Indian Industrial School's newspaper, *The Red Man*, was subtitled "Games With The Big 4," and its eight pages

Skulking Indian, *New York Journal 10-24-1897*

contained reprints of articles from newspapers around the country. Typical was the editorial from the *Boston Herald*, "The statement in our account of the football game on Saturday between the teams of the Carlisle school of Indians and Harvard, that, if the men making up the former had scientific training added to the strength, quickness and endurance which they now possess, no college team in the country could stand against them, is a conclusion endorsed by most of the college graduates and undergraduates who are experts in football and who witnessed the game." That scientific training wouldn't arrive for a few more years, but Carlisle competed while waiting.

The Indians sported a new look for 1897: uniforms in their school colors. A committee headed by former student then vocal teacher, Mary Bailey, researched the issue of school colors over the summer of 1896 and students voted to accept the committee's recommendation at the first Saturday evening meeting of the 1896-97 school year. Too late to obtain football uniforms in school colors for the season about to start, 1897 was the first year the Indian first team was clad in Red and Old Gold. Not too late for 1896 was "Carlisle Indian School March," composed by former student and then current bandmaster, Dennison Wheelock. It was played at football games and other events. Carlisle was also honored with another march that year. Celebrated pianist Robert Tempest of Philadelphia, who had recently visited the school, wrote "Roosters of Carlisle," borrowing an Indian melody that had been printed in the school paper for the refrain.

The football program was generating considerable revenue for the school by this time. *The Indian Helper* of April 17, 1896 reported on one use of the proceeds: "The 28 shower baths in the gymnasium are well patronized. These are not to take the place of the tub bath, but are in addition to the weekly scrub all hands are required to take."

Carlisle played, and lost, to three of the "Big Four" in 1897 by respectable scores, ending up at 6-4-0 again. Carlisle once again suffered four losses in 1898, coming up short against three of the "Big Four" for a 6-4-0 record. However, the team took another post-season road trip, beating Illinois, Cincinnati and The Ohio State University Medical College in seven days. In five short years, Carlisle had established itself as one of the better teams in the country just below the "Big Four." The Indians were very close to achieving what Pratt had directed them to do.

1899 was a pivotal year for Carlisle football because Pratt's first choice for head coach, Glenn S. "Pop" Warner, finally became available. Pratt, not knowledgeable about football himself, had asked Walter Camp, the country's foremost authority, to recommend a coach. Camp suggested a young, innovative coach by the name of Glenn Scobey Warner, better known as "Pop." However, Warner was not available until internal politics convinced him to leave his alma mater, Cornell. When Warner asked for $1,200 for the season plus expenses, Pratt didn't blink. After some minor negotiations, they shook hands and a new era started. The football world would be forever changed when "The Old Fox" took the coaching reins of this up-and-coming team of undersized footballers and embarked on a grueling schedule. Carlisle players gained their first victory over one of the "Big Four" when they defeated the Penn Quakers 16-5 in Philadelphia. *The Red Man* was so proud of that victory that it put "WON" in all capital letters by the score for that game. Carlisle students, led by their band, began a tradition of parading through town in their nightshirts after important victories.

They lost to two of the "Big Four" that year, Harvard and Princeton. The 22-10 loss to Harvard happened without the services of team captain and star player Martin Wheelock, who was too ill to play. The players were treated to a post-season rail trip to San Francisco (they always traveled first class) where they defeated the University of California 2-0 on Christmas Day. This road trip may have been the longest taken by a football team up to that time. The Warner era at Carlisle had begun with a 9-2-0 season, their best so far, a victory over one of the "Big Four" and capped with a win over previously unbeaten Cal. On the way back, Warner agreed to play an exhibition

1902 Carlisle football team. *Cumberland County Historical Society, Carlisle, PA*
Front row (left to right): Nikifer Schouchuk, James Johnson, Charles Williams, Frank Yarlott, Frank Beaver, Ely Parker
Second row: Arthur Sheldon, Antonio Lubo, Joel Cornelius, Albert Exendine, Walter Matthews, Johnson Bradley
Back row: Wilson Charles, Charles Dillon, James Phillips, Joseph Saunooke, Nicholas Bowen, William White, Coach Glenn Warner

game with the Phoenix Indian School team that was coached by a Harvard alum. Because Harvard had switched to leather uniforms that year, so had the Phoenix coach. The players roasted in the leather suits and were soon exhausted. The Carlisle team stayed on for a few days and shared pigskin tricks with the locals. At season's end, Isaac Seneca was named to Walter Camp's All-America team, the first Indian to receive the honor and one of the few players outside the "Big Four" to be selected.

The 6-4-1 1900 season was a bit of a letdown for the Red and Old Gold with losses to the three of the "Big Four" they played and, for the first time since 1895, there was no post-season road trip. The undersized 1901 team lost a close one to Penn 16-14 and, crippled by injuries, was beaten by Harvard 29-0. However, Carlisle did not have another losing season for over a decade.

Carlisle returned to winning ways in 1902 with an 8-3-0 season, splitting with the "Big Four" by losing to Harvard and beating Penn for the second time. The *Philadelphia Press* summed it up, "There was no doubt about the victory as the Red Man outplayed his palefaced foe at all points of the game and tied the second Red and Blue scalp firmly to his belt by the decisive score of 5-0." On defense much of the game, Carlisle scored a touchdown early in the second half, missed the extra point and played field position the rest of the way in an extremely hard-fought game with the improving Quakers.

The 1903 squad led by All-America quarterback James Johnson was probably the best Carlisle squad to date. The Indians lost to Princeton and Harvard but beat Penn again 16-6. The one-point 12-11 Harvard loss was a heartbreaker for the players, coming oh so close but still losing. It was also the game in which big Charles Dillon, a Carlisle guard, scored the touchdown using the famous "hidden ball" play. Mose Blumenthal has often been given credit for sewing a piece of elastic in the hem of Dillon's jersey to keep the ball from coming out, but Freddie Wardecker, owner of Blumenthal's former menswear store, does not believes that Mose did the actual sewing. Although Blumenthal's store, also known as "The Capital," had sewing machines, the proprietor did not know how to operate them. He probably supervised the project. Quarterback James Johnson received the kickoff and placed the ball under Dillon's jersey while the team huddled. The Carlisle backs faked having the ball and then raced downfield to retrieve the ball from under the back of Dillon's jersey to touch the ball down for the score. Pop Warner later wrote that he was glad that Harvard outscored Carlisle that day because he didn't like to win on a fluke. The *Boston Sunday Post* had this to say about the game: "With a team outweighed nearly forty pounds to the man, crippled, bruised and battered from other contests, and on a foreign field, the Indians gave an exhibition of football that has no parallel in the annals of Harvard football."

After finishing the season 11-2-1, Pop Warner returned to his alma mater, Cornell, to coach the 1904-6 seasons. Richard Henry Pratt, then a colonel, was relieved of his command because of his most recent negative comments regarding the Bureau of Indian Affairs. Major William A. Mercer, a cavalry officer, was selected to replace him as superintendent of Carlisle. Former Carlisle stars Bemus Pierce and future hall-of-famer Edward Rogers were brought back to coach the 1904 Indian team. Their only losses in this 9-2-0 season were shutouts by two of the "Big Four," Harvard and Penn.

Likely because of the turmoil surrounding Pratt's departure, Carlisle did not participate in the St. Louis World's Fair. The band did play there, however, as part of the Pennsylvania exhibit. In the fall, the school got a second chance. Promoters were unable to get the Army-Navy game relocated to the Fair to coincide with President Roosevelt's visit, but they were able to arrange a Carlisle-Haskell Institute game on the Saturday after Thanksgiving. A Thanksgiving Day game previously arranged with Ohio State became a warm-up on the trip to St. Louis. The Indians' second team beat the Buckeyes 23-0 two short days and a few hundred miles away before overwhelming Haskell 38-4. President Roosevelt didn't see the game but a large crowd of the curious did. Nine Haskell players were so impressed with the Carlisle program that they later enrolled there.

1905 saw Carlisle coached by committee. George Woodruff, the renowned former Penn coach, was advisor to the coaching team of Bemus Pierce, Siceni Nori, Frank Hudson and Ralph Kinney. The Indians again lost to Penn and Harvard in back-to-back games but did beat a team that gave them much satisfaction, the "soldiers" at West Point. In an 11-day period, with permission from the War Department, the Indians beat Army 6-5, then demolished Cincinnati 34-5 and lost games to two semi-professional teams, Canton A. C. and Massillon A. C., 8-0 and 8-4, respectively. A decade later the

Canton-Massillon rivalry would be the stuff of legends and would provide a place for Carlisle stars to continue their football careers and change football history.

The Carlisle Indians had gained a national reputation for excellence in football, and athletically-inclined boys on the reservation were becoming increasingly aware of it. Some boys aspired to attend Carlisle to play football with this heroic bunch. Other boys dreamed of playing in the Carlisle band. Still other boys, and some girls, too, wanted to attend Carlisle because of the educational opportunities. While no one would confuse the education that was provided at Carlisle Indian Industrial School with that of an Ivy League college, Carlisle provided opportunities that were not otherwise available to most boys and girls on the reservation. Students returning from Carlisle used their educations to move into leadership positions, a fact that did not go unnoticed by children on the reservation.

Before the 1906 season started, Pop Warner tutored Carlisle coaches, former stars Bemus Pierce and Frank Hudson, in the new rules instituted to keep President Roosevelt from banning the game. The neutral zone was established, the distance needed to make a first down was increased from five to ten yards, and the forward pass was legalized. The rule changes eliminated some of the disadvantages Carlisle teams had faced previously, including lack of size, and allowed them to capitalize on their strengths – speed, agility and conditioning. Warner developed a new offensive scheme to exploit Carlisle's strengths, speed and deception, and offset their weaknesses, size and depth. Warner's system, known to us as the single-wing, revolutionized football.

The two Indian coaches led their charges to a 24-6 victory over Penn but were outplayed by the Crimson in a 5-0 loss at Harvard. They unexpectedly lost to Penn State on a field goal, the only score in the game. Not reported by *The Arrow* (Carlisle's school paper changed its name in 1904) or Steckbeck was a Thanksgiving game hastily arranged with Vanderbilt while the team was on the road for games with Minnesota, Cincinnati and Virginia. The Champions of the South wanted a crack at the slayers of the Champions of the West and beat the Indians 4-0. Three victories against one defeat in 12 days isn't bad. Neither was a 9-3-0 season with a tough schedule.

On September 21, 1906, *The Arrow* reported, "Carlisle Indian football management decided to have its eleven directly coached by full-blooded redskins of intelligence. This was done largely because the Indian will work harder for an Indian coach than for the average college expert trainer. Coach Glenn S. Warner is undoubtedly the only white man who has ever been able to hold fast the attention of the redskinned footballist and teach him better things." At the end of the season, the *New York World* opined, "Bemus Pierce by skillful handling of the Indians has placed them in the front rank of the college world… Carlisle has done so well that the team is rated as one of the high class organizations of the year." The December 21 *Arrow* announced

FULL OF PERSONAL LIBERTY

that Warner would return as athletic director in charge of coaching all sports. Bemus Pierce and Frank Hudson were praised but were not available year round. It was probably not coincidental that Mrs. Warner visited Superintendent and Mrs. Mercer over Thanksgiving.

1907 was Carlisle's strongest team to that time and, in Pop Warner's opinion, one of their best teams ever. The high points of the 10-1-0 season were another victory over "Big Four" foe Penn and their first ever over Harvard. Frank Mt. Pleasant, whom Walter Camp later snubbed by naming him only to the Honorable Mention All-America team due to a perceived lack of ruggedness, led the Indians to victory with his passing and a 75-yard touchdown run in the 23-15 triumph. A parade of students in their nightshirts greeted the team upon their return to Carlisle. Hundreds of townspeople turned out with them to welcome the victors. Warner savored the 18-4 victory over Chicago and their coach, Amos Alonzo Stagg, considering it one of the high points of his career. The only loss in the otherwise perfect season was a 16-0 shutout in a downpour of rain by "Big Four" nemesis Princeton. Little Boy, one of Carlisle's best linemen, explained why the Indians usually did poorly in inclement weather, saying, "Football no good fun in mud and snow." Jim Thorpe sat frustrated on the bench his first year on the team as Mt. Pleasant punted and threw 50-yard spirals, the first person Warner saw do this.

Mt. Pleasant's snubbing by Walter Camp was not an isolated incident. Writers not infrequently found ways to disparage the Indians' successes by focusing on their infrequent losses. Detractors portrayed Carlisle's defeats as character flaws held by people of the Indian race. Reasons given included lack of discipline, disinterest in training, and being too close to their aboriginal state. These writers' theories conflicted with Warner's observations. Furthermore, they would soon have an Indian to both deify and denounce.

Jim Thorpe vaulted to the position of starting left halfback in 1908. In his first year as a starter, Carlisle lost only to Harvard and Minnesota and tied Penn. Carlisle won the other ten. The Indians either lost to or tied the national champions, depending whether one thinks Harvard or Penn best that year. Jim Thorpe had a good year showing much promise, so much that Walter Camp ranked him a third team All-American. Thorpe then left school to play minor league baseball. Pennsylvania was the only "Big Four" team scheduled for 1909. That game accounted for one of Carlisle's losses, the first one in four years to the Quakers, in this 8-3-1 Thorpe-less season.

Moses Friedman, a civilian educator, replaced Major Mercer as Carlisle superintendent in 1908, but little changed with regard to the athletic program. Penn and Princeton were the "Big Four" teams Pop Warner scheduled for 1910. For reasons unknown, Harvard Law School replaced Harvard on the 15-game schedule. Western Maryland College mercifully canceled their game; otherwise the Indians would have had to play 3 games in seven days. A combination of injuries and bad luck resulted in a disappointing season with no "Big Four" victories and an 8-6-0 season.

Jim Thorpe, no longer a skinny kid, returned for the 1911 season. Pop Warner viewed this team as his greatest at Carlisle as it began the best three-year run in Carlisle's Football Trail of Glory. Gus Welch, Alex Arcasa and Lone Star Dietz all scored touchdowns in the win over Penn while Thorpe nursed an injury on the bench. Thorpe used his heavily bandaged leg to kick a field goal in each quarter for the victory over Harvard. This 11-1-0 season was their second and last two "Big Four" win campaign. The Indians picked up where they left off in 1912 but let up in their loss to Penn, the only member of the "Big Four" on that year's schedule. The scoreless tie was to a very good Washington and Jefferson team. However, it was not the one that was rewarded with the honor of being the Eastern representative in the New Year's Day game in Pasadena, California as has been reported elsewhere. It was in the much-written-about game against West Point that Pop used the double wingback offense to thwart the Soldiers 27-6. Trouncing Brown 32-0 on Thanksgiving Day was a fitting capstone to Thorpe's career at Carlisle and the 12-1-1 season. Again in 1913, Penn was the only one of the "Big Four" on the schedule, but this time it was a 7-7 tie. The other blemish to their 10-1-1 record was a 12-6 upset by Pitt. Carlisle completed a three-year run of 33 wins, 3 losses and 2 ties against the toughest teams with only ten home games, and those were the warm-up games.

Carlisle Indian School teams were so well-known and respected that youth teams sometimes named themselves in their honor, much as kids' teams are called the Yankees or White Sox today. For example, a Syracuse, New York YMCA league named their basketball teams Syracuse, Harvard, Rutgers and Carlisle.

Some think that the vaunted Carlisle Indian School football program ended in August 1918 when the school closed, because Carlisle Barracks, its home, was used as a hospital to treat soldiers wounded in The Great War. While it is true that the Red Peril of the East would take the field no more, Carlisle's competitive football ended before that. In his seminal work on Carlisle Indian School football, *Fabulous Redmen*, John S. Steckbeck places the end of Carlisle's football trail of glory at February 25, 1915, the date of Pop Warner's farewell dinner. I mark the end a year earlier. On February 6, 7, 8 and March 25, 1914, a joint commission of Congress under the direction of Inspector E. B. Linnen conducted an investigation of the Carlisle Indian School. The changes brought about by the commission led to the demise of the Carlisle football program. Although the U.S. Army technically brought the program to an end when it took back Carlisle Barracks in 1918, the football program was already dead, though still staggering from 1914 to its official demise.

Judge Cato Sells, new Commissioner of Indian Affairs, apparently at the urging of the Indian Rights Association and a student petition, began an investigation of Superintendent Moses Friedman's management of the Carlisle Indian Industrial School in January 1914. It seems that Cumberland County Judge Sadler (it is not clear whether it was Wilbur, the father, or Sylvester, the son, because the hereditary judgeship was transferred from father to son in that year) meted out a 60-day jail sentence, possibly at Friedman's urging, to an Indian girl and boy for an infraction punishable only by a fine under Pennsylvania law. The infraction was not stated but debauchery is a definite possibility. This did not sit well with the Philadelphia-based Indian Rights Association. There were also accounts of arrests of Indian boys found drinking alcohol in the town of Carlisle. According to Indian School staff and other students, "negro bootleggers" were to blame, not tavern owners. The timing could not have been worse for Carlisle as the walrus-mustachioed Judge Sells was on a rampage to stop the scourge of alcohol on his wards while trying to clean up the corrupt government agency.

On Friday, February 6, 1914, a joint commission of Congress arrived unannounced in Carlisle to interview staff and students at Carlisle in an attempt to get to the bottom of the situation. It was not a pretty sight. Superintendent Friedman made an unauthorized trip to Washington to plead his case, blaming Gen. Richard Pratt, founder of the Carlisle Indian School, with meddling but was told to get back to his post. Local newspapers ran editorials supportive of Friedman but several students and faculty members criticized his leadership. Meanwhile Inspector J. Linnen interviewed witnesses.

Rosa B. LaFlesch, outing manager, testified that discipline: "… is better now than when I first came here, although it is lax yet." She went on to say, "They [students] have no respect for him [Supt. Friedman]." Wallace Denny, assistant disciplinarian (and Pop Warner's long-time trainer) gave four reasons or causes for student dissatisfaction:

1. Superintendent Friedman reduced the number of receptions and sociables per month to one each.
2. Students were given more difficult [academic] work.
3. Food was of a poor quality.
4. Employees did not work in harmony with Superintendent Friedman.

John Whitwell, principal teacher, reported that Mr. David H. Dickey, outing agent, found Pop Warner drunk with Gus Welch. Whitwell also claimed that students wrote "the Jew" and other such things on a blackboard in reference to Moses Friedman. He accused Friedman of carrying almost 200 students who were no longer at the school on the roll. Angel DeCora, native art teacher, presented the commission with a list of twenty-eight girls who had been "ruined" and sent home. Band director Claude M. Stauffer was accused of beating a 17-year-old female student, Julia Hardin, at the insistence of Hannah H. Ridenour, a matron.

Pop Warner was accused of mishandling athletic funds. One of the charges was that the athletic association paid Hugh Miller, sports editor for the *Carlisle Sentinel*, and E. L. Martin to publicize the Carlisle team in the cities in which they played. The fact that hundreds paid out for PR resulted in thousands in gate receipts seemed to escape the commission. Or, it appeared unseemly to the senators and congressmen for the school to pay for publicity when they had franking privileges and reporters constantly asked them for stories. Warner was found to have kept scrupulous records but was criticized for how some of the money was spent. He argued that he was getting the best value for the school when he purchased canned goods from his family's Springfield Canning Company. The coach also mentioned disbursing some of the money to the players. "At the close of the season the boys are given a $25 suit of clothes and a $25 overcoat; that is, the first team. And the first team also gets a souvenir of some kind." This explains some of the $25 and $50 chits at Wardecker's Men's Wear (formerly Blumenthal's). Warner was also criticized for recruiting star athletes from reservations, something he adamantly denied. He countered that many of his best players had never seen a football before arriving at Carlisle.

Commissioner Sells dismissed Friedman and Stauffer, bringing charges against Friedman for theft of funds. Oscar Lipps was brought in as acting superintendent. During his trial, Friedman claimed it was Chief Clerk Siceni

J. Nori who embezzled the money and destroyed the records. State charges against Friedman were then dropped and moved to federal court when it was learned that Nori needed the money to make support payments for his estranged wife and children. Friedman was acquitted, resigned, and took a job that paid $3,000 a year. A cook was suspended for taking an Indian boy into a saloon and buying him liquor. That infraction was worth a fine and imprisonment for the cook. Pop Warner was allowed to stay on as athletic director.

A result of the Congressional Investigation was a change in the curriculum and stricter requirements for admission. A number of the faculty changed and many students did not return in the fall. The investigation brought out the fact that, although Angel DeCora and Lone Star Dietz had not been teaching native arts for about two years due to curriculum changes, Superintendent Friedman had kept them on because he thought they were assets to the school. Dietz was teaching mechanical drawing but DeCora had no specific duties. The commission apparently agreed with Friedman and did not recommend their dismissal. Complaints of students loitering in the former Native Art Department led to the Leupp Art Building being reassigned to the new alumni association. Students would no longer make or decorate things to be sold by the school. Resale items were to be purchased in NY.

At the beginning of the 1914 football season, an article, probably written by Hugh Miller or E. L. Martin, titled, "Carlisle Indian Stars Are Teaching the Palefaces How to Play Football Game," was printed in newspapers around the country. Bemus Pierce, Albert Exendine, Frank Mt. Pleasant, Frank Cayou, Wiliam Gardner, Wilson Charles, William Garlow, Emil Hauser (better known as Wauseka), Pete Hauser, Charles Guyon (also known as Wayoo), Fritz Hendricks, Ed Smith, Antonio Lubo, Joseph Shoulder and Thomas St. Germaine were or had been coaching football at colleges and high schools around the country. Jimmie Johnson, Gus Welch, Lone Star Dietz and several others had or were assisting in Carlisle by 1914.

After the great 1911-1913 run, things changed drastically football-wise in 1914 and not for the better. Pop Warner described the 5-9-1 1914 season as disastrous. Some excellent players, Gus Welch and Pete Calac for example, were back but the team lacked the depth of talent it had enjoyed in former years. The season started off with the usual victories in three warm-up games, but the margins of victory were smaller than the previous year. The next four games were played against tougher opponents. All four were lost. In 1913, the Indians went 2-1-1 against the same four teams: Lehigh, Cornell, Pitt and Penn. Next they were pummeled by Syracuse, a team they had beaten the previous year, by a score of 24-3. They then played to a scoreless tie with Holy Cross, an opponent Carlisle defeated the only other time they played. The big game of the year was against the Fighting Irish of Notre Dame at White Sox Park in Chicago. Carlisle put up a good fight until Gus Welch was injured making a tackle. Notre Dame swamped Warner's charges 48-6 in the only time the teams from the two legendary programs met.

Carlisle easily handled cross-town rival Dickinson College 34-0 without Gus Welch, who stayed behind in Chicago's Mercy Hospital, but the annual Thanksgiving opponent, Brown, was a tougher match. Carlisle outplayed and outgained the Bears 3 to 1 but fumbled away a 20-14 loss. Three postseason games were arranged this year. The first was a charity game for the Children's Charitable Hospital of Marblehead, Massachusetts just two days after the Brown game. The opposition was an all-star team composed primarily of former Harvard players. The All-Stars prevailed 13-6. A week later the Indians were in Birmingham, Alabama where they beat the University of Alabama 20-3. *The Carlisle Arrow* mentioned that a third postseason game, a game against the University of Georgia, was to be played in Atlanta the following Wednesday but did not report on the game. However, contemporary newspaper accounts show that Carlisle played Auburn in Atlanta and lost 7-0. This game has not been forgotten by the Auburn faithful because it figures prominently in their folklore regarding the origins of the "War Eagle" battle cry.

Auburn supporters recalled the game this way:

"The 1914 contest with the Carlisle Indians provides another story. The toughest player on the Indians' team was a tackle named Bald Eagle. Trying to tire the big man, Auburn began to run play after play at his position. Without even huddling, the Auburn quarterback would yell 'Bald Eagle,' letting the rest of the team know that the play would be run at the imposing defensive man. Spectators, however, thought the quarterback was saying 'War Eagle' and, in unison, they began to chant the resounding cry."

The only problem is that the Carlisle roster included neither a Bald Eagle nor a War Eagle. However, it did include a Hawk Eagle – the star right guard. Given that Hawk Eagle sounds more like War Eagle than does Bald Eagle and Hawk Eagle was a very good player, the essence of the story may well be true. It's just the details that are muddled.

The National Archives' file for Charles Guyon contains a footnote to the Carlisle-Auburn game. Apparently Wahoo underwrote that game and, due to Carlisle having an off season and a short time to effectively promote it, lost $2,897.75. His lawyer requested that Oscar Lipps return half of the loss. Lipps blamed the season's results on Carlisle having an "off" year and predicted that, after all accounts were finalized, Carlisle would show a small loss for the season. So, Guyon was out the money.

Even though the congressional investigator had wrested control of the athletic funds from Warner, many things continued to operate pretty much as they had. But now it was Superintendent Lipps sending chits to Blumenthal's to pay for the players' citizen clothing.

Those were the happy days!
The Providence Journal 11-28-1915

The Auburn game was the last one Pop Warner and Lone Star Dietz coached for Carlisle. After their game with the Indians, University of Pittsburgh officials began discussions with Pop Warner to head their football program. At season's end negotiations concluded, Warner was feted at a farewell banquet attended by former Carlisle lettermen and friends. The death of Carlisle football formally honored, all that remained was for the corpse to die.

The University of Pittsburgh offered Warner, and he accepted, a salary of $4,500 which was very good money in 1915. However, one of the most ardent supporters of amateur athletics and outspoken critics of professionalism in sports, tenured Amos Alonzo Stagg, was paid $6,000 by the University of Chicago in 1905, a full decade earlier. It is no wonder that Carlisle's 1907 thumping of Chicago was one of the victories Warner savored most.

Carlisle needed a new football coach. As soon as Warner's impending departure was made public, speculation ran rampant in newspapers across the country. First, Al Exendine was to take Warner's place if he could be released from his contract with Georgetown. Next it was Frank Mt. Pleasant, who chose the University of Buffalo instead. Pop's protégé, Lone Star Dietz, was an obvious choice, but he opted to leave the Indian Service and took his first head coaching job at Washington State College, establishing the Carlisle-Washington State connection. Gus Welch was at least one writer's choice if Dietz wasn't available. Several former players, including Charles Guyon, Bemus Pierce, Frank Hudson and Frank Cayou, applied for the job. But none of the Carlisle stars was chosen or would accept the job, probably the latter in most cases. In March, newspapers reported that well-known Indian lawyer and former Texas A & M quarterback, Victor M. "Choctaw" Kelley (often spelled Kelly) had been selected for the job. Before leaving for Pullman, Dietz predicted that Kelley would not be successful as the new Carlisle head coach. Gus Welch later charged that Kelley's hiring had been a political decision. The fact that Kelley's appointment was made by the Commissioner of Indian Affairs, Cato Sells, supports Welch's contention.

Leaving his former job at the University of Texas, Coach Kelley arrived in late August to take the reins of the Carlisle football team. Gus Welch, who had had a successful year of coaching at Conway Hall, a preparatory school in Carlisle, agreed to assist Kelley with the varsity. Although stars like Welch were gone, the season started encouragingly enough with a 21-6 defeat of Albright College. But the scoreless tie the next week with Lebanon Valley College, a team that had not scored on them in their 14 meetings, threw cold water on Carlisle's dreams of mediocrity. The following week at Lehigh the competition improved, and Carlisle doomed its fate by making errors, losing 14-0. Rousing speeches by "Choc" Kelley and former Carlisle great Al Exendine may have boosted the Indians' performance against Harvard but mistakes, such as penalties, destined their defeat, even though they outgained the Crimson 275 yards to 175. Harvard prevailed 29–7.

Next up was Pop Warner's new and undefeated team, the University of Pittsburgh. Pittsburgh, considered by some to be the best team in the country, pounded Carlisle to the tune of 45-0, their worst defeat of the year. The next week neither team played well when the Carlisle-Bucknell contest ended in a scoreless tie, Carlisle's second of the year. Unable to move the ball inside the opponent's 20 or defend the forward pass, Carlisle lost to a West Virginia Wesleyan team that it had hoped to beat. A week later, looking like the Carlisle of old, the Indians scored 23 points in the first half, but the breaks went Holy Cross's way in the second half. Carlisle had to hang on for a 2-point victory. Dickinson College was ready for the Indians this year and fought hard to the end. But the Indians fought back and pulled out a 20-14 triumph on Dickinson's home field. Two Carlisle fumbles spelled defeat in their 14-10 loss to Fordham. A fumbled punt on Fordham's 15 was returned 85 yards for a touchdown, and a fumble at Fordham's 3 near the end of the game sealed the Indians' fate. Last up on the schedule was the annual Thanksgiving game in Providence, Rhode Island against Brown.

What happened off the field was, perhaps, more interesting than what happened in the 39-3 shellacking at the hands of a strong Brown team featuring Fritz Pollard. One of Lone Star Dietz's friends at Carlisle informed him that, to get even with Dietz for the statement he had made about Victor Kelley, Kelley had given a copy of Carlisle's playbook to Brown. Brown had been invited to Pasadena, California to play an East vs. West game on New Year's Day against Dietz's team after the town's little floral parade was over. An editorial in *The Providence Journal* considered the statement to be absurd, saying that Brown coach Robinson had played Carlisle so often that he knew their plays better than Kelley and needed no assistance from him. Besides that, it asserted, when Brown played Carlisle it thought it was going to be playing against the University of Washington, not Washington State. Someone in Providence had confused the schools.

The Thanksgiving game was such a resounding defeat for Carlisle that *The Providence Journal* ran a cartoon depicting the then current state of Carlisle's program as having seen better days. A week later *The Journal* ran two articles about Carlisle on the same page. In one article, Gus Welch blamed Victor Kelley for the poor season, saying, "There was a meeting three weeks before Thanksgiving at which Superintendent Lipps, Manager Meyer, Kelley, Capt. Calac and myself were present. It was decided then that Kelley was to be dismissed as head coach. Now they want to make me the goat of the whole affair. I want the public to know the facts." This chaos was a far cry from Carlisle during its glory years. The other article reported a decision made in Washington, DC that would subordinate football at Carlisle to the point at which the team would not be competitive.

Rumors circulated in newspapers across the country that intercollegiate football at Carlisle was to end. Carlisle's team was not disbanded but came close. The 1916 schedule wasn't in place until late October because football wasn't allowed on campus for a month. When the schedule finally came out, it had only five games on it and those were not with top caliber teams. Victor Kelley resigned and physical education instructor M. L. Clevett took over the coaching duties. The first game was against Conway Hall with the Indians winning 26-0. Susquehanna University, a team for whom 24-0 was the closest they could get in eight previous tries, was the next opponent. The 12-0 loss to Susquehanna was a blow to the Indians' ego because they knew they had lost to a weak team. Carlisle then traveled to Conshohocken to play their Athletic Association. Tied at 6-6, Coach Clevett withdrew his team at halftime due to the brutal treatment his team was receiving. Clevett was thrown into jail for refusing to return half the guarantee money. Eventually the money was returned and Clevett was released, but the game was never finished. Two weeks later former Carlislians Joel Wheelock and William Winneshiek helped Lebanon Valley College defeat the dejected Indians 20-6 for the Dutchmen's first victory in the long series. Carlisle closed the 1-3-1 season with a 27-17 loss to Alfred University in New York City.

Leo F. "Deed" Harris, Carlisle High School alum and former Warner scout, took the coaching reins for the 1917 season. He tried to prepare the team for a nine-game schedule similar to those Carlisle was accustomed to playing. Unfortunately Carlisle's players were young and small. Also, a quarantine to prevent the spread of an epidemic on the school's grounds forced the team to relocate to one of the school's farms for much of the season, preventing organized practice. Carlisle started the season like Carlisle of old with 59-0 and 63-0 shellackings of Albright and Franklin and Marshall, respectively. Things went downhill quickly with seven successive losses, including the worst defeat in Carlisle's proud history at the hands of Joe Guyon's current team, Georgia Tech, in Atlanta, 98-0. Their last game both of the season and ever was a 26-0 loss to Penn, bringing the in-state rivalry and Carlisle Indian School football to a close.

When the United States entered the First World War in 1917, allowing or encouraging students to enlist became a topic of discussion among school superintendents. Hervey B. Peairs of Haskell Institute in Lawrence, Kansas and John Francis of Carlisle discussed the ways they were dealing with the issue in their correspondence in April, 1917 concerning Gus Welch's application for the athletic director position at Haskell. Peairs began the discussion with a question:

> "What policy are you adopting with reference to the enlistment of boys in the army? There is quite a demand here among the boys to be allowed to enlist, but at least 50% of the parents object. Probably about 50% are very willing to have their sons enlist and do their part. I have felt that I ought not to allow any of the boys or young men to leave the school and enlist in the army without the consent of the parents, even though the boys are of the age when they can lawfully enlist without such consent."

Francis responded:

> "With reference to the enlistment of boys here that are over 21, I have permitted them to go without the consent of the parents; under that age I required them to obtain the consent of their parents. I have also tried to avoid anything like a wave of wild excitement sweeping through the school, but on the other hand I have let them understand that where, after careful consideration, they felt they wished to enlist in the Army or Navy the school was proud to have them go and would do everything possible to help them go, and those of our boys who have enlisted have gone in this spirit."

Several former Carlisle football players were quick to join up. *The Carlisle Arrow and Red Man* issues of that time contained lists of former students and, if known, where they were stationed. Those who had attended college after leaving Carlisle were often commissioned as officers. Because of their athletic prowess, some were given the opportunity to represent their units in athletic competitions. *The Carlisle Arrow and Red Man* also included a former student's recollection of being treated as an oddity:

> "An Indian officer writes: "In the army one has splendid opportunities to make acquaintances, and being the only Redskin officer in camp, people want to meet me just for curiosity's sake."

The U.S. Army prevented further embarrassment to the once-proud school by taking the facility back to be used as a hospital to treat soldiers wounded in World War I. The mantle for Indian athletics was passed to Haskell Institute in Lawrence, Kansas, where football again flourished before Depression-era government funding cuts ended the Indian football trail of glory forever. In 1920 after the war was over, Society of American Indians passed a resolution demanding that the government reopen Carlisle or that another, comparable facility be established. Carlisle Barracks was instead used for the Medical Field Service School.

In 1931, Pop Warner planned a reunion of Carlisle Indian School football players at the 1932 Summer Olympics held in Los Angeles. He wanted to have a scrimmage with former stars, but it was necessary for Jim Thorpe and other Carlisle luminaries to attend for it to be successful. Jim Thorpe, then strapped for cash, did attend the Olympics courtesy of Vice-President Charles Carter and was seated in the Presidential box. He received a standing ovation from the 105,000 present for the opening ceremonies in the Los Angeles Coliseum when his name was announced. The Federation of American Indians also proposed that a reunion of former Carlisle students be held, presumably in Carlisle. It is not known if either of those reunions materialized, but the one proposed by former player Isaac Lyon did, at the New York State Fair in Syracuse in 1941. Pop Warner attended, along with a large number of former students. Attendance at the fair jumped largely due to interest in seeing the Carlisle Indians.

In early 1937, a newspaper article datelined Philadelphia discussed the unusual accents of many former Carlisle students: "American Indians with a Pennsylvania Dutch dialect may confuse visitors to western reservations, but William 'Lone Star' Dietz, assistant coach of the Temple University football team, can explain it…. 'For years hundreds of Indian boys and girls were brought from the reservations to Carlisle, and after they had become oriented to the institutional surroundings, they were sent to farms in Dauphin, Lancaster, Lebanon and other predominantly Dutch counties. There they were reared with the farmers' children, went to their schools and learned the topsy-turvey Pennsylvania Dutch dialect. They naturally acquired the accent and never lost it.'"

Thorpe and Warner died in the 1950s and were soon followed by many others. The last of the great football players died in the 1970s. The last surviving Carlisle student died a few years ago, but memories of the school linger on.

In 1910, Superintendent Friedman mailed a questionnaire to former football players no longer at Carlisle, as Pratt and Mercer had done before him, apparently to refute the widely held belief that athletes "never amount to much after leaving school" was a myth. Who received the questionnaires is unknown as is who returned them. What is known is some players returned them, and some of these responses still exist in student files. The results found comprise no scientific study but do represent the thinking of some individuals. Charles Guyon responded, "I owe my success to the training I have received in the two schools I have attended, and to make it short – I am working for something higher – to the highest goal." Caleb Sickles frankly stated, "From my own experience I think that the pupil who has attended Carlisle should never go back to the reservation to live. If he has holdings I would advise him to sell them, put the money in the bank and seek employment or attend a school and obtain a professional or technical education." Ed Rogers answered, "What little degree of success I have attained I attribute entirely to my early training at Carlisle" and offered, "I might add although the subject is not mentioned nor no opinion is requested that to abolish non-reservation schools is a mistake and would be a serious detriment to the progress and welfare of the future young Indians."

The next chapter discusses what several of the players did immediately after or, in a few cases, while attending Carlisle. Carlisle Indians played significant roles in the development of the early professional game. This book tells their stories along with numerous others.

"REVENGE!"

Celebrating an early Carlisle victory;
Pennsylvania Engraving Company

Although Carlisle generally played college teams, the Indians sometimes lined up against independent or professional teams.

Carlisle Indians Turn Pro

Professional football took a very different developmental path than did baseball. Football in America evolved much like rugby had in England in that both games were born at the elite schools in their respective home countries and grew to become interscholastic sports. American inter-scholastic sports began when Harvard and Yale, modeling themselves after what they viewed as their British counterparts, Oxford and Cambridge, competed in rowing. It was natural that the elite schools would be among the first to compete against each other in football (soccer and rugby) in this country. In the 1880s, Yale's Walter Camp, "Father of American Football," instituted the rule changes that differentiated American football from its English cousins when he was a student playing the game. Camp continued his involvement with football long after graduation and dominated the rules committee until 1905.

In the earliest days of American football, players were amateurs associated with the colleges they attended. Soon graduates played. It wasn't long before gypsy players matriculated at a school just long enough to play in an important game. Some were never students of the institutions they represented or, in at least one case, were students at other or both institutions. Ruling elites such as Theodore Roosevelt promoted sports to young men of his class as a means of preparing them for leadership. It was not for money that these amateur athletes were to compete, but for roles in leading the country. The brutal contests of strength, speed and wit helped determine who would later be making the major decisions for the nation. Requiring that college sports be amateur events for the most part restricted participation in them to the scions of the wealthy and powerful because few others could afford the luxury of paying college tuition while making no income.

Charges of professionalism started early on when players for other schools, of course, were paid outright, with free clothing, or for jobs which required little work. Professional (paid) coaching was soundly criticized as well. William Rainey Harper, President of the fledgling University of Chicago, set a precedent in 1893 when he offered and Amos Alonzo Stagg accepted a tenured position as associate professor in charge of the Athletic Department for $2,500 per year. Stagg had a good salary and a job for life, or at least until mandatory retirement age. The often sainted Stagg was an ardent supporter of amateurism and a constant critic of professionalism in athletics.

In those days college athletics were seldom under the control of college administrators. Student and athletic organizations generally raised the money to field a team and pay the coach. Football also generated profits that the associations could use to support other athletics at the school. Walter Camp, who also espoused the merits of amateurism, accumulated $100,000 for Yale's athletic fund over a ten-year period even while using some of the money to pay athletic tutors. Camp, however, was not paid for his efforts as he had a good-paying job as an executive of the New Haven Clock Company. But then, he was merely an advisor and not the coach.

Athletes were not to be paid, and this restriction was not just for playing football. Scholarships and part-time jobs were considered to be marks of professionalism. However, student-athletes from humble backgrounds, if they were good enough athletes and businessmen, sometimes found ways to afford playing college amateur sports. Some found paying jobs with alumni or supporters of the school's teams. Ace Clark, captain of the Washington State College 1916 Rose Bowl team, took entire years off to work at manual labor to save up enough to pay his way through school. In 1900, Penn State became one of the first colleges to officially authorize athletic scholarships to cover tuition, room and board. There were no set eligibility standards. It was not uncommon for the managements of two squads about to play a game to negotiate player eligibility in the week leading up to a game. There weren't even set rules regarding professionalism. Some schools allowed their athletes to play professional or semi-pro baseball over the summer. As a practical matter, it would have been difficult policing hundreds of baseball teams across the country, especially considering that players often played under assumed names.

Carlisle Indian School, being a government facility with students who were wards of the government, had an unusual situation. Neither its academics nor its economics resembled those of a prestigious university; nor were the views of its faculty and administration. Providing ways for students to earn money was an important issue for school administrators. Pratt instituted outings as a central part of his system, in part because they gave students the opportunity to make and save some money of their own. Later, the Native Art Department provided a venue to sell the objects that students created in the classroom. Even after Warner's departure, Superintendent Oscar Lipps signed chits for athletes to redeem for clothing at Blumenthal's Men's Wear. So, even though Carlisle's athletes were at least the equal of their counterparts at elite institutions, their financial status was definitely not. Few Carlisle students had affluent parents, whereas college students of the day largely came from the upper classes. While some, such as Jim Thorpe, received modest incomes from their allotments of tribal lands, many did not. Even if they had money in an account at the reservation, getting the Indian agent to release it was a challenge.

High schools also picked up the game and played according to college rules, but those students not wealthy enough or so inclined to attend college found their playing days ending at graduation. Soon town, neighborhood or company teams gave ordinary people with athletic ability an opportunity to play football as young adults, sometimes longer. Because they were not affiliated with schools, these teams were dubbed independents. For some reason, independents sprang up in the Great Lakes region in mill towns from New York to Wisconsin. Mill workers did not attend college and often worked at least part of Saturday, making it impossible for most to attend college games, assuming they had the money or interest in doing so. Sunday was when the working class could play or watch football, and that is when they did it. Cities often had blue laws that prevented games being played on Sundays, so the city teams that existed had to play mostly road games.

Independent games were often hard-fought with neighboring towns over bragging rights for the superiority of one locale over another. Partisans bet on their teams, often in large amounts. Team managers brought in ringers to ensure their teams' success and to protect their wagers. On November 12, 1892, the Allegheny Athletic Association of Pittsburgh (AAA) paid former Yale All-American William "Pudge" Hefflefinger $500 to play guard against Pittsburgh Athletic Club (PAC) in what is acknowledged as the game involving the first professional player. It is not unlikely that other players were paid prior to this, but AAA's financial records documented the fact that Hefflefinger had been paid to play. In 1895, David Berry, manager of the Latrobe YMCA team and editor of the *Latrobe Clipper*, paid John Braillier $10 more than expenses to play quarterback for his club. Braillier used the money to purchase a pair of pants that he wore proudly at Washington and Jefferson College, where the future dentist also played football. Braillier is the first known college player to also be playing on Sundays for pay. Independent football had become semi-pro as teams began paying a star or handful of stars to augment their local boys who played for the fun of it.

Complaints of professionalism of college players were widespread, but Carlisle probably had fewer instances, or at least reports, of its players playing on Sundays than did many football powers, due to logistics if nothing else. Because Carlisle played most of its games on the road, nearly all after the early season warm-ups, players were generally at distant cities on Saturdays, returning home late Saturday night or heading off to another city for a midweek game. This made travel from Carlisle to another city for a Sunday game difficult. Also, Carlisle players were under closer watch by their coaching staff and administration than were college students. Carlisle officials had tighter control and would not have been pleased to have their stars injured in a Sunday game and unable to play the next Saturday. However, under certain circumstances it appears to have happened. Keith McClellan, author of *The Sunday Game*, discovered that Frank Mt. Pleasant played for the Altoona Indians in 1905 and recruited some of his teammates. Warner wasn't at Carlisle in 1905. It seems unlikely that Pop would have allowed his players to risk injury playing for another team - at least during the season. Gus Welch related a story much later about having played for a professional team in Pottstown, Pennsylvania and having recruited some teammates to join him. However, a decade later Carlisle and Notre Dame were reputed to have more former or current players involved in the professional game than any other schools.

Western Pennsylvania was an early hotbed of independent football. Going into the 1900 season, the Duquesne Country and Athletic Club (DC&AC) was the dominant team but was burdened with a bloated (for its day) payroll. The Homestead Library Athletic Club (HLAC), supported by Carnegie Steel money, was on the ascendancy. HLAC hired Bill Church away from Georgetown University and loaded up on stars, including former Carlisle star Bemus Pierce and several DC&AC players. Historians disagree on the details of what happened in this time period. The NFL position is that William Chase Temple became the first owner of a professional team by taking over the DC&AC in 1900. Another historian believes that Temple left DC&AC between the 1899 and 1900 seasons and joined HLAC as its

Caught along the sidelines in Philadelphia-Homestead game, *Philadelphia Inquirer* *11-24-1901*

football chairman. Greensburg and Latrobe also expected to contend in 1900. The Greenies, financed by local stockholders, brought onboard Carlisle All-American Isaac Seneca and some other stars.

The 1900 season proved to be a financial disaster for the western Pennsylvania powers. The DC&AC and Greensburg teams folded. Latrobe returned to being a town team. HLAC was the only one of these teams to return the next year at full strength. That year it played several college teams and a few independents. Hawley Pierce, Bemus's brother, was on the roster of this undefeated team. Unfortunately, rain fell on almost all of its games, dampening enthusiasm and creating box office losses. William Temple had had enough of football. He later moved to Florida where he was credited with developing the Temple orange.

In 1902 baseball's upstart American League was plucking stars from the National League, creating a bidding war for players, with perhaps the most intense competition being found in Philadelphia between the Athletics and Phillies. Phillies owner Col. John I. Rogers responded to this threat by forming a football team. Athletics owner Ben Shibe followed suit and put his baseball manager, Connie Mack, in charge of the new football team. Rogers and Shibe felt that winning the football championship of Philadelphia would help their baseball teams. And if one of them beat Pittsburgh, that team could claim the world's championship. So, they contacted Dave Berry who agreed to reassemble the old Homestead team, thus forming the National Football League. The two Philadelphia owners so distrusted each other that they made Berry president of their new league. They contacted New York and Chicago about joining the league but were unsuccessful.

David Berry recruited a number of the best players available for his team including Artie Miller, a former Carlisle star, who spent his summer working as a lumberjack in Wisconsin. Berry had recruited so many stars that he called his team the Pittsburgh Stars. The Philadelphia As roster included wacky lefthander Rube Waddell, who had just finished his first season with the club, going 24-7 after joining the club on July 1. Manager Connie Mack found it necessary to dispatch two Pinkerton agents to the West Coast to accompany the "sousepaw" to Philadelphia. He had been pitching quite well for the Los Angeles Loo Loos. Waddell was a great talent but his eccentric habits made it necessary for Mack to keep him close during the off-season. Connie did not risk injuring Waddell by playing him in a football game, but he might have been an asset to the team as he had played rugby in the off season for several years. Several excellent games were played by the new league's teams, but much money was lost in this inaugural year of the NFL. The league standings were so muddled that it was difficult to determine which, if any, had a legitimate claim to the championship. Enter Tom O'Rourke, manager of Madison Square Garden, in need of a New Year's event.

Needing to fill the Garden, O'Rouke came up with a grandiose idea about holding a World Series of Football. Unfortunately for him, the college teams weren't interested, so he turned to the independents. The four best independents that year were the three NFL clubs and the Watertown, New York Red and Blacks. The Red and Blacks had already claimed the World Championship of football in spite of having lost to the Athletics, at home no less. O'Rourke invited three of the four teams, figuring that New York fans wouldn't be interested in watching a team from Pittsburgh. Watertown refused to risk its self-proclaimed championship and the Philadelphia teams weren't coming, at least not as the Phillies or Athletics.

The clever O'Rourke put together a five-team tournament: the New York team, an amalgam of the best of the Phillies and Athletics players; the New York Knickerbockers; the Orange, New Jersey Athletic Club; the Warlow Athletic Club; and the Syracuse Athletic Club, rechristened the All-Syracuse team, with the addition of the Pierce and Warner brothers plus the Watertown backfield. O'Rourke optimized the schedule to promote the greatest interest (read box office). New York was supposed to easily dispense with All-Syracuse in the first night's contest, but O'Rourke was unaware that Syracuse had loaded up his team. Pop Warner later wrote that his brother, Bill, talked him into playing this game, the only pro game he ever played. Warner's head injury probably caused him to miss an extra point and three field goals. Syracuse won anyway. Two nights later they defeated the Knickerbockers 36-0, without the elder Warner, to win the first World Series of Football.

The NFL disbanded after the season was over. In 1903 the Franklin team in Venango County, Pennsylvania loaded up with every talented player it could find and there was no real competition to test them. O'Rourke invited Franklin to the second World Series of Football at Madison Square Garden, and the team accepted. This time Watertown agreed to come but was pummeled by Franklin in a game most notable as the one in which the officials were in full evening dress, including top hats and white gloves. Some opined that they were officiating a funeral. In a way they were because this was football's last World Series. The Franklin team was disbanded after the game and other Pennsylvania teams didn't pick up their high-priced players.

As Western Pennsylvania football declined, Ohio football ascended in places like Canton, Akron, Shelby and Massillon. However, this ascendancy moved forward, and sometimes backwards, in fits and starts. Carlisle played the vast majority of its games against college teams but did occasionally play athletic clubs. Because athletic clubs and other independent teams did not have the opportunity to practice as often as college teams, they were viewed as being a notch below them. In 1905 for some strange reason – most likely for money – Carlisle scheduled both Canton and Massillon clubs as part of a 6-games-in-19-days suicidal road trip. The Indians beat the four college teams but lost to the much heavier Canton and Massillon squads by respectable scores. Playing, and beating, Carlisle improved the stature of these rivals.

In 1906, as interest and support in the game was increasing, an event happened that set the professional game back for almost a decade. The problem started to brew when Canton lured several players away from rival Massillon for higher pay. Rumblings about crooked work during the game erupted after the Massillon newspaper, *The Independent*, accused Canton coach and captain, Blondy Wallace, of having someone on his team throw the game. Wallace sued for libel but withdrew the suit, most likely because *The Independent* had enough evidence to prove its claim. Tensions ran high because a lot of money had been bet on the game. A brawl at the Courtland Hotel Bar erupted among Canton followers that put an end to pro football in Canton and Massillon – at least for a while. Ohio football descended into what historian Milt Roberts called the "Unglamorous Years." Football continued but without the high pay and fanfare of the preceding years.

As Carlisle Indian School football improved to a high level in 1907, critics complained of professionalism at the school. Pop Warner responded with a letter he circulated to newspapers and college football programs. He claimed that 52 of the 54 players on the 1907 roster were regularly enrolled students; the other two were employees. However, some students were enrolled at places like Conway Hall, Dickinson College or Dickinson School of Law. Warner accepted that allowing students to play on the varsity more than four years and allowing employees to play might not be cricket. So, he announced that, in the future, Carlisle would only allow students to play and for a maximum of four years.

Something neither Warner nor his critics mentioned is that Carlisle stars sometimes played for college teams after having played for Carlisle. Jim Thorpe did mention being approached by a number of schools who wanted him to play for them. James Johnson, Ed Rogers, Frank Cayou, Joe Guyon, Mike Balenti and Frank Mt. Pleasant, for instance, played for Northwestern, Minnesota, Illinois, Georgia Tech, Texas A & M and Dickinson College, respectively, after finishing their studies at Carlisle. Lehigh University raised concerns about the eligibility of these players in 1908 when that school refused to play Dickinson College if Mt. Pleasant was on the squad. No other complaints have been found for Carlisle Indians playing for more than four years, when the surplus was for a college or university. There were some complaints about players shifting to Haskell Institute, though. Some of these men were named to All-America teams at the schools where they played after leaving Carlisle.

Professionalism with regard to baseball had been an ongoing problem for Carlisle for a number of years when Pop Warner eliminated it as an intercollegiate sport in 1910. The Indians, of course, excelled at its replacement, lacrosse, and produced All-Americans in that sport, but providing Carlisle students the opportunity to compete in a truly American sport was not the reason for the shift. Star athletes, many of whom were football players or track stars, would leave school to play baseball for pay. Carlisle student files contain several entries for students leaving to play baseball. Some did not come back and others' eligibility to play intercollegiate sports became an issue. At that time hundreds, if not thousands, of minor league and semi-professional baseball teams needed players. Although the pay was low, it was attractive to young men who loved to play the game and who had little money. That former Carlisle student, Albert "Chief" Bender, had been a huge success in major league baseball surely encouraged others to aim for the big leagues even if they didn't have Bender's talent.

Jack Cusack considered 1912 the Renaissance year for professional football because so many teams began to blossom that interest in the game increased dramatically in a large part of Ohio. A Canton team was organized that year as the Professionals to distance itself from the 1906 Bulldogs scandal. Cusack, then 21, took the job as team secretary-treasurer as a favor to team captain Roscoe Oberlin. He did the job for free. The alternative was to take a share of the profits – should there be any. After some internal squabbling and tactical maneuvering on the part of Cusack, he took over as manager.

After a 6-3 season, Jack Cusack felt he needed to attract more former college players to compete, and to do that he needed to pay them. He switched his players from a profit-split basis to salaries. Cusack and Oberlin backed the team financially as partners. Even with several of the college men on the 1913 roster, Canton still lost to Akron, its then arch rival. Cusack believed that, if football were to become profitable, it had to live down the 1906 scandal and regain the public's trust. A major obstacle, Cusack thought, was the constant jumping from team to team by players wanting to make a little more money. He approached the owners and managers of the other Ohio teams who agreed verbally to treat players who had signed with another team as that team's property until the other team released him. This collusion resulted in increased respectability and lower player salaries. Even with that agreement, Canton still lacked something – a strong rival in neighboring Massillon.

Canton-Massillon contests had been quite popular earlier, but Massillon dropped its team after the 1906 scandal. In 1914 the Massillon Chamber of Commerce invited Cusack to a meeting, during which they proposed to start a team by enticing away the Akron Indians' best players. When Cusack refused to play the team if it were formed that way, the backers decided against it. Canton sorely needed a rival in Massillon to be financially stable. In 1915, a group of Massillon businessmen, led by Jack Whalen and Jack Donohue, formed a team. Knowing that he would have to upgrade his team to compete, Cusack contacted every All-American he could think of and landed some of them. However, many would only play under assumed names to protect their primary employment. Coaches in particular were in jeopardy of losing their jobs because colleges and sportswriters were generally opposed to professional football. One of his best catches was the former Carlisle star, Bill Gardner, who soon figured in an historic event.

Canton, then known as the Bulldogs again, opened the 1915 season with a 75-0 shellacking of the Wheeling Athletic Club, followed by a hard-fought 7-0 victory over the always tough Nesser brothers' Columbus Panhandles. A 9-3 road loss to the Detroit Heralds, a team they had beaten the previous two years, was followed by a 41-12 win over the Cincinnati Colts, a team that was better than the score indicated. The Bulldogs then easily dispensed with the "Champions of Pennsylvania," the Altoona Indians, that included Carlisle players Alex Arcasa, Joe Bender, Joe Bergie, H. Brennan, Furrier, Fritz Henderson, Hoffman, Ted Pratt, Stilwell Saunooke, Shipp, George Vedernack, Hugh Wheelock, Joel Wheelock, Winneshiek and Woodring. (First names of some of these players are unknown.) Several of these names never appeared in accounts of Carlisle games, so it is likely they never started for the varsity or got enough playing time to mention. Also, some may have been playing under assumed names. For instance, Stilwell Saunooke had last played on the varsity in 1903, making it questionable that he could still play competitive football. Current players may have taken others' names to mask the fact that they were playing on Sundays.

Next up on the schedule were the Massillon Tigers. Cusack didn't know exactly who was on that team because so many played under assumed names. One who played under his own name was Notre Dame star end, Knute Rockne. Notre Dame quarterback Gus Dorais was Rockne's passing partner on both teams. Through painstaking research, Keith McClellan has determined who were most of the players on the Massillon roster, and the team was loaded with talent. Cusack knew he was up against a very tough team and needed to do something. Anyone who read the papers knew that Jim Thorpe was assisting Indiana University that fall. Some may have even known that he was playing on Sundays for the Pine Village Athletic Club. Cusack dispatched Bill Gardner to Bloomington to talk with his old teammate. Gardner returned with a signed contract under which Thorpe would play for Canton for $250 a game.

Jack Cusack's financial advisors thought he would put the Bulldogs into receivership by committing to the unheard of sum of $250 a game. Sure, a few players had been paid even more than this for the odd game, but never had anyone made a commitment to pay this much game after game. Cusack estimated that attendance at his team's games had averaged about 1,200 people up to that point in the season. The peak was the game at Detroit which drew 2,900. Home games against Columbus and Altoona drew 2,500 and 2,400, respectively. 6,000 attended the Canton-Massillon game at Massillon, and 8,500 turned out for the standing-room-only rematch in Canton. Cusack's gamble paid off in spades. Thorpe's hiring was a watershed event for professional football. His ability to attract large, for that time, crowds made football an economically viable business, even if paying stars handsomely. And two Carlisle stars had played prominent roles in making this happen.

Canton and Massillon split with each other and tied for the Ohio championship in 1915, but Canton was a stronger team in 1916. Cusack added three more Carlisle Indians: Pete Calac, William Garlow and Gus Welch. Jack added additional All-Americans to his roster as the schedule toughened. Thorpe returned to captain the team when the baseball season ended. At times Canton had four or five All-Americans warming the bench; the team was that strong. In 1968 Cusack stated that he felt his 1916 Canton Bulldogs could stand up against any of the pro teams of the current era. The Bulldogs went 9-0-1, giving up a single score all season and that one on a blocked punt. Canton was "Champion of the World" again. 1917 was a similar story. With Thorpe and Calac leading the way, Canton finished 9-1, splitting with Massillon. By this time, the U.S. had entered WWI and professional football was stopped until after the Armistice.

Jack Cusack took a job in the Oklahoma oil fields during the war and wasn't around when it was time to restart the team. A friend of Cusack and Thorpe, Ralph Hay, offered to take over the Bulldogs and Cusack let him. Hay basically reassembled the 1916-17 Bulldogs for 1919 and signed former Carlisle Indian and Rambling Wreck, Joe Guyon, who some thought was better than Thorpe. Given the age difference, he may well have been at that time. However, when the chips were down, Big Jim carried the Bulldogs on his back to important victories. Canton won the championship again in 1919 but struggled financially. The Black Sox baseball scandal that year cast a pall on all sports, but professional football was hurt more than the others.

Red ink, team-jumping by players, skyrocketing salaries, fickle fans and the Black Sox scandal haunted the professional teams. Something had to be done, and a regular league sounded just like the ticket. On the evening of August 20, 1920, Ralph Hay held a meeting of team owners and two players, Jim Thorpe and Stanley Cofall, in the office of his Hupmobile dealership in Canton. This meeting gave birth to the American Professional Football

Oorang Indians coming to town, *Baltimore News 12-6-1922*

Conference (APFC). Membership rules that first year were so vague that no one is certain exactly which teams were in the league and which weren't. The league did have some rules, or at least understandings. Members voted not to recruit undergraduate college students, not to lure away other teams' players with offers of higher salaries, to cooperate in making up schedules and, most importantly, to put a cap on player salaries. Unfortunately, only four teams were represented at the meeting: Canton, Akron, Dayton and Cleveland. Three other teams had written to Hay before the meeting, most likely to arrange games with Canton. Hay chose to include these teams as league members. However, exactly which teams wrote him is murky.

On September 17, a second meeting was held. In addition to the four original members, six other teams were represented: Rochester Jeffersons, Hammond Pros, Decatur Staleys, Rock Island Independents, Muncie Flyers and Racine (Chicago) Cardinals. Due to the heat, the meeting was held in the showroom and then-illegal cold beer was distributed to the owners, who sat on running boards of new Hupmobiles. New members were accepted and the league name was changed to the American Professional Football Association (APFA). Jim Thorpe was named President, more likely for name recognition than any presumed executive skills. Missing was one key component: a viable Massillon team for a rivalry with Canton. Membership fees were set at $100, but there is no record of any team actually paying it. Rules were not discussed, so they defaulted to the college rules then in force. Three more teams joined the league in 1920: the Detroit Heralds, Columbus Panhandles, and Chicago Tigers, none of whom were required to pay the $100 fee.

Teams played warm-up games in September against non-league teams and began their league schedules, such as they were, in October. A *retired* Jim Thorpe played only when it was necessary for the Bulldogs to win or tie. The league finished its first season unable to name a champion or to keep all of its teams. A league meeting was held in Akron on April 30, 1921. By a vote, the undefeated Akron Pros were awarded the "World's Professional Football Championship." Joe Carr of the Columbus Panhandles was elected President, a move that turned out to be an inspired choice.

Twenty-one teams were listed as being in the APFA in September but only 13 were listed in the final standings, largely due to having played too few league opponents. Thorpe, Guyon and Calac were in Cleveland's backfield that year and, after playing two games, the Decatur Staleys moved to Cubs Park in Chicago. At year's end, both Chicago and Buffalo, who had a slightly better record, claimed the league championship. After George Halas and Dutch Sternaman were awarded the Chicago franchise – well, not the only Chicago franchise as the Cardinals also had one – Halas was given a seat on the league's executive council. A council meeting naturally awarded the 1921 championship to the Staleys. Halas wanted to name the team the Cubs because they were playing in what folks today call Wrigley Field, but cubs are cuddly creatures, not exactly the image of a ferocious football team. So, Halas picked the grown up version of the animal for the team we know as the Bears.

The day before the January 1922 league meeting, nine University of Illinois players were banned from college athletics for having played for Taylorville, Illinois in a game against Carlinville, whose management had hired Notre Dame ringers. Headlines demanded action by the pro teams to end the practice of enticing college players to play for pay. The pros needed a scapegoat but not one who would cost the other teams the loss of a large gate. The Green Bay Packers fit that bill perfectly and agreed to withdraw from the league and be refunded their $50 franchise fee. The team owners then discussed, but did not pass, a salary cap. Two days later the fledgling football association got the most publicity it had to date when the Chicago *Herald and Examiner* headline blared across eight columns, "Stagg Says Conference Will Break Professional Football Menace." Knute Rockne announced that Notre Dame would treat harshly any of its players who had played for Carlinville. The Associated Press said Rockne had "…long been known as a staunch enemy of professional football." That is, since he had last played for Massillon. Eventually eight players were dropped by the Irish, necessitating that four sophomores, Stuhldreher, Miller, Crowley and Layden, start in the backfield the next year.

At the June meeting, owners felt they needed a grander name to reflect their grandiose ideas and renamed themselves the National Football League, even though they had no team on the Atlantic seaboard and the westernmost team was on the east bank of the Mississippi. Among the teams that were added – teams came and went so fast in those days that the league had trouble keeping up with them – were teams from Green Bay, Wisconsin and LaRue, Ohio. The Green Bay Blues, coached by former Irish backup Earl "Curley" Lambeau, were soon redubbed the Packers by the press. The LaRue team, the Oorang Indians, featuring Thorpe, Guyon and Calac, is worthy of a chapter of its own.

In the off-season, league President Joe Carr borrowed the reserve clause from baseball. Players who played for a team one year were reserved for it for the next year. This kept players from jumping from team to team for better offers. Carr also had 15% of players' salaries withheld until the end of the season. That also caused players to stay put, especially later in the season.

After winning the 1922 championship, Canton Bulldogs' owner Ralph Hay, the man most responsible for establishing the NFL, wasn't selling enough Hupmobiles to offset the Bulldogs' financial losses and sold the team to a group of local businessmen. The Bulldogs continued their championship ways under the new ownership but would continue to hemorrhage money.

After winning another championship while losing $13,000 in 1923, the new owners of the Bulldogs had had enough and sold the franchise, players and all, to Sam Deutsch, owner of the Cleveland Indians franchise. Had Deutsch decided to field both teams, the league would have had problems. Instead, he merged the two franchises into the Cleveland Bulldogs to represent both the team's location and its players. The Bulldogs won the 1924 championship, despite a 23-0 December loss to the Bears, because of a league rule sponsored by George Halas; the rule allowed only those games played between NFL teams before November 30 to count toward championship consideration. So, Halas's rule cost him a championship. The 1925 season was extended to December 20.

Chicago won the league championship in 1925 but this time it was the Cardinals, not the Bears. However, the Bears won something more important near the end of the season. On the Monday before Thanksgiving, Harold "Red" Grange signed a contract with the Bears two days after finishing his college career with the University of Illinois by gaining 192 yards against the Buckeyes of Ohio State. During his college career, Grange set records not yet equaled. The "Wheaton Iceman's" performance against the previously unbeaten Michigan Wolverines in 1924 is the stuff of legends. All he did was to return the opening kickoff 95 yards for a touchdown, then race through the Michigan defense for three more long touchdowns in the first twelve minutes of play. "The Galloping Ghost" returned briefly in the second half to run for one touchdown and throw for another.

A *Chicago News* reporter, apparently no fan of professional football, wrote, "He is a living legend now. Why sully it?" University of Michigan coach Fielding Yost said, "I'd be glad to see Grange do anything else except play professional football." Grange's college coach, Bob Zuppke, was opposed to professionalism and told him, "Football just isn't a game to be played for money." Recognizing the hypocrisy, Grange replied, "You get paid for coaching, Zup. Why should it be wrong for me to get paid for playing?"

Grange's business manager, C. C. ("Cash and Carry" to some) Pyle, arranged a 10-game-18-day exhibition tour for the Bears and their new star. The tour was to open on Thanksgiving Day as a home game against the cross-town rival Cardinals. 36,000 people, by far the largest crowd to attend a professional football game to that time, packed Wrigley Field in spite of a snowstorm that hit that day. It was still snowing on Sunday when 28,000 showed up to see Grange and the Bears host Columbus. Only 8,000 hearty souls turned out in St. Louis the following Wednesday, due to a continuing snowstorm and 12 degree temperature. The following Saturday a rainstorm didn't discourage 35,000 from attending a game in Philadelphia. The next day 65,000 paid plus an estimated 8,000 gate-crashers watched Grange and the Bears play the New York Giants at the Polo Grounds. That game turned around the Giants' season financially, turning a loser into a winner. This game was one of the most important games in the history of pro football, not because of what happened on the field but because so many fans were in the stands and because it was New York. Professional football was now important.

The next game was in Washington, DC, where President Calvin Coolidge, not a sports fan, when introduced to Grange and Halas of the Bears, said, "Glad to meet you young gentlemen. I always did like animal acts." 25,000 Bostonians watched the Bears play the Providence Steamrollers on Wednesday. The next day in Pittsburgh, Grange suffered a blood clot as a result of a torn muscle caused by being kicked in the arm. 20,000 Detroit fans requested refunds because he was unable to play and 18,000 cheered him in a token appearance in a home game against the Giants to end the tour. He was beaten up and worn out but $150,000 richer. They started a second tour of nine games on Christmas Day in Coral Gables, Florida, playing games in other Florida cities, New Orleans and up the West Coast from San Diego to Seattle, all to large crowds. Attendance and money had reached new levels in the NFL. Jim Thorpe raised semi-pro football to a professional level in 1915 and Red Grange took it a step higher in 1925.

When asked about his contributions to pro football in later life, Indian Joe Guyon responded:

> "Take like when I went to the New York Giants in '27. I must have been about thirty-five then. But I spearheaded the Giants to their first world championship. Spearheaded them, yeh. Did everything. I kicked kickoffs clear through the uprights. I could still outrun those pro ballplayers. That was my last year of pro football, because that baseball injury ruined everything, but gosh-darn, I enjoyed New York."

Thorpe, Calac and Guyon completed their professional playing careers before the end of the decade, but Carlisle's participation in the NFL was not over. Lone Star Dietz was hired to coach the Boston Braves in 1933. A controversy over the team's name change to the Redskins to honor Dietz continues long after his departure after the 1934 season. The importance of Carlisle players to the birth of professional football was not forgotten by Jack Cusack, one of the midwives. In a 1968 interview, he told Bob Curran, "Consider such giants of the game as Big Jim Thorpe, Doc Spears, Milton Ghee, Carp Julian, Bill Gardner, Pete Calac, Dr. Hube Wagner, Robert Butler, Howard (Cub) Buck, Greasy Neale, Fred Sefton, P. C. Crisp, Bill Garlowe, Costello, and Ernie Soucy; if they were not real 'professionals' – well, what were they?"

3

All-Indian Teams

After finishing at Carlisle, many of the football players wanted to continue their on-field participation. Relatively few athletes of any era are good enough at their sport to support themselves playing a boy's game. This was especially true in the years during and immediately following Carlisle's all-too-brief foray into the world of big-time college athletics. However, some of the Indians, as discussed in previous chapters, were talented enough to support themselves by working as athletes. Many who were top-notch athletes and still wanted to play couldn't make enough money at it to consistently put bread on the table for their families. So, some Carlisle alums started teams of their own to give themselves and their former teammates further opportunities to play and, if lucky, to make a few bucks. This chapter covers Carlisle Indian School football players who later played on teams that were comprised of all Indian players, or at least advertised to be so. But first a little background about those teams is needed.

The earliest All-Indian team which was formed to provide a place for former Carlisle students to play was the Detroit Carlisle Indians, or ex-Carlisles or Braves as they were often called. However, the 1915 Altoona Indians and 1916 Pitcairn Quakers could both boast of having many former Carlisle players, the exact number of which may never be known due to the practice of using assumed names, sometimes multiple names, when playing professionally. Current and former Carlisle students working for the Ford Motor Company created the Detroit team in 1916 to give themselves an opportunity to play football on their day off work. Creating an alumni team may not have been an original idea: also operating in Detroit around that time was a team of Harvard alums who, not surprisingly, called itself the Harvards. The Altoona and Pitcairn teams were sponsored by the respective Pennsylvania Railroad operations where many of the players worked during the week.

The Detroit, Altoona and Pitcairn teams played many of the professional teams that later formed the National Football League (NFL). However, not all former Carlisle players still active in professional football played for All-

1922 Oorang Indians NFL team included several former Carlisle Indians: Leon Boutwell, Joe Guyon, Stillwell Sanooke, Bill Winneshiek, Bemus Pierce, Nick Lassaw, Elmer Busch, Jim Thorpe, Thomas St. Germain & Pete Calac; *Cumberland County Historical Society, Carlisle, PA*

Indian teams. Some, such as Jim Thorpe, Pete Calac and Joe Guyon, played for the Canton Bulldogs alongside All Americans from major universities.

In 1922 an all-Indian NFL team, the Oorang Indians, was formed. Although it listed a number of excellent players on its roster, its primary purpose was to promote and sell Oorang Airedales, a breed of dog sold nationwide by owner Walter Lingo who operated out of that football capital, La Rue, Ohio, the smallest town to ever have an NFL franchise. Lingo loved his dogs more than anything. However, American Indian lore fascinated him. As the story goes, in the winter of 1921, he, Jim Thorpe and Pete Calac were possum hunting on Lingo's expansive farm when the idea struck him to sponsor a professional football team to promote his enterprise. Speculation has it that alcoholic beverages may have played a part in the decision.

It is accurate that Thorpe was an avid sportsman who loved to hunt and fish and kept hunting dogs throughout most of his adult life. It is also accurate that Lingo was a tireless promoter of his Oorang Airedales and often took famous people hunting as a way of getting publicity. It is likely true that he took Thorpe hunting. However, it is unlikely that the team was born at the end of a day's hunting near La Rue, Ohio.

On February 16, 1922, a report came out of Milwaukee that Joe Plunkett and Ambrose Clark of Chicago had acquired an NFL franchise to replace

OORANG INDIANS

No.	Name	Pos.	College	Tribe	Wgt.
30	WHITE CLOUD	L. E.	CARLISLE	TUSCARORA	175
22	LONE WOLF	L. T.	CARLISLE	CHIPPEWAY	190
7	HILL	L. G.	CARLISLE	IROQUOIS	200
3	WINNESHEIK	C	CARLISLE	TUSCARORA	185
20	BUSCH	R. G.	CARLISLE	MISSION	220
14	LONG TIME SLEEP	R. T.	CARLISLE	FLATHEAD	195
4	COLAC	R. E.	W. VIRGINIA	MISSION	195
8	BONTWELL	Q. B.	CARLISLE	CHIPPEWAY	188
10	GUYON (Capt.)	L. H.	GEORGIA TECH	CHIPPEWAY	190
6	ATTACHE	R. H	SHERMAN	MISSION	185
32	EAGLE FEATHER	F. B.	CARLISLE	MOHICAN	215
9	F. BROKER	FULLBACK	CARLISLE	CHIPPEWAY	190
11	H. BROKER	QUARTERBACK	CARLISLE	CHIPPEWAY	175
12	SANOOK	END	CARLISLE	CHEROKEE	180
26	WAR EAGLE	GUARD	FLANDEAU	CHIPPEWAY	210
5	EARTH	HALFBACK	CARLISLE	MISSION	180
2	J. THORPE	HALFBACK	CARLISLE	SAC & FOX	190

	1st	2nd	3rd	4th
CHICAGO				
OORANG INDIANS				

CHICAGO VS.
ROCK ISLAND
SUNDAY, NOV. 19TH AT 2:15 P. M.

the one in Green Bay that had recently been dropped from the league. Jim Thorpe was reported both to have signed with the team and to have recruited such luminaries as Al Nesser of the Akron Pros, Ed Conley of Valparaiso University, and several players from Notre Dame.

A week or two later, Jim Thorpe announced that he was retiring from football: "I've sung my swan song in football. I have laid aside a tidy sum and feel that it is about time I retired from active football playing. My decision is not influenced by a desire to avoid the hard knocks of the game, for I love it above all others, and am confident I could continue in the game for five years longer without appreciable letdown in my play. It is simply that I feel that I have played long enough and mean to turn my attention to hunting and fishing and less strenuous sports." That didn't sound like a man who had agreed to form a team earlier that winter. Maybe he had something up his sleeve.

On March 18, Walter Lingo and Jim Thorpe announced the formation of a new NFL franchise called Jim Thorpe's Indians of Marion, Ohio, better known as the Oorang Indians, from Thorpe's home in Yale, Oklahoma. Lingo put up the $100 franchise fee which was less than the price of one of his Airedales. Thorpe, as well as a number of other sportsmen, was a shareholder in the Oorang Kennels Company. The primary purpose of the team was to promote Oorang Airedales, not necessarily to win football championships, but a few wins would be nice. And, by the way, almost all the games would be played on the road, a situation Carlisle and Haskell players would find familiar. The team was to be composed entirely of Indians because Lingo had somehow convinced himself that a supernatural bond existed between

Airedales and Indians. So Thorpe and Lingo set about recruiting former Carlisle and Haskell stars as well as some others.

The roster included names like: White Cloud, Lone Wolf, Hill, Winneshiek, Busch, Long Time Sleep, Calac, Boutwell, Guyon, Attache, Eagle Feather, Fred and Henry Broker, Sanooke, St. Germain, Downwind, Running Deer, Strong Wind, Thunder, Big Bear, War Eagle and Earth. Some of these names should be familiar from earlier chapters, but others were coined by Walter Lingo to give the players what he thought were more Indian-sounding names. Attache and War Eagle were listed as having attended Sherman Institute and Flandreau Indian School, respectively. The rest were supposed to have attended Carlisle. It's hard to tell exactly who all of these guys were.

Jim Thorpe was paid well – $500 a week to be exact – but his duties were not confined to football. Besides practicing during the week, he and the rest of the team were involved in the daily operations of the kennel. They also had to practice their pre-game stunts. The team required three special train cars to travel to games because they took dogs with them to show off for the crowds. Some credit Walter Lingo with having invented the half-time show. And the dogs didn't perform by themselves; the players were an integral part of the entertainment. Skits included Airedales retrieving targets that Indian marksmen had shot; dogs trailing and treeing a bear; Indian dances; tomahawk, knife and lariat throwing; and Indian scouts demonstrating their war-time exploits with Airedales in WWI, including war veterans delivering first aid in no man's land. Sometimes before a game Nick Lassaw, dubbed Long Time Sleep by his teammates due to the difficulty in getting him up in the morning, wrestled a bear.

The other teams – their owners at least – liked the Oorang Indians because they filled stadiums. Their on-field performance was unfortunately not as good as their theatrics. Most likely they were too tired to play well. Chicago Bears' tackle Ed Healey thought Thorpe was a poor coach, especially with discipline. Healey also thought the players were rough. "I have a vivid recollection of how they used the 'points.' By that I mean the elbows, knees and feet in their blocking and tackling. They'd give you those bones and it hurt. They were tough S. O. B.s but good guys off the field."

However, their off-field antics are the stuff of legends. In one story, a bartender in Chicago wanted to close up shop but some Indians put him in a phone booth and turned it upside down so they could drink until morning. Of course, the Bears killed them on the field the next day. Late at night in St. Louis, several players left a bar to find the trolley they wanted to take going in the opposite direction. Not wanting to wait forever or walk back to the hotel, they picked up the trolley and turned it around to head in the direction they desired. Sometime quarterback Leon Boutwell put it into perspective: "White people had this misconception about Indians. They thought we were all wild men, even though almost all of us had been to college and were generally

more civilized than they were. Well, it was a dandy excuse to raise hell and get away with it when the mood struck us. Since we were Indians we could get away with things the whites couldn't. Don't think we didn't take advantage of it."

After two years of seeing his team play uninspired football and coping with shrinking crowds due to having already seen the dog stunts, Walter Lingo mercifully pulled the plug on the Oorang Indians' football team. But he wasn't done with using Indian athletes to promote his dogs. In 1926, the Oorang Indians baseball team, featuring Jim Thorpe, Pete Calac and several of the same players who had formerly played on the football team, barnstormed across Ohio. Although the All-Indian NFL franchise was gone, the concept of all-Indian football teams did not end with the demise of the Oorang Indians.

In the early 1920s, former Carlisle great Pete Hauser coached the Hominy Indians. Based in Hominy, Oklahoma, the Indians criss-crossed the country playing, and beating, most teams that dared to book a game against them. After two successful years, Hauser stepped down. Former Haskell great John Levi took over as player-coach and the team continued to win. The team reached its zenith on the day after Christmas in 1927 in Pawhuska, Oklahoma, the capital of the oil-rich Osage tribe. Their opponents were the new NFL champion New York Giants who featured former Carlisle and Oorang star, Joe Guyon. The Indians won 13-6 and again defeated the Giants two weeks later in San Antonio, Texas. Few Carlislians would have been young enough to have played for Hominy, so it was largely a Haskell outfit. (An early Hominy star was a John Martin who, better known as the Gashouse Gang baseball player Pepper Martin, was eventually discouraged from playing by the St. Louis Cardinal management.) The Great Depression took its toll on such luxuries as barnstorming Indian football teams, causing Hominy to fold its tent in the early 1930s.

Histories of these all-Indian teams are sketchy but Robert L. Whitman wrote a book about the Oorang Indians. One of the biggest problems facing researchers, like Whitman and the author of this book, is determining exactly who played for these teams due to the use of fake names either to disguise players' involvement or to make them sound more colorful. Those players that have been determined to have strong ties to Oklahoma are included in this book. Surely, some will be overlooked for various reasons, the inability to find information on them being the greatest. The author hopes enough information surfaces after publication of this book to make additional chapters necessary.

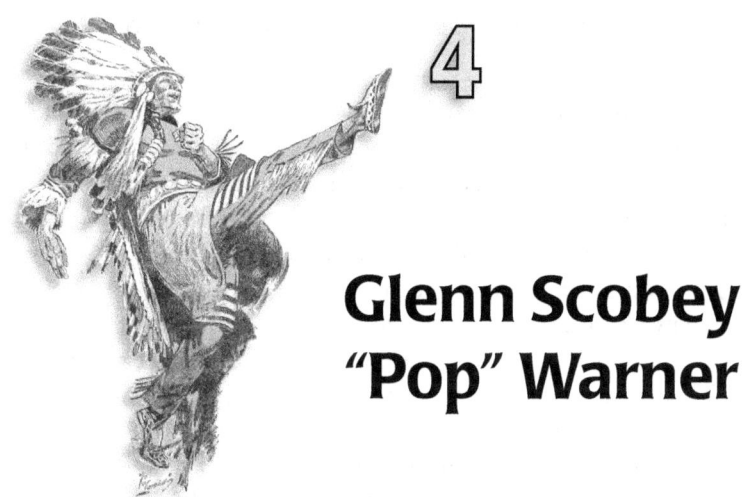

Glenn Scobey "Pop" Warner

Coach of All the Ages

Pop Warner, the Carlisle Indians' coach and athletic director in their glory years, was not an Indian and never claimed to be one. The closest Warner would ever get to being an Indian was when he was made an honorary Sac and Fox. It is necessary to know a little about Warner because he was an integral part of the team and of the players' lives in Carlisle and, in some cases, in later life. This chapter is intentionally short; readers wanting to know more about "the Old Fox" can read the biographies already written about him. The purpose of this chapter is to provide the reader unfamiliar with Warner a brief overview of his life with an emphasis on his time at Carlisle. It hopefully includes a few nuggets rescued from the dustbin of history unknown even to those knowledgeable about Warner.

Glenn Scobey Warner was born on April 5, 1871, on a farm near Springville, New York, the first-born son of William H. and Adaline Scobey Warner. The family moved into town when Glenn was 10, a relocation that made playing baseball on a daily basis more practical. He also played what passed for

---

Name: Glenn Scobey Warner   **Nickname:** Pop; The Old Fox
DOB: 4/5/1871   **Height:** 6' 0"
Weight: 205   **Age:** 28
Tribe: N/A   **Home:** Springville, NY
Parents: William H. Warner; Adaline Scobey Warner
Early Schooling: Griffith Institute
Later Schooling: Cornell University
Honors: College Football Hall of Fame, Charter Member 1951; Helm's Athletic Foundation Hall of Fame, 1951; Stanford Athletic Hall of Fame; Greater Buffalo Hall of Fame, 2001

football at the time, but baseball was his game. He was a fireball pitcher and could hit the long ball. After he completed high school, he moved with his family to Wichita Falls, Texas, to work on their wheat farm and cattle ranch. After a year of working on the ranch, he spent two more years in Texas learning the tinsmith trade and making some money. However, his 1892 vacation in his old hometown changed the direction of his life.

At 21 years of age, he returned to Springville just in time to play baseball for the town team in a series of games against the hated rival town's team. Both teams hired ringers and he established a friendship with one of his town's ringers, John McGraw, that paid off in later life. After some success betting on harness races, he convinced himself that he was an expert and followed the Grand Circuit the rest of the summer. He lost $150, all he had previously won plus everything else he had except his return trainfare, on the first day. Broke and not desiring to explain to his father what had happened to his money, Warner considered pursuing the course his father had wanted him to follow from the start. His father wired him the $100 necessary to enroll in law school at Cornell.

Money in hand, he caught the day train to Ithaca and, on the ride, made the acquaintance of football captain Carl Johanson who, upon seeing Warner's size (200 pounds), ordered him to attend football practice that afternoon. Despite having little experience, having missed the two previous weeks of practice, and having to play in a game the next day, Warner was made starting left guard. He did not relinquish that position during his playing career at Cornell. However, he was still more interested in baseball. On the first day of spring practice, Glenn tried to impress the coach even though he had been told to take it easy, and he developed a sore arm. The next day, in spite

Warner coaching; *U. S. Army Military History Institute*

of the pain, he threw at full speed again, ruining his arm forever. His baseball career over, he dabbled a bit with boxing and track but found that his best opportunities were then in football.

Shortly after arriving at Cornell, he acquired the nickname "Pop" because he was three years older than his classmates. The name stuck to him like glue the rest of his life. Pop played football and studied law for two years, then graduated. He was elected captain for the following year but, since he had completed his law degree, he had to take some graduate level courses to be on the field. His father couldn't be expected to pay, so Warner solved that problem by selling watercolor landscapes he painted.

Some consider Glenn Warner to have been Cornell's greatest guard ever. However, after starring for three years, his playing days were essentially over. He passed the bar examination and was ready to litigate at season's end. After finding a law firm in Buffalo that was willing to accept him, he went to work in January 1895. Before his slim body of clients could grow to provide him a decent income, an opportunity to supplement his income by coaching football appeared. While pondering the idea of making $25 a week in the fall, he got another offer for $35. Not wanting to let an opportunity escape, Warner negotiated with Iowa Agricultural College (today's Iowa State) to prepare its team for the season by working with it for five weeks at $25 a week. His assistant worked with the team the rest of the season while Warner coached the University of Georgia for $35 a week for the whole season. So, in Pop's first year as a head coach, he mentored two college teams, a feat that has seldom been duplicated. It should be noted that Warner lost the entire $125 salary from Iowa State in a wager on their first game. This two-team scheme worked well enough that Warner prepared the Iowa State team for five seasons running while coaching elsewhere during the season. After two successful years at Georgia, Warner's alma mater beckoned. He also had on-field success in his two years at Cornell, but internal politics made staying there unwise if not impossible.

The Carlisle Indian School football team had been described by sportswriters as a fine set of athletes sorely in need of first-class coaching. Superintendent Pratt took that to heart and looked for the best coach he could find. Walter Camp recommended Warner, thinking that this innovative young coach would be a good fit with the Indians. Warner asked for a salary of $1,200 plus expenses and Pratt didn't blink. So, when Pratt offered him the job, he jumped at it.

The 1899 Carlisle team, Warner's first at the Indian school, was loaded with fine players, several of whom may have already been first team All Americans had they played for one of the Big Four. Warner soon found that the methods he had used previously, and those under which he had played, would not work with the Indians. Pushing players hard and swearing at them was the norm for coaches at that time, but the Indians did not respond well to what they considered abuse. He recalled that a near mutiny resulted and several good players stopped coming to practice because of his tactics. Pop observed that they were not used to being sworn or cussed at and found the experience to be humiliating. Ives Goddard, a noted language expert, offers this opinion:

> "For one, Indian languages do not have the equivalent of using the name of deities in legal or religious oaths and hence do not have the use of 'God' etc. in what is called profanity in the narrow sense, taking the name of God 'in vain.' Secondly, they typically do not have slang words for sexual and other intimate functions and body parts, so there can be no equivalent of using 'four-letter words' in English. (Some speakers of some languages may avoid some words or use jokey substitutes, though.) Probably all languages have offensive ways of talking about people or cussing people out, considered serious or even 'fighting words.' In general, however, there are unfortunately few details available about the specific usages in these areas in various languages.
>
> "My guess would be that the Carlisle students who objected to swearing did so because of Christian upbringing in Protestant churches whose missionaries condemned such language in English."

Warner called a team meeting for all the players, including the ones who had stopped coming to practice. He explained that his verbal outbursts were meant to emphasize points and were not intended to demean players. He promised to tone down his language and asked them to come back to practice. "The next day, the Indians returned to practice and I went on to coach without using a lot of profanity to motivate my team. I soon found out that I would get better results from them by this method. Once this problem was settled, the Carlisle team began to concentrate on football. And the results were impressive."

The 1899 team with Warner at the helm was Carlisle's best to date. It was the first Indian team to beat one of the Big Four, Penn. The only losses were to that year's national co-champions, Harvard and Princeton. The Indians also defeated that year's West Coast power, California, on Christmas Day. For the first time ever, Walter Camp named an Indian, Isaac Seneca, to his All America first team at halfback. He also named Martin Wheelock to his second team at tackle and Frank Hudson to the third team at quarterback. Hudson was also the preeminent kicker of his day and others on the team, including Wheelock, were pretty darn good. It was reported in the press that, "Warner, the Carlisle coach, attributes the skill of the redskins in kicking to the fact that the lower part of the leg is hung straight from the knee, instead of slightly curving, as is the case of Caucasians."

Major Pratt allowed the long football trips because he thought the travel was educational for the players. That the school usually made a good bit of money couldn't have hurt. It was upon the team's return from the California trip that Major Pratt made Warner an offer to be the school's athletic director. The $2,500 salary was an offer he couldn't refuse. Because he then had a full-time position at Carlisle, Pop closed out his off-season law practice. However, he occasionally used his knowledge of the law to draft a contract for a player who was turning pro. Because the athletic director was responsible for all sports, Warner had to bone up on track, something he had never coached. Gaining a rudimentary knowledge of coaching track from books and conversations with experts, Warner inaugurated Carlisle's first ever track team in 1900. The track on which the Carlisle teams raced still circumnavigates Indian Field, the site of the Indians' football battles on Carlisle Barracks, current home of the U. S. Army War College.

Glenn made an interesting observation regarding his athletes: "And it was a noticeable fact that the Indian football players were often the brightest students at Carlisle and their teachers frequently remarked on how much quicker they were to learn than the other students."

Warner's 1900 team went 6-4-1 against a tougher schedule than was played the previous year. The 1901 team was weak over all and was one of the few losing seasons Warner experienced at the Indian school. Wanting to rest his first-string halfbacks for the upcoming game with Penn, Warner left them home when the team went to Michigan to play Fielding Yost's point-a-minute team. The backups, Louis Leroy and Edward DeMarr, decided Detroit was close to home and ran away, leaving Carlisle without running backs for the game. Their absence didn't materially affect the outcome of a game Warner had little hope of winning.

A junior player on that year's squad was a young man by the name of Charles Albert Bender. He would likely have turned into a good football player if he had persisted, but Connie Mack, manager of the Philadelphia Athletics from 1901 to 1950, beckoned. The young Chippewa left Carlisle to play in the big leagues where the future Hall-of-Fame pitcher was often called "Chief."

Things improved football-wise in 1902 when, by beating Penn again and losing only to Bucknell, Harvard, and Virginia, the Indians again had a winning record. After the season, Pop's younger brother and sometime assistant, Bill, talked him into agreeing to take what turned out to be the princely sum of $23 to play for a professional team in the World Series of professional football held at Madison Square Garden over the New Year. The Warner brothers held up one side of the line at guard and tackle. Carlisle Indians Bemus and Hawley Pierce held up the other side of the same line. In the first game, Pop received a bad cut on his head but didn't leave the game. After the injury, he missed a kick after touchdown and three field goals in a winning effort. As he told it, "The next morning – following the game – I awoke feeling very stiff and could only move my tired body with great difficulty. I even had to call upon my brother, Bill, to help me get dressed that morning because of the tremendous pain that I was suffering. After that single game, I decided to retire from my career in professional football."

The team improved considerably in 1903, having its best team yet, beating Penn again and losing only to Princeton and Harvard. The single-point loss to Harvard featured the much-written-about hidden ball or hunchback play that gave the Indians a lead. Warner later wrote, "In a way, I'm glad that Harvard was able to come back to win because I never liked to win a game on a fluke, although the hidden ball play was within the rules at that time."

Cornell alumni were upset over their football team's performance in the last four games of the 1903 season. The coach with whom they were dissatisfied was one William Warner, Pop's younger brother. After being approached by a Cornell faculty committee, the elder Warner agreed to return to coach his alma mater in 1904. Knowing that Superintendent Pratt would likely be forced out of his position at Carlisle, due to public statements he had made which would make conditions at Carlisle uncertain, surely made Pop's decision to leave easier. His results in 1904 and 1905 at Cornell were slightly better than his brother's had been, from a won-lost perspective. 1906 was much better but he was involved in a campus controversy.

In early 1907 after an 8-1-2 season, Warner resigned to make peace at the school. He had found it necessary to drop a star player from the squad. "But my disciplining of this player nearly caused a campus riot. The player was a hero among the school's student body, and naturally my action created an uproar with them and caused a lot of trouble and unrest.... I had felt in my heart and mind that I was right in regards to my handling of the matter, because I had done what any coach would have done if he has any *backbone* to him."

Pop Warner apparently didn't sever all his ties to Carlisle when he departed for Cornell. In 1906 Carlisle's new superintendent, Major Mercer, invited Warner to help prepare the Indians for the upcoming season. Radically new rules had been adopted after the outcry over the large number of deaths of football players experienced in 1905. The new rules shifted the advantage from bulk to speed and deception as well as legalization of the forward pass. Warner spent a week coaching Carlisle's coaches with his new innovations. One of the things Warner imparted to Bemus Pierce and Frank Hudson, former players then coaching the Indians, was the earliest incarnation of his new formation. He later wrote to football historian Col. Alexander M. Weyand, "As to the single wing formation I started using this in 1906. That was the year the rules were radically changed making it necessary to have seven men on the line of scrimmage and making it illegal to help the ball carrier by pushing or pulling. Walter Camp in his writings often referred to it as the <u>Carlisle</u> formation. I do not remember what team it was first used against. I also originated the double wing formation but I believe I used it before the Dartmouth game of 1912 [Carlisle only played Dartmouth one time. That game was played in 1913]. Although it sure worked havoc on Dartmouth I think I used it two or three years before 1912."

Perhaps it was seeing Frank Mt. Pleasant throw 40-yard spiral passes or it was seeing how well the Indians ran his offense under the Indian coaches, but Warner agreed to come back to Carlisle for the 1907 season. He later recalled:

> "Carlisle played good football from the first, but it was in 1907 that the Indians rounded into true championship form., downing Pennsylvania by a score of 26 to 5, Minnesota by 12 to 0, Harvard by 23 to 15 and Chicago by 18 to 4. With the exception of the unbeaten Pitt team of 1916, it was about as perfect a football machine as I ever sent on the field. Typically Indian, too, for among the first-string men were Little Old Man, Afraid of a Bear, Lubo the Wolf, Little Boy, Wauseka, [Frank] Mount Pleasant and [Mike] Balenti. The boys clicked into shape early in the season, and the very first game convinced me that a big year was ahead.
>
> ...
>
> "The Carlisle eleven of 1907 was nearly perfect. Jim Thorpe, by the way, made his first appearance that year, subbing now and then for [Fritz] Hendricks. The forward pass had just been permitted by the new rules and we were about the first to see its value and develop its possibilities to the limit. How the Indians did take to it! Light on their feet as professional dancers, and every one amazingly skillful with his hands, the redskins pirouetted in and out until the receiver was well down the field, and then they shot the ball like a bullet. Poor Pennsylvania, among the first to experience Carlisle's aerial attack, finally reached a point where the players ran in circles, emitting wild yawps. The one defeat of the 1907 season was handed to us by Princeton.
>
> ...
>
> "Few things have ever given me greater satisfaction than that Chicago victory. Stagg's team up to then, was laying claim to the championship and sports writers refused to concede that poor Lo had a chance. The game, in fact, was to be a field day for the great [Chicago quarterback Wally] Steffen, famous for his twisting, dodging runs and educated toe

Emil Hauser, James Johnson, Al Exendine, Pop Warner;
Cumberland County Historical Society, Carlisle, PA

... Steffen did kick one field goal but that was his only pretense to glory. [William] Gardner and [Albert] Exendine were on him every time he tried to run back a kick.... I remember that Carlisle's share of the gate was $17,000, an almost incredible sum in those days.

...

"Our ends that year were Gardner, a Sioux [sic], and Exendine, an Arapahoe [sic], and I still maintain that they have never been surpassed for sheer brilliance. Pete Hauser, who did the kicking for us, was a big Cheyenne with a powerful toe, his punts averaging 60 yards, and under instructions he always raised them sky high. Gardner and Exendine were off at the swing of his leg, and it was rarely that they failed to keep up with the ball. In the game with Chicago they made life miserable for Wally Steffen, invariably nailing him in his tracks, although [Chicago coach Amos Alonzo] Stagg finally assigned three men to block each end."

1907 was not the end of a team's great runs; it was just the continuation of what Warner started in 1899 and continued for some years. Warner observed that some of the tougher teams became reluctant to schedule Carlisle now that they were often beating Penn and had defeated Harvard. Never again would they be able to schedule three or four games against the Big Four; even scheduling two Big Four opponents became less common.

The undersized Indians and Warner's offenses that capitalized on speed and deception were a perfect match. The combination was so effective that other coaches copied it. Warner started marketing a correspondence course on the rudiments of football in 1908. Soon the Warner system dominated American football.

Carlisle peaked with three straight one-loss seasons in 1911, 1912 and 1913. Warner considered the 1911 team as the best, having defeated both Penn and Harvard. It should be noted that Jim Thorpe had departed before the 1913 season, so Carlisle wasn't a one-player team as some have suggested. The outcome of the government investigation into improprieties at the Indian

Reno Gazette 12-9-1915

school in early 1914 made it impossible to field a competitive team, so Warner left.

Much has been written about Warner's role in the stripping of Jim Thorpe's medals, so that needs no repeating. However, what may be new information is that student records from the Carlisle Indian School contain numerous mentions of students leaving to play summer baseball. Even the school newspaper mentioned individuals and their teams. No mention was made of pay, but it was common knowledge which teams were professionals. It is highly unlikely that Superintendent Friedman and Coach Warner were unaware of this. They probably knew Thorpe left to play minor league baseball but didn't expect to see him return and, if they did, they certainly did not expect him to become the physical specimen who did return.

The most famous football referee of the period, Mike Thompson, officiated many Carlisle games and said this about Warner:

> "I first saw the Indians in 1902, when I refereed their game against Cornell. Bill Warner, Pop's brother, was captain of the Cornell team that year, as Pop had been in 1894... Pop knew his Indians. He walked and acted like one, and came to be a man of few words, mostly grunt, until his boys really believed that he had Indian blood. He knew an Indian's strength and limitations, capitalized on the former and avoided the latter. Warner showed each man his job individually, demonstrating it, not talking it. Perhaps he gave his quarter a little theory, but for the most part he depended upon their native cunning, skill and love of the game to do the rest. The Indians loved trick plays. Pop gave them plenty and knew just when to pull his tricks. I doubt that any other coach could have approximated his success at Carlisle..."

Warner himself learned that coaching the Indians required a different approach than coaching white players. "While at Carlisle, I had developed a theory that the Indian boys had been trained by their forefathers to be keen observers. Often when the Indian boys were exposed to a new sport or game they would usually refuse to participate. Instead, they would stand and watch the older, more experienced Indian boys, who were participating in the new sport or game, demonstrate how it was to be played. Then after having studied the play or actions, or motions of their elders, they would attempt to mimic those same actions, or motions, and would usually be almost as accomplished as those who they had just observed."

Warner shared some other insights into his Carlisle players in a 1933 interview. "Carlisle was a school where the Indian would come as a mere boy and stay there a number of years obtaining his education. I had a chance to develop him from the ground up and to use his ability during his best athletic years.... Some of my boys came to Carlisle entirely uneducated and it took them years to get through, meaning I had them on my teams when they were more mature." When asked what the optimum age for a football player was,

Warner responded, "It is hard to lay down a general rule because one man may be at his best at 27 and another at 20. On the whole, however, I would say that 23 is a fine age for a football player. He is old enough to know some of the tricks of the trade and young enough to have plenty of speed and fire."

After leaving Carlisle, Warner went on to coach at Pitt, Stanford and Temple, to win national championships and to win the Rose Bowl but he always loved the Indians:

> "Great teams, those Carlisle elevens that I coached, and what was even finer, sportsmen all. There wasn't an Indian of the lot who didn't love to win and hate to lose, but to a man they were modest in victory and resolute in defeat. They never gloated, they never whined, and no matter how bitter the contest, they played cheerfully, squarely and cleanly.
>
> "Whenever I see one of those all-America teams, I cannot help but think what an eleven could have been selected from those *real* Americans who blazed such a trail of glory across the football fields of the country from 1899 to 1914. One might go a long way before he found a better line-up than this:
>
> | | |
> |---|---|
> | Exendine | right end |
> | Wauseka | right tackle |
> | Bemus Pierce | right guard |
> | Lone Wolf Hunt | center |
> | Martin Wheelock | left guard |
> | Hawley Pierce | left tackle |
> | Ed Rogers | left end |
> | James Johnson | quarterback |
> | James Thorpe | right halfback |
> | Joe Guyon | left halfback |
> | Pete Hauser | fullback |
>
> "And for substitutes, if substitutes were ever needed for these iron men, how about such players as Bill Gardner, Lone Star Dietz, [Antonio] Lubo, Afraid of a Bear, Little Boy, [Isaac] Seneca, [Jonas] Metoxen, [Pete] Calac, [Frank] Hudson, [Frank] Mount Pleasant and Gus Welch?"

As great a coach as Warner was, he was no better at predicting the future than anyone else. In an article for Baseball Magazine, Pop looked into his crystal ball and saw a limited future for football:

> *Football will never be a great national game, for a variety of reasons. The season is shorter, not so many games are possible as in baseball, for instance; and the game is not so open or spectacular. But, in my opinion, one of the main reasons why it will never be a popular sport, is the fact that it depends too much on careful coaching.*
>
> Glenn Warner

Michael Balenti

Pikey

Cheyenne Belle, as she was commonly known, was the daughter of Charlie Rath, founder of Dodge City, and Roadmaker, full-blood Cheyenne. Actually, Rath married Making-Out-Road after the death of his second wife. He quickly shortened her name to Roadmaker. Their only child was born around 1861 near Bent's Fort in present-day Colorado. He named his daughter Cheyenne Belle because her mother had been considered the Belle of the Cheyenne, as she was vivacious as well as beautiful. A little explanation is in order lest the gentle reader be misled. Roadmaker was no debutante. She had four children from her three previous marriages: the first was to Kit Carson whom she threw out after a year of violent quarrels; the second was to Flat Head; and the third was to Wolf Man. She divorced both Cheyenne husbands, according to the tribe's custom, by moving back into her parents' tipi. Charles Rath believed that there were two ways to get along with the Indians: sell them liquor or marry into the tribe. He chose the latter despite Roadmaker's disposition. Neatha Seger, daughter of John H. Seger, said, "Her name meant 'laid down the law' as many a man learned over the years." However, Seger didn't think she was more beautiful than other Cheyenne women. So, Rath laid rich gifts at the door of her lodge and they were duly accepted by a male

---

Name: Michael Richard Balenti **Nickname:** Pikey
DOB: 7/3/1886 **Height:** 5'11"
Weight: 175 **Age:** 24
Tribe: Cheyenne **Home:** Calumet, OK
Parents: Michael Balenti & Cheyenne Belle
Early Schooling: Seger Indian Industrial School, Colony, OK
Later Schooling: Texas A&M
Honors:

Mike Balenti;
Cecilia Balenti-Moddelmog

relative. He made a wise choice for a licensed Indian trader because she knew all the important people. Those who knew her said, "Nobody pushed Roadmaker around." Rath pursued his business interests; Cheyenne Belle seldom saw her father after she was about two years old when he left her with her mother in the Cheyenne camp.

Cheyenne Belle survived the Battle of Washita of 1868 in which George Armstrong Custer's 7th Cavalry attacked Black Kettle's band who were wintering along the Washita River. The Cheyenne women, children and old people hid in a pit at Sand Hill for protection. The soldiers found them there and opened up with a Gatling gun. Fortunately, the sand piles protected Cheyenne Belle from the bullets and she was able to escape during a thunderstorm that night by swimming across an unguarded pond.

At age 13, Cheyenne Belle enrolled in the Indian boarding school operated by Col. and Mrs. John H. Seger in Colony, Oklahoma. She lived in the Segers' home and cared for their children to free up Mrs. Seger to perform other duties around the school. When Belle arrived, she knew no English but learned quickly. A year later, she was assigned the duty of teaching a "camp class" of newly-arrived students who knew no English. Seger observed that she could teach these children English more effectively than could the white teachers. The following year she was given 50 children to teach and had them reading from the first reader and singing gospel hymns inside of four months. She was also learning practical things at the Segers' school. Belle learned how to bake bread and operate a sewing machine, at which she became quite proficient. For some months she was in charge of the children's dining room. After four years at the school, at age 17, she made one of her periodic visits to the Cheyenne camp to see her mother but did not intend to leave the school.

Belle arrived home just as Michael Balenti, a soldier originally from Austria then stationed at Fort Reno, was negotiating to buy her older half-sister, Shaking Herself (aka Mandy Whitewolf). As soon as he saw Belle, Balenti shook his head and told Roadmaker, "This is the one I want." After arriving at the price, the two were married. Roadmaker probably made out better on the deal because Belle was 12 years younger and pretty. Although Belle was not well prepared for keeping a house, she learned quickly. After their first child, Willie, was old enough to travel, her husband suggested that they visit her father and show him his first grandchild. This happened around 1880. Charles Rath put them up in a hotel near where he lived at that time in Mobeetie, a wild town in the Texas panhandle. Apparently their first meeting since she was a small child was pleasant.

As soon as Balenti's enlistment was up, he left his position as orderly to Col. Lewis and took a job as a tailor at the Indian school. Belle assisted him and quickly became a skilled tailor and dressmaker. She also became skillful at making Cheyenne fancy work (quillwork and beading), some of which was later acquired by the Oklahoma Historical Society and displayed in their museum. Children came quickly: four sons, William, George, Michael and John, came first; they were followed by a sister, Hattie, and brother Jesse was the last. The Balentis took Belle's allotment on North Fork bottom (North Canadian River), built a neat frame cottage, and lived there well past the time their children were raised. Belle was a believer in the power of education. She sent Willie to a boarding school in Halstead, Kansas that was under the charge of Rev. Criss Crabel. George, Mike and John went to Carlisle Indian Industrial School. Hattie attended public school in Calumet, Oklahoma and in the district school near her home. Belle used the proceeds from the sale of cattle to buy a piano for Hattie to play. In 1913, the *Colony Courier* editorialized, "We favor Cheyenne Belle for the Indian lady candidate for a free trip to the Panama Exposition. We do not believe another Indian woman in Oklahoma having the opportunities has accomplished so much." This was evidence of how highly esteemed she was in both white and Indian communities.

Michael Richard Balenti must have applied himself at the Seger Indian School at Colony, Oklahoma before coming to Carlisle because he was advanced enough when he arrived to allow him to graduate when he finished his enrollment. Exactly where he began his education is not known, but an agency school or the local public schools are possibilities. At Carlisle, he was a star pupil in the classroom and worked as a baker. Perhaps his mother influenced this choice of occupations. His name first appeared, briefly, in print in

The Arrow in the spring of 1905 as being on the baseball team and participating in the Standard Literary Society. As the summer wore on, he got more playing time, mostly in right field. In the fall, Mike made the varsity football team and got some playing time in the opening game, a 71-0 drubbing of the Pennsylvania Railroad YMCA team from Columbia, Pennsylvania. Mike was the victim of unfortunate timing: he had to compete with Frank Mt. Pleasant and Archie Libby, both excellent players, for the job of starting quarterback. Mike had to settle for a mop-up role and some time as left halfback. As the opposing teams became tougher, his playing time diminished to an amount too little for him to letter that year. Mike led Carlisle's Third Team to victory over Shamokin, and Frank Mt. Pleasant was selected as the quarterback of the *New York Evening Sun*'s All-Eastern Eleven. That still wasn't bad for his first year on the varsity. He was also active in the Standard Literary Society and was elected Editor. He was also a frequent debater.

Beginning shortly after commencement in March 1906, Mike's brother, George Balenti, Carlisle '04, returned to the school for a time and taught a course in mechanical drawing, a subject he had been studying at Drexel Institute in Philadelphia. Mike surely studied with him. Mike competed in the Seventh Annual Contest, placing second in the 100-yard dash behind Archie Libby. Baseball season started about that time, which was none too soon for Mike. It was on the diamond that he shone most brightly, athletically speaking. He started the season playing shortstop and batting clean-up. He later shifted to right field and moved around in the top three positions in the batting order. Some Carlisle students headed off to play minor league baseball for the summer, but not Mike. In July, he attended the Northfield Conference as a member of Carlisle's YMCA contingent and found the experience to be a positive one for him, spiritually. In the fall, he was also promoted to 1st Lieutenant and Adjutant of one of the cadet squadrons and was on hand for the first day of football practice.

Probably to adapt the Indians' strengths to the revolutionary rule changes that went into effect for the 1906 season, Frank Mt. Pleasant was shifted from quarterback to left halfback. Archie Libby moved up to the first string at quarterback while Mike and Louis Island vied for playing time behind him. He got significant playing time as quarterback of the Second Team in the games they played against local teams. Mike started the late-season game against Cincinnati as several of the regular starting team sat out this relatively easy opponent.

Balenti started the 1907 baseball season playing 3rd base and batting 3rd for the Indians. He finished the season playing for Hagerstown. The Hagerstown *Herald* had much to say about him in its writeup of the game in mid-August between Hagerstown and Carlisle:

> "Balenti hit everything that came over the plate and ran the bases like a deer."

> "One of the prettiest plays of the game came in the seventh, when Balenti scooped up Heagy's grounder and fired it to Newashe in time to retire the runner."
>
> "The DuBois team, with which Balenti played before its disorganization a few weeks ago, won the pennant and Mike closed their season with a home run to his credit."

Mike's play and deportment were both praised in a letter from J. Frank Ridenour of the Hagerstown Baseball Club. That letter is included in William Newashe's chapter.

Mike's brother John arrived at Carlisle in September with Emil and Pete Hauser who were also Cheyenne from Oklahoma and who both played on the football team. John ran away within two weeks of arriving and returned. It's not clear from the records if he left Carlisle for good in November of 1908 or in March 1909. The 1907 Carlisle team would be the school's best to that time and one of its best ever as it was loaded with star players. Mike spelled Mt. Pleasant for a while in the Villanova game and found himself competing again with Louis Island for the position of backup quarterback. Both of them played against Bucknell and got weak reviews from *The Sentinel*:

> "Mt. Pleasant was not in the game and Island filled his position most of the time, until replaced by Balenti. The former ran the team fairly well, but was poor on running back punts and was responsible for some heavy losses. Balenti also was weak in handling the ball. Both seemed to be anxious to get in the lime-light by kicking drop kicks, and Island did succeed in scoring in this manner."

Frank Mt. Pleasant broke his thumb in the game against Minnesota and was too banged up otherwise to play the final game against the Champion Chicago Maroons. William Yankee Joe told what happened in *The Arrow*:

> "Every student thought it was up to Island who had been backing up Mt. Pleasant during the season. But when we learned the line-up and with Balenti in at quarter back some of the students were a little shaky.
>
> "We all know that Balenti was unable to score against the Bucknell team here this fall, but we must consider the plays, for he was only allowed to use three different plays. On Saturday's game was when his real test came against the Champions of the West. Balenti filled the position well and could not be criticized by anyone.
>
> "As we heard the news coming back from the Chicago field, our quarter back was running back the punts for 20 and 35 yards before being thrown to the ground by the Chicagoans. He seemed to know how to hammer the westerners' line. The students who were shaky at the start were surprised by the work of Balenti. It will be long remembered the work that Balenti did in our closing game at Chicago. 'Pop' knows what he is doing in the line of football."

"The Game by Wire" column, also in *The Arrow,* implied that the game's plays were being communicated by telegraph to Carlisle and that students were assembled to follow the game. It reported, "Balenti's good work was especially well received and applauded." The injury that kept Frank Mt. Pleasant out of the game also kept him from being named to Walter Camp's All America First Team due to "a lack of ruggedness."

Mike made the September Merit Roll for having the highest average, 9.2, in the Junior Class. He raised the bar in October with a 9.4 average. Balenti remained active with the Standards, apparently preferring to speak and debate rather than serve as an officer. In December he gave a talk about his "…exciting experiences on his Western trips. He is a Western boy and carries all the characteristics of the so-called 'Wild West.'" Family lore had it that Mike was paid $150 a month for the 1907 season and was offered $250 for 1908. He may have received money from the Athletic Association or for "work" performed elsewhere, but $150 a month for a backup quarterback seems high. There may have been some exaggeration.

By late January, Mike, who had been elected captain of the 1908 baseball team, was already "hustling" his teammates for position. He also had the team working out every day. At the athletic banquet held in late-February, Mike got his first letter "C" for football and another one for baseball. In mid-March, he wrote a column for *The Arrow* in which he explained the recent cuts of baseball players down to 26. The reduction was necessary because he didn't have enough uniforms for all those who tried out. He defended what was surely his most controversial decision by saying, "Men who have played on the squad in former years with little or no improvement have been dropped to make room for new and untried material. In order to have a good team, year in and year out, the men who are to stay for several seasons must get the preference over men who have only one season more at school here." A week later *The Arrow* reported on an inter-squad game used to help identify the best players. The article exhorted players to try out when it said, "Captain Balenti has hopes of a winning team and he is going to pick the *best* men, irregardless [sic] of what was or has been, and if you want to play ball you have to play good ball or none. Go after a place on the first nine!"

A piece in the May 15 *Arrow* summed up how the baseball season went:

> "The baseball team made a very poor showing on the Eastern trip, losing to Holy Cross 6-0, and to Brown 11-0. Whether it is a case of too much individual playing, lack of determined spirit, swelled head, or no head at all, it is hard to say. The base ball team started out with good prospects, but as in former years, the team seems to get worse instead of improving and it is possible that this branch of sport my yet find itself and brace up and finish the season with a creditable record."

On May 29, *The Arrow* was singing a different tune:

> "The baseball team has finally found itself and the game with Dickinson on Monday showed that they can play ball when they make up their minds to do it. Everyone in town picked Dickinson to win, but the way the Indians played made the Dickinson team look like a high school bunch."

Apparently, the Dickinson hitters found William Garlow's pitching to be unhittable. His detractors said that all he had was speed. Perhaps they didn't know about his spitter. The Indians won 5-0 even though, after driving in Newashe with a triple, the Captain forgot the third baseman had the ball and was put out with the old hidden-ball trick. The team improved but was inconsistent and finished 13-14. Mike Balenti was re-elected captain for 1909. Shortly thereafter he left for Bridgewater, New Jersey to play summer ball. He ended up playing for Myerstown in the Lebanon County League.

1908 was Mike Balenti's break-out year at Carlisle. Not only was he the starting quarterback on the vaunted football team, but he was President of both the Senior Class and the Standard Literary Society, and he was captain of the baseball team. In addition to that, he wrote several articles for the school newspaper. To top it off, he even had a serious girlfriend.

The football team lost several of the stars from the great 1907 squad and had to rebuild. A major improvement was that Jim Thorpe, now at left halfback, knew the plays. Previously, Albert Exendine told Jim what to do before each snap. There was also an unusual addition to the team. Victor Kelley, who had played the three previous years for the Agricultural and Mechanical College of Texas, transferred to Carlisle and backed up Balenti at quarterback. He didn't get a lot of playing time but surely learned a lot from Pop Warner. The team went 10-2-1, losing only to Harvard and Minnesota and tying with Penn. Overall, it was a very good season. Warner considered Mike to be as good a passer as Frank Mt. Pleasant and, after the Navy game in which he kicked four field goals, he started getting mention in the press for All America consideration. The losses and tie probably doomed any chances he had in that direction. Walter Camp did place his teammate, Jim Thorpe, on his All America Third Team. In later years, Balenti claimed to be a faster runner than Thorpe in football togs but not in a track suit.

About six weeks before commencement, the Junior Class gave a reception in honor of the graduating seniors. As class president, Mike Balenti was called upon to say a few words. Later in the evening, he and Cecilia Baronovitch, Haida from Alaska, were awarded second prize, presumably in a dance contest. As part of the week-long commencement festivities in early April, 84 students put on the comic opera, "The Captain of Plymouth," in which Michael Balenti played the role of John Alden. Of his performance, *The Indian Craftsman* said, "…his natural diffidence made him a perfect Alden."

Bandmaster Claude M. Stauffer explained, "I was moved to attempt this through reading an editorial in *The North American* on the civilizing influence of opera. I thought if Oscar Hammerstein can spend $1,000,000 to civilize Philadephians, we could spent a few weeks for the same civilizing influence on the wards of the nation. And say, do you know that I believe we got the better results." Newspapers across the country ran a wire story about the play.

Mike spoke as the representative of the Class of 1909 at the annual alumni reception as they were the incoming class to the Alumni Association. He also gave a declamation titled "The Seven Lamps of Architecture" to a student assembly. *The Arrow* opined, "He expressed Dr. Hillis's beautiful thought on character building so clearly and forcibly that all understood and enjoyed the effort very much." "The Class Prophecy" printed in *The Arrow* predicted Cecilia Baronovitch's future: "She is down in Oklahoma keeping house for one of the world's greatest athletes. She is noted for the fine bread she bakes. Michael Balenti took a course in civil engineering. He is now a bridge builder in Oklahoma." It appears that the classmates were more than just dance partners. Cecilia could be regarded as the female counterpart of Mike Balenti. She was active in the Susan Strongstreth Literary Society, played first mandolin in the mandolin club, sang in the choir organized by the Sisters of Saint Katherine, sang solos at club meetings, and gave talks at student assemblies. After receiving her certificate from the Normal Department, she headed for her home in Alaska. Mike received his bakery certificate and headed in a different direction.

Shortly after commencement, the ambitious baseball schedule of 33 games started in earnest. A new coach, Mr. Eugene E. Bassford, had been hired, and great things were expected because he had turned out championship teams at Fordham the three previous years. Captain Balenti played shortstop and batted at several spots, generally in the upper half of the line-up. The team only went 10-17 (some scheduled games were rained out), but Coach Bassford was optimistic because the team was composed of mostly new men. Philadelphia newspapers rumored that Mike would be playing for the Philadelphia Athletics that year. The story went that A's ace and Carlisle alum, Charles Albert "Chief" Bender, got Mike to agree to sign with his team. After Balenti tried out with them, Connie Mack inked him and immediately turned him over to Milwaukee of the American Association. Manager John McClosky sent him directly to the Dayton Veterans of the Central League without a tryout. After getting some time in the starting line-up, he was released in mid-July, but his contract reverted to St. Paul.

The fall of 1909 found Mike Balenti back on the gridiron again. This time he was in College Station, Texas playing for the Agricultural and Mechanical College of Texas. He was no doubt recruited by Victor Kelley who was back at A&M and by assistant coach Charley Moran. Students collected enough money to buy out the head coach's contract after a disappointing tie in the second game of the season. Moran was then promoted to head coach. With Kelley at quarterback and Balenti at left halfback, the Aggies went 7-0-1, including a win over Oklahoma and two over Texas. The last game against Texas, which was played in Austin, illustrates the Indians' value to the Aggies. The only score of the game was made on a halfback pass from Balenti to Kelley, who was stopped short of the goal line by Kirkpatrick. As aiding the ball carrier was still legal, Balenti threw off the tackler, allowing Kelley to cross the goal line and score the winning touchdown. Although Mike missed the kick after Kelley's score, he was invaluable as a placekicker that year. As a side note to this game, he surely attended the first on-campus Bonfire in A&M history as a member of the football team. After season's end, A&M was deemed All Southwestern Champions. With that honor came the right for the head coach to select the players for the All Southwestern Team. Charlie Moran named Mike as All Southwestern left halfback and Kelley as one of the quarterbacks. This ended his football career but he still had lots of baseball in front of him. After the season, he was mentioned alongside Frank Hudson and Jim Thorpe in an article that discussed the all-time great kickers who had played the game. He may have played baseball for A&M but game accounts discovered to date didn't mention him.

In the summer of 1910, Mike Balenti played minor league baseball again, this time for Savannah of the Sally League. At the end of the season, he was drafted by the Atlanta Crackers but was missing at the start of 1911 spring training. Demonstrating one of his grandmother Roadmaker's traits, he held out for more money. After coming to terms with the Crackers, he joined them in spring training. He was considered one of their brightest prospects. At the end of the tryouts, he was assigned to the Macon Peaches of the Sally League. In July, he was called up by Cincinnati of the National League and played in eight games for the Big League club, hitting .250 for the stint. Renowned scout Hugh Nicol went on record as saying that he thought Mike had what it took to make it in the major leagues. Before the October 8 game, he participated in an eight-event meet with St. Louis players but didn't win his event, the 100-yard dash. Perhaps his mind wasn't on the race.

Newspapers across the country announced that Mike was soon to wed. Cecilia Baronovitch had traveled all the way from Kasaan, Alaska where she had been teaching to marry the man she called "Pikey." Shortly after the close of the season, they were wed but when and where are not known. They spent the winter in Calumet, Oklahoma, probably with or near his family. The Cincinnati club released him at the end of the 1911 season, but he was picked up by Chattanooga of the Southern League for 1912. In September, after having a pretty good year with the Lookouts, he was drafted by the St. Louis Browns of the American League. After the season was over, Mike finally got to see his son. Michael, Jr. was born on July 11 in Alaska, so Cecilia must

HELLO! HERE COMES MIKE BALENTI FROM THE NORTH POLE FOR SPRING TRAINING

It is reported that Mike Balenti, the Alaskan Indian baseball player who has signed up with the St. Louis Browns, is on his way south for spring training.

have returned home to her family to have the baby. Once the baseball season started, Mike was on the road much of the time. Just before spring training started for 1913, a cartoon of Mike mushing his way down from Alaska on a dogsled ran in papers across the country.

The Browns played Mike in 70 games that summer but he only hit .180, which is far too low an average to make it in the Big Leagues, even for a shortstop. In early September, newspapers announced that he was taking the job of assistant football coach at St. Louis University. If he actually took the job, he may not have returned to Alaska that winter. Or he only assisted for a couple of weeks to help get the team ready for the season.

His first three children were born in Seward's Ice Box. Newspapers announced that the Chattanooga Lookouts would be paying for his $200 railroad ticket to come to spring training, but he would have to leave home on February 1. In February of 1914, *The Sporting News* reported, "It takes so long for Mike Balenti, the Indian ballplayer, to travel to and from his home in Alaska, that he has decided it isn't worthwhile for him to try to play ball. In fact, if he plays, he doesn't get any time off at all. He hardly gets home after one baseball season before he has to turn right around and start back. Mike lives somewhere with his wife's tribe a thousand miles from the railroad. It took him two months to get home last fall and he would have to start back about New Year's to get back to Chattanooga, where he was booked to play this year, in order to escape a fine for reporting late." This article may have been planted to help with salary negations because Mike was back in uniform in spring training.

Mike broke his leg sliding into second base in June 1914 and was out for the rest of the season. After the team's management obtained approval from the rest of the teams in the Southern League, Chattanooga agreed to pay him his salary although he was unable to play. The incident had a sad note to it as *Sporting Life* reported that Cecilia arrived on the train from Alaska just in time for the game, rushed to the ballpark to see him play, and got to her seat in time to see him get injured. He healed faster than expected and was able to play in a few games at the end of the year. While nursing his wounded limb,

Mike negotiated a contract to become athletic director and football coach at the University of Chattanooga. That work wouldn't interfere too much with summer baseball, particularly one in which he was laid up. His Chattanooga team went 5-4, scoring 143 points while giving up 222. Pummelings by Sewanee (46-3), Tennessee (67-0), and Alabama (63-0) accounted for most of the points given up. The Lookouts wanted him back for 1915 if he would take a pay cut. Instead, he signed with the San Antonio Bronchos of the Texas League. After a good year with San Antonio, he was sold to the Galveston Buccaneers, for whom he played in 1916. Before the 1917 season, he wrote them that he was retiring from baseball after receiving a higher paying offer in another line of work. He eventually signed with and played for the Buccos.

Mike Balenti continued his football coaching career while playing baseball for San Antonio and Galveston. In the fall of 1915, he began coaching Baylor's backfield as an assistant to C. P. Mosely and, according to Baylor University's records, continued doing that to 1920. This coaching gig may have been opportunity to which he referred in his negotiations with Galveston or it may have been something else. He and his brothers were doing some inventing at that time. In 1915, he and George filed a patent application for an "Attachment for Jumping Standards." Patent number 1,193,972 was awarded to the brothers on August 8, 1916. "This invention relates to standards used for determining the height of high jumps, pole vaults, or analogous athletic endeavors, and the primary object of the invention is to provide an attachment for standards of this nature, which will accurately record substantially the exact height of the jump." It's doubtful that they made any money on this one, but he and John may have done better a few years later. In 1919 they applied for a patent for a "Pancake Machine." The purpose of the machine was described as follows: "This invention relates to an improved pancake machine and the principal object of the invention is to provide a machine in which pancake dough may be mixed and held while being used, improved valve means and actuating means for the valves being provided for controlling passage of the pancake dough out of the outlet opening in the bottom of the receptacle or container." The patent was awarded on December 28, 1920. The device they designed looks a lot like devices used in pancake restaurants today.

Somewhere between 1917 and 1920, Mike and Cecilia moved their family to Oklahoma. The three older children, Michael, Jr., Mary, and Richard, were born in Alaska; and the two younger ones, Kathleen and Thomas Edgar, were born in Oklahoma according to the 1930 census. It's not clear exactly how long Balenti played minor league baseball, but it was longer than most. After his playing days were over, he managed a number of sandlot teams. In 1922, he managed the Guthrie entry in the Oklahoma State League to a 48-59 record. In 1934 he managed the Altus Advertisers. It's anyone's guess how many other teams used his talents. It is known that he officiated games. The most unusual one was the 1937 game between Texas Tech and Texas College of Mines when Mike, Jr. was a star fullback for the Miners. (Mike, Sr. wasn't one of those tragic figures who excel in athletics and die in poverty.) In 1920 he worked as a bookkeeper in a garage and it is believed that he later worked in the construction industry. He must have done pretty well because, in the early 1950s, he cut a fine figure on the Amarillo golf courses, apparently enjoying his retirement. He died on August 4, 1955 of a heart attack at 69 years of age in Altus, Oklahoma.

According to Mike's granddaughter, also named Cecilia, he was called "Mikey" until a little boy with a cold was unable to pronounce his name correctly. From that time on, his wife called him "Pikey" and he called her "Lady." It is not know which child dubbed her that. They addressed each other by these names the rest of their lives.

Mike's athletic ability didn't die with him. Sons Michael and Richard were high school and college football backfield stars at Texas College of Mines. During WWII they were Marine fighter pilots. Richard received the Distinguished Flying Cross for his heroics.

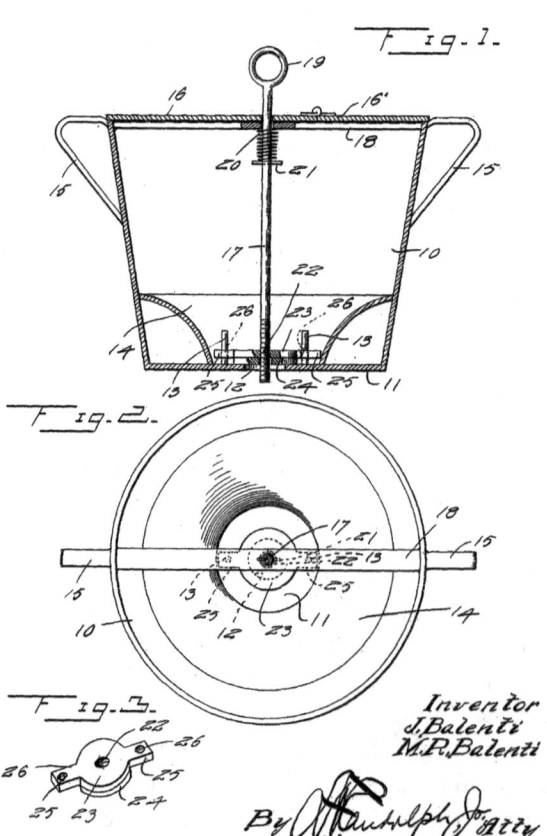

Frank Cayou

Strongheart

Francis Mitchell Cayou was one of the more colorful of the Carlisle Indians, and that is saying something. Frank first came east to Chicago from the Omaha Reservation in Nebraska in the summer of 1893 to work as one of the hundreds of Columbian Guards at the World's Columbian Exposition. Seeing what white men had accomplished caused him to think his people were ignorant and degraded. Three years later he spoke about that experience:

> "Drunkenness and laziness is their curse. The white people keep the Indians on reservations. This degrades them. They are environed by civilization, but they are not of it. The government sends my people money, and they drink it up. It was almost as bad to give them rations so freely, for they would eat in a short time what they had and go hungry without a thought for tomorrow. I was that way, but I saw what the white people

Frank Cayou (right), Athletic Director of Illinois Athletic Club; *Chicago History Museum*

had done, and the desire possessed me – the ambition, I should say, to raise myself up and help my race. Their only hope is to live among the whites, be educated and adopt their ways."

His arrival at Carlisle on October 8, 1893 nearly coincided with Superintendent Pratt's rescission of his ban on inter-scholastic football. His later career path suggests that he might have been the orator who presented the students' arguments so well, but his age, 15, and newness at the school argue against it. Regardless, he was soon immersed in the school's athletic programs. Although small at age 17, Frank starred on the football and track teams, due in part to being a very fast runner. He soon made a splash in the big city papers. 1894 was Carlisle's first full season of football but it was already producing stars – and Frank Cayou was one of them.

The Saturday before the 1895 season started, he won a competition that was not exactly of an athletic type, but he won it in a cake walk – literally. In its article on the Standard Debating Club's first sociable of the year, *The Indian Helper* reported, "In a cake walk, Mr. Frank Cayou and lady, Miss Julia Long, won the prize of a handsome cake for the most graceful marching." Cupid's bow may have misfired as Julia returned to nursing school in Philadelphia two days after the dance. But Cayou didn't sulk. Instead, he threw himself into school affairs. He was active as an orator both as an officer for the Standards and in giving talks to the entire student body.

Frank completed his studies at the Indian School and graduated in March 1896. A month after commencement, consumption (tuberculosis) struck close. Fellow class member Edward Spott died of consumption a month after graduation and Cayou served as a pallbearer. Both graduates were still in town because they were enrolled in the Dickinson College Preparatory School.

1896 was Carlisle's first winning football season. Although enrolled in the prep school, Frank continued to play for the Indians. The speedy left

Name: Francis Mitchell Cayou	**Nickname:**
DOB: 3/7/1878	**Height:** 5' 9.2"
Weight: 142	**Age:** 20
Tribe: Omaha	**Home:** Omaha reservation north of Decatur, Nebraska
Parents: Fred Cayou, white, probably French; Me-umba-the (Moonbeam)	
Early Schooling: Omaha Agency boarding school, possibly the Presbyterian Mission School	
Later Schooling: Dickinson College prep school; Dickinson College; University of Illinois	
Honors: Wabash College Athletic Hall of Fame, 1982	

halfback stood out in the Yale game played in New York City. His 45-yard run around end was the play of the game for Carlisle. As a token of her esteem, the wife of financier Russell Sage and future philanthropist, Olivia Sage, who had watched the game with the Pratts, gave the Carlisle players bunches of mums and roses in their school colors. Mrs. Sage tied Frank's bunch with the ribbon she wore during the game because of his outstanding run.

The *New York World* had a lot to say about Cayou's performance against the previously unscored upon Yale team:

> "It was a heaving, twisting, squirming mass of men. Suddenly men in blue began to fall. Bass, the famous, and Rogers, pride of Yale's rush line, went down like ninepins. Between them sprang an Indian. He had the ball in his arms and he was free. One after another of the Yale men sprang after him, only to be bowled over by the stocky Indians who protected him. It was the business of Chauncey, the New Haven half-back, to stop this handsome Indian. The Yale man made a dash for him. Cayou shook him off and never checked his pace. Cayou ran sixty yards and made a touchdown. The Indians had scored against Yale in the first ten minutes of play. The 'bleachers,' the 'bridges' and the 'deadheaders' were drunk with excitement. People in the covered grand-stand even awoke to fine enthusiasm. The Indians along the side lines danced around. Now and then one would give an ear-splitting yell. The Yale men looked at each other as if they were not sure what had happened."

Frank made an interesting acquaintance at that game. William C. De-Mille, an undergrad at Columbia University at the time, became familiar with Frank and his background when they met after the game. Cayou's life story formed the basis for a major literary work by DeMille less than a decade later.

During the week after the Penn game, *The Indian Helper* reported on something that had previously been a secret: "Frank Cayou surprised everybody with a solo. But a very few knew that he possessed such a rich, true voice. In fine baritone, he rendered 'Yearnings,' by Rubenstein, in a manner that showed study and cultivation; the song was enthusiastically encored." This would not be his last vocal performance.

The 1896 football season included a post-season trip to Chicago for a night game in the Coliseum against Intercollegiate Conference of Faculty Representatives (today's Big Ten Conference) power Wisconsin. The Indians defeated the Champions of the West, of course. Note that the Big Ten was often called the Western Conference in those days. Ever wonder what "Champions of the West" referred to in *Hail to the Victors*? Well, the Indians beat them a few times.

Frank represented the Indian School in the spring as captain of the track team. His primary events were the short dashes and the mile relay. Perhaps the most exciting race was the relay run in a meet at Dickinson College, in which the normal schools also participated. When Frank, who ran the anchor leg, received the baton, he was 20 yards behind the leader. He rapidly made up the ground and won going away on the home stretch.

Frank left for Northfield Summer School for Bible Study in June 1897 as one of the contingent from the Indian School's YMCA. The Bible conference was held on the grounds of the Northfield Seminary for Young Ladies which was founded by evangelist Dwight Lyman Moody in 1879 in his hometown, Northfield, Massachusetts. Religion was a key theme throughout Cayou's life.

Frank played football for the Indians again in 1897 while studying at the Dickinson College Preparatory School. 1897 featured a three-games-in-eight-days road trip to the Midwest in which they played Illinois, Cincinnati and Ohio State Medical College. The first of the three was a night game in the Chicago Coliseum. It was in that game that John Steckbeck thought protective headgear was first worn in the West when some Carlisle players donned them.

The day after winning the game, Frank and David McFarland, who had been injured in the game the night before, headlined a meeting of the Hyde Park YMCA. The *Chicago Daily Tribune* reported, "Frank Cayou, the substitute left halfback, was the principal speaker. He showed the pale faces how the same skill in mass play and line bucking and the same dogged endurance which won the Carlisle boys their great victory at the Coliseum had scored many a touchdown in the contest with Indian superstition and inbred depravity." He talked at length about the situation at Carlisle and quoted scripture. He also talked about the uphill battle against popular conceptions they fought. "Many of the whites have queer conceptions of the Indian. 'The only good Indian is a dead Indian,' expresses the general sentiment, apparently. There were no dead Indians at the Coliseum last night, but I think they are pretty good boys." He also spoke out against the reservation system and said winning by tricks was not necessary.

Frank also did some speaking at the football banquet held in January at Dickinson College when he gave a talk entitled, "Past, Present and Future of the Carlisle Indian School Team." After summarizing Carlisle's very short history at playing the game, he prematurely predicted victory over one of the Big Four in the upcoming season.

1898 again found Frank Cayou at Dickinson College, not in the prep school but in the college proper as an unclassified student. However, he still played football for Carlisle and continued to shine both off and on the field. After the Williams College game in Albany, New York, the team visited public schools where Cayou gave a speech, toured the Capitol, where the players were introduced to the governor, and cruised the Mohawk and Hudson Rivers on the *Yale*.

The Illinois game, Frank's last in a Carlisle football uniform, was a bittersweet experience. Sweet because it was a victory but frustrating in its ending as reported by the *Chicago Chronicle*:

> "There were twenty-five seconds of time left when the signal was given for the last assault of the day. Cayou caught the pass, hesitated the fraction of a second and then gave a leap. The impetus carried him off on top of the struggling pile of players and his body swayed over the line, but before he could reach the earth and call down the whistle had blown. The game was over with the ball on the Illinois six inch line, half a foot from another touchdown."

However, Frank wasn't done with football for the year because Dickinson College still had a game left to play and it was a big one against Penn State. *The Dickinsonian* justified his appearance:

> "Two new faces appeared on the home team, Rodgers [sic] at left-end and Cayou at left half-back, both of them star players for the Indians, but *bona fide* students of the College and as such entitled to a place on our eleven. They played in their usually brilliant style, Rodgers especially distinguishing himself by fine tackling."

In the spring, Cayou was competing for Dickinson College in track. He won a gold watch at the Penn Relays, repeating his success of the previous

Cayou elopes, *Sandusky Evening Star* 12-28-1903

year when competing for Carlisle. That spring he also sang baritone solos accompanied by the renowned Carlisle Indian School band under the direction of Dennison Wheelock.

After spending the summer in Boston, perhaps playing baseball or working, Frank returned to Carlisle long enough to gather up his things and head west. He moved to Champaign, Illinois where he enrolled in an electrical engineering program at the University of Illinois, played football and ran track. In a meet between Illinois and Chicago, Cayou and his competitor finished in a dead heat with both tying the intercollegiate record for the 220-yard dash of 22 seconds. The April 29, 1900 *Chicago Daily Tribune* reported that, on the previous day in a local meet in Champaign, he had won both the 440-yard dash and the 220-yard dash. Someone by the name of Brundage came in second in the 220. This was not be the last time a Brundage would finish behind a Carlisle Indian. Frank starred in football, of course, and ran 85-yards for a touchdown against Purdue.

Cayou also spent some time in Arcola, Illinois the next summer, supposedly to train the Arcola Volunteer Fire Department Hose and Hook and Ladder teams for the Illinois and national championship competitions, both of which they won. *The Daily News* reported, "Handsome, an athlete, a knobby dresser, he won his way into the best society of the city, and was a marked favorite of the young women of the city… A graduate of the Carlisle school, he presented a most pleasing appearance, was a splendid conversationalist and had hundreds of friends."

In 1901, he continued playing in Illinois' 18-0 victory thumping of Indiana in spite of breaking his nose shortly after entering the game. In July 1902, *The Red Man and Helper* quoted Frank as writing, "The musical training received at Carlisle has enabled me to hold a position as bass singer in a quartette choir in the largest church in Champaign. I have been captain of the track team this year and my time in running for the quarter mile race has been fifty seconds."

In the summer of 1902, Frank's days of competing for Illinois came to an end, most likely because he and three teammates raced for Arcola in the state firemen's tournament held in Blue Island in mid-August. The Central Illinois AAU disqualified Cayou, his teammates and a Taylorville athlete from college athletics. All were accused of accepting pay for competing, and all denied the charges, saying they could prove their innocence. It does not appear that Frank competed for Illinois after that. During the 1911 season, a New York sports writer who wrote under the Monty byline listed Frank Cayou among the best fullbacks who ever played the game. That was something considering he played halfback.

That fall found Frank Cayou coaching, still in Champaign but now coaching the Champaign Central High School football team. A 6-2-2 record for his first year of coaching wasn't too bad considering that the first loss, a 29-0 beating by Danville, was quickly avenged in a rematch 5-0 later in the season. The only other loss was by one point to Bloomington. Two ties were the only other blemishes on their record. The next fall, in 1903 still in Champaign, he was in charge of the University of Illinois freshmen. However, football did not take up all of his time; he had some left for other matters.

In mid-November, according to *The Daily Record*, "Monday he arrived in this city and said he desired to take Miss Anna Snyder to Champaign, where 'The County Chairman' was to be presented. No one objected to the arrangement, and he took the young lady to the hotel to dinner. Some friend managed to steal all the wearing apparel of Miss Snyder while the dinner was in progress, and the pair took the fast train north for Tuscola. Arriving at Tuscola, Cayou hunted up County Clerk Hawkins, where a marriage license was secured, and the marriage occurred at the Methodist parsonage, Rev. William Brandon officiating. Immediately after the ceremony the happy young people left on the late train for Chicago." A later illustrated article distributed nationally identified the bride's age, 18, as the only objection her wealthy parents had to their socialite daughter marrying a penniless Indian. *The Daily Record* reporter was apparently quite enamored with the winsome Miss Snyder when he wrote, "His bride is regarded as one of the most handsome young women of Douglas County, a county famous for fair women." He was quite supportive of the groom. "During the summer months Mr. Cayou spent in this city he conducted himself with great credit, and many think he will make a name and fortune for himself and bride."

Indications are that the newlyweds set up housekeeping in the bride's home town and Frank took a job "traveling for a Chicago mercantile house." It isn't known if Frank's influential father-in-law arranged the job or if he got it using his own contacts in the sporting world. Regardless of how he got the job, he seems not to have stayed with it for long.

On May 6, 1904, *The Decatur Review* announced that Frank Cayou would be taking the helm of the Wabash College football program that fall. Because Wabash's home, the town of Crawfordsville, Indiana, was not terribly far from Arcola, Illinois, it is likely that the young couple maintained their household in Arcola while he shuttled back and forth to the campus as his schedule dictated. Before football season started, several of the best track men in the country, including Frank, were permanently suspended by the Western Association of the AAU for participating in the firemen's hose reel games in World's Fair Stadium in St. Louis in August. Reasons for the suspensions were not provided. Frank was likely more concerned with fielding a winning football team than running races at this point in his life.

The Scarlet of little Wabash College faced a daunting schedule for 1904. Included in its opponents that year were Illinois, Purdue, Notre Dame and Indiana. Only 300 students attended what is one of the few remaining all-male institutions of higher learning today. Fewer attended during Cayou's time. While watching his undersized team, which averaged a little over 140 pounds per man, battle the much larger opponents, Cayou remarked that they fought like little giants. Reporters picked up on it and Wabash's teams have been known as the Little Giants ever since. So pleased was the College's administration with Frank's performance that they awarded him a three-year contract as physical director and football coach. He then had a full-time job as athletic director in charge of all sports at the Indiana school. As another reward for the 4-4 season in which he lost only to the four large schools on the schedule, Frank was presented with two more majors to play: Northwestern and Chicago. The Little Giants beat one of them, Notre Dame, which wouldn't lose another home game until 1928. For little Wabash to go 6-5-1 against this schedule was quite an accomplishment.

1906 was considerably lighter with only three majors to play: Indiana, Purdue and Illinois. Cayou's charges lost only to Indiana, holding Illinois to a scoreless tie and beating the Boilermakers, the derogative name given to the Purdue teams in 1891 by Wabash fans who believed ringers from the Monon Shops were brought in to play instead of students. Having a good year, an open date and perhaps a lot of confidence in his team, Cayou telegraphed Carlisle in hopes of setting up a Thanksgiving Day game. That was not to be, so the 5-1-1 record was Cayou's best at Wabash. Perhaps sensing that their "famous Indian" coach, as reporters liked to say, was a valuable commodity, in March of 1907, before his contract ran out in June, the Wabash Board of Trustees authorized an extension to his contract accompanied by a substantial raise. Immediately after completing a successful spring track season, Cayou set about preparing his men for the upcoming gridiron campaign with pre-season practices in mid-June. Getting and keeping his men in peak playing condition was a key to his success because his players suffered fewer injuries than average as a result.

In September, an advance man promoting a road tour of William C. DeMille's hit play, *Strongheart*, which was to be staged in Crawfordsville, let it be known that the title character was based on the life of local football coach and athletic director, Francis M. Cayou. The playwright and the athlete had kept in touch during the years since they met in New York City. Cayou's well-publicized romance, his experiences at Carlisle and Dickinson College, and his athletic achievements formed the basis for the plot. DeMille fabricated incidents for dramatic effect but maintained the essence of Cayou's life in the play. The Broadway smash got much press regarding the then controversial topic of inter-racial marriage. Strongheart was the son of a chief who, like Cayou, had been sent first to Carlisle and then to college. Where Cayou attended Dickinson College and the University of Illinois, his theatrical counterpart attended Columbia, the playwright's alma mater. While starring on the football team, Strongheart and the sister of a teammate fell in love. The life and art differ in that the play's hero returned to his tribe to give them the benefit of his education. Sports and art would mix soon in Crawfordsville.

After a grueling practice that sportswriter and former Chicago star, Walter Eckersall, came to town to observe, Frank treated his players to a production of *Strongheart*, very likely staged in the coach's honor. A movie version of *Strongheart* was filmed in 1914 and was remade as *Braveheart* in 1926. The name change was likely to avoid confusion with the famous dog, Strongheart, whose picture can still be found on dog food cans in the grocery store. William C. DeMille's younger brother, Cecil, directed the remake at his own studio.

In the country edition of that morning's Chicago *Tribune*, Eckersall wrote, "Under-the tutelage of Frank Cayou, the famous Carlisle Indian and subsequent University of Illinois athlete, Wabash has developed in all branches of athletics, and every western university has been compelled to look upon them as contenders in every line of sport. Their practice shows grim determination and that aggressiveness which has won for them the place they hold as the foremost college, outside of the 'Big Nine,' in western athletics. On Oct. 19 Wabash will meet Michigan at Indianapolis. Great interest is being manifested in the game throughout the state, and Coach Cayou is confident a surprise is in store for the Wolverines. The famous Indian has innumerable plays of an intricate nature, which may prove bewildering to the Michiganders. Wabash seems rather light for Michigan, but the Wolverines will have to work for every point they get. The 'Little Giants' will play Purdue the Saturday previous to the Michigan game. This may prove a handicap, for some may not be in the best of shape for the big game. It should be understood that the Purdue game will be no criterion to what the Michigan game will be, as Cayou has new plays and different men for that contest."

The 1907 Little Giants beat Purdue again but lost to Michigan 22-0 and to Michigan Agricultural College (today's Michigan State) 15-6 on successive Saturdays. The Michigan game took a toll on the team, physically. Captain Gipe was treated by an Indianapolis specialist for an unnamed serious injury. Right guard Sunderland was "out of his head for several hours and it required the attention of a physician to bring him around." Hess's back was badly wrenched and Sohl's ankle was strained. *The Lake County Times* reported, "The whole team shows the effect of the great weight of Michigan, who outweighed, according to inside information, Wabash, almost thirty pounds to the man." In spite of these injuries, Wabash ended up a more than respectable 5-2-0. The Little Giants rose to the task but that would be Cayou's last football team at Crawfordsville.

While he was preparing the track team for its spring 1908 season, "Chief" Cayou, as reporters loved to call him, submitted his resignation effective the end of the school year. A reporter for the *Fort Wayne Daily News* was sympathetic to his position when he wrote, "The graduate system of managing athletic teams was installed at the local institution this college year. Upon adoption, Athletic Director Cayou in reality became practically nothing more than the coach of the team." He also opined that students would rally to convince the "wily coach" to stay. He didn't stay. Friction between coaches, students and alumni was not infrequent in those days due to the closer involvement of the student body with the management of the team. Coaches often left schools when the meddling became too great. "Chief" Cayou had worked wonders at the tiny school and was ready for new challenges.

In the summer, Coach Cayou became "Umps" Cayou when he took a job umpiring Eastern Illinois League baseball games at locations such as Staunton and Mattoon. Also reported was that he had taken the head coaching position at Washington University in St. Louis starting in the fall. He was the first full-time football coach to be hired by that school in its relatively short history of fielding a team in that sport. When the school year arrived, he was off to the Mound City, but his bride remained in her home town.

Prior to football season, *The Indianapolis Star* opined, "Wabash is somewhat of a doubtful quantity this year. The 'Little Giants' have lost their football wizard Cayou. The wonderful Indian coach is gone. In his place Ralph Jones will handle the football candidates. Jones, while not a football player, has made a remarkable career as a basketball coach." The veteran team Frank left behind finished 2-6.

Sports reporters didn't expect much from the Washington U. Bears in 1908 because, in the opinion of *The Indianapolis Star*, "he has practically no good material to work with." That was likely the case, but Frank did his best and turned in a .500 season. After opening with a scoreless tie with Carleton College, Cayou's new charges lost to Kansas, Missouri, Vanderbilt and Tulane while beating the likes of Shurtleff College (today's Alton Campus of Southern Illinois University at Edwardsville), Knox College, Rose Poly (Rose-Hulman Institute of Technology) and Millikin University.

A fan from Decatur, Illinois at the Rose Poly game observed, "He [the quarterback] made some small mistake in the first half and when the final whistle sounded, Coach Cayou, the Indian, ran out on the field, threw his arm roughly about the little man's neck and fairly dragged him back to the training quarters. I heard Cayou say afterward that he read the riot act to that youngster until he shed tears. Needless to say, in the final half, the lad played great ball." Apparently he felt the need to resort to applied psychology to motivate his players.

Frank started off 1909 by playing in a charity game on New Year's Day between the Walter Eckersall's Chicago All-Stars and Rube Waddell's St. Louis All-Stars indoors in the Coliseum. Eckersall starred for Chicago, kicking three field goals in the first half. Cayou drop kicked a field goal in the second half for St. Louis. These were the only points scored by either team. The most erratic and talented lefthander and probably the most difficult player to manage regardless of position in baseball history, Rube Waddell was then pitching for the St. Louis Browns, and surprisingly, played a good game at guard. More surprising was that he was still on the field when the final whistle blew and had not run off to chase a fire engine.

For ten days in September, Frank Cayou assisted Pop Warner prepare Carlisle for the 1909 campaign. This may have been a more or less annual practice but has not been documented for other years. Frank surely put Warner's formations in his bag of tricks. The Decatur, Illinois *Daily Review* looked forward to its home team playing Washington U, predicting, "As St. Louis turns out monster crowds to see Coach Cayou's football machine in action, the J. M. U. [James Millikin University] should clear from $75 to $100 on that game."

Cayou had a lot of vacancies to fill on his 1909 team, the largest being the two tackle positions. A number of other veterans also did not return. Any hopes for a good season were squashed when West Point Cadet Eugene A. Byrne died as a result of injuries suffered in a mass play on tackle by Harvard. The parents of Washington U's best player reacted to this tragedy by refusing to let their son play football. The Decatur *Daily Review* reported, "[Alvin] Durr according to Coach Cayou of Washington, is the most valuable man on his team and he is despondent as a result of this notification." Injuries during the season added to the misery. Washington U beat Shurtleff, Millikin and Knox while losing to Kansas, Missouri, Vanderbilt and Arkansas. For the second year in a row, the Bears lost to Missouri and Kansas, the two Missouri Valley Conference foes they played, ending up 0-2 in conference.

Wabash experienced something unusual in football that year: a coaching loss in mid-season to another school. In late October, Coach Jones, Cayou's successor, left Wabash, quite likely for reasons similar to those that convinced Cayou to leave. Jesse Harper, who later gained fame at Notre Dame, took over the reins.

Just prior to the start of the 1910 season, Anna Snyder Cayou filed for divorce from her husband of almost seven years on the grounds of desertion. She is said to have told a *St. Louis Post-Dispatch* reporter that she had great admiration for him and wished him success, but their temperaments were so different that they couldn't hope to get along.

The 1910 season was almost a repeat of the previous year but with some minor details changed. Washington U lost to Shurtleff, Missouri, Arkansas and Iowa, defeating Westminster, Rose Poly and Drury. Once again they went 0-2 in conference. On Sundays, the wily Indian coached the Staunton, Illinois town team with some success. Reporters attributed much of the success to the "crafty redskin's" coaching.

Minnie Weaver, whose family folklore led her to believe she was related to Pocahontas, became Frank's second wife in May 1911. They decided to marry in Louisville to avoid the publicity their wedding would receive in St. Louis, but they were thwarted because the bride was only 19 and the minimum age in Kentucky law was 21. So, they crossed the Ohio River and married in Indiana. They spent much of the summer in Michigan with Minnie's sick aunt. In September they returned to St. Louis for football season.

At 4-2-2, 1911 would be Cayou's best Myrtle and Maroon team, his only over .500 team with Washington U. The losses to Indiana and Arkansas were closer than usual, and conference foes Missouri and Drake were tied. He had improved the team but in following seasons it wasn't better than its competition.

1912 would be a near repeat of Frank's first season at Washington U. His team went 4-4 (0-2 in conference) defeating the lesser schools and losing to the larger ones. Frank turned in his resignation in the spring as he was unable to produce winning teams in any of the sports he coached at Washington U. The football team was 18-18-3, exactly .500 under his tutelage. He did leave St. Louis with something of value though. His son, Francis Jr. was born there, possibly in October 1911.

Before leaving town, Frank made his feelings known about the treatment of Jim Thorpe at the hands of the AAU and U. S. Olympic Committee. A St. Louis newspaper reported him as saying, "This entire rumpus about James Thorpe was started by a jealous bunch of pigs who wanted something sensational to snort about. If every athlete is to be ousted from the AAU who has played professional baseball, we will have no college or preparatory school baseball at all. In more than half the schools in the country men are admitted on various athletic teams when at least a dozen persons may know that they have received money for their services at some previous time. Jim is the greatest athlete the world has ever known. They'll all have to go a long way to find another who will accomplish what he has. The AAU is run in a slipshod manner. The officials know that nine-tenths of the supposed amateurs play ball in the summer and receive pay for it, yet nothing is said. Then comes the world's greatest athlete, who won so much glory for the United States at the Olympic games, and they put him out of amateur contests forever."

Rather than hitting the gridiron for another campaign in the fall of 1913, Frank, then 35, started to work with sporting goods giant A. G. Spalding & Bros. in Chicago. He was likely assigned college accounts because of his background and fame. That summer his daughter, Louisa, was born in Michigan, where Minnie may have been spending the summer. Frank made what appears to have been a first step toward an eventual career change when he directed 25 Objiway in a production of Longfellow's "Hiawatha" at the Fifth Annual United States Land Show from November 20 through December 7. President Wilson opened the Land Show by pressing a button connected to an electric wire. This was quite a production. A stage over 100 feet long was built in the balcony of the Chicago Coliseum to accommodate the actors and scenery used in this drama.

At the winter baseball conference in January 1914, probably as an offshoot of his job with Spalding, Frank designed new uniforms for the Indianapolis Indians minor league team that changed ownership at that meeting. The uniforms used Carlisle's colors, red and old gold, as stripes on a black band on the socks. The socks' background colors matched the pants and shirts – white for home and gray for road. "Indians" was emblazoned on the front of the shirt and copper-colored Indian heads were placed on each sleeve.

Immediately after hearing that Pop Warner had resigned from Carlisle, Cayou wrote Acting Superintendent Oscar Lipps a lengthy letter in which he applied for the athletic director's position that would soon be open. Included was an extensive list of references that included names like Walter Eckersall and Andy Smith. Lipps informed him that only a coach for the football season was going to be hired.

When not promoting Spalding's products directly, Cayou promoted the business indirectly by officiating track meets and football games. He sometimes opined on the merits of teams. In 1915 he was particularly impressed with the Ann Arbor, Michigan town club. In 1917 he shifted to the upstart Thomas E. Wilson Company for whom he worked a year. After the U. S. entered WWI, he offered to "… join any regiment organized at any of the Indian reservations for work on the border in case Mexico tries to take over Texas or New Mexico." He claimed that several other Indians from Chicago would follow suit. Nearing 40 years old he was not a candidate for the draft. However, his offer wasn't as frivolous as it might sound. Apparently German agents had been hard at work in Mexico.

Frank returned to coaching as the athletic director of the Illinois Athletic Club (IAC) in Chicago where he stayed until 1920. The IAC, located in the 18-story classical/Beaux Artes skyscraper at 112 S. Michigan Avenue in Chicago's Loop, was built for the club and is still used for a similar purpose but under a new name. His next assignment was a similar position with Great Lakes Naval Training Center that he held through 1923.

In 1919 the Illinois State Legislature designated the fourth Friday of September as American Indian Day. That day was first celebrated in 1920, the same year that the Indian Fellowship League was founded. Frank Cayou was active in the IFL and was involved in the annual celebrations of American Indian Day. He even served a few terms as president. The 1922 IFL convention, at which he was re-elected president, passed a resolution calling on President Harding and Congress to grant full rights of citizenship to Indians. On "Indian Day," his photo in full regalia appeared in newspapers across the country.

By 1926 Frank Cayou was reported to have had embarked on a new career as a lecturer who talked about Indian religions and lore. Pop Warner interpreted his career change a little differently, "I understand he has since gone into vaudeville under another name with considerable success, doing an Indian skit. He was a very good singer, which was quite an unusual accomplishment for an Indian." At age 49 Cayou remarried again, this time to Pearl Murray Buffalo who was Osage. Both could have been widowed or divorced. The great influenza epidemic of 1918-19 could have taken their spouses or their marriages could have failed or one of each. That same year, 1927, Frank was named Head Chief of the Omaha Pow Wow. At some point he joined the Native American Church, a distinctively American religion that combines Christianity with the use of peyote. In 1935, he was president of the church and was living with Pearl in Hominy, Oklahoma where both were registered Republicans. Pop Warner thought he was in vaudeville but other accounts had him on the lecture circuit. Because he may have worked under a stage name, it is difficult finding out precisely what he was doing. Frank died on May 7, 1948 at the Claremore Indian hospital in Oklahoma. Apparently a widower in later life, he was living with a stepdaughter in Hominy, Oklahoma at the time of his demise.

Al Exendine

Ex

Albert Andrew Exendine arrived in Carlisle in 1899 at age 15. He was born in Cherokee Indian Territory near present day Bartlesville, Oklahoma, 10 to 12 miles from the closest neighbor. He was the son of Jasper Exendine, reputedly a half-blood Cherokee, and Amaline Exendine, a full-blood Delaware. Jasper must have been quite a character, serving for a time as a deputy marshal for "Hanging Judge" Isaac Charles Parker. He later became a prosperous merchant and rancher whose spread encompassed what is now the city of Bartlesville. The first oil finds in Oklahoma have been attributed to Jasper and George B. Keeler. Apparently, Jasper passed on an interest in the law to his son.

Prior to coming to Carlisle, Al had some formal education at the Presbyterian Mission School near Anadarko, Oklahoma, often referred to as Mautame, as the natives called it. Exendine described his early education to John L. Johnson in 1962: "We would plough, harrow and cut broom corn a few hours a day and attend classes the rest of the time. While attending Mautame,

Name: Albert Andrew Exendine	**Nickname:** Ex
DOB: 1/7/1884 or 1/27/1884	**Height:** 5'10"
Weight: 174	**Age:** 22
Tribe: Delaware	**Home:** Bartlesville, OK
Parents: Jasper Exendine, half-blood Cherokee; Amaline Exendine, Delaware	
Early Schooling: Mautame Presbyterian Mission, Anadarko, OK	
Later Schooling: Conway Hall; Dickinson School of Law	
Honors: College Football Hall of Fame, 1970; American Indian Athletic Hall of Fame, 1971; Oklahoma Athletic Hall of Fame, 1972	

Albert Exendine;
*Cumberland County
Historical Society,
Carlisle, PA*

my friend, Joseph Tremp, and I read an ad in the Anadarko newspaper which stated: 'Students wanted for Carlisle Indian School.' Joseph Tremp turned to me and said, 'Albert, let's go to Carlisle.'" Tremp was able to get permission so he left almost immediately, but when Albert learned he had to commit to a five-year enrollment, he cooled on the idea. A few months after arriving in Carlisle, Tremp wrote his friend a letter extolling the school's virtues. Eventually, the letter prevailed.

Ex's first official recognition at Carlisle came in January of 1902. It did not come from his work on the football field or track. It came from his command of the language and his ability to frame his argument logically, skills that came in handy in later life. He debated successfully for the negative side against the question, "Resolved that Indian schools should be abolished." In May, he was acknowledged for his athletic ability: "Albert Exendine of the Freshman class was the best that took part in the sports for the Freshmen in a high jump, hammer throw, and shot putting." He wasn't able to win or even place against the upperclassmen yet, but he was ready to deliver an oration to a joint meeting of the freshmen and sophomore classes. His football work to this point was just to prepare him for bigger things. After all, he had never played the game before coming to the Cumberland Valley.

Making the football team wasn't a sure thing. He later related getting a cool reception from Warner: "He told me that I should have played football my first year there, and that it would be pretty tough for me to make the team because I had not. 'Pop' expected all the boys at Carlisle to play football, and conducted an excellent football program to attract them. He finally consented, and turned me over to an assistant coach on the field. He knocked me all over the field for an hour and a half before I learned to defend myself. By then I was wringing wet and so was he, but 'Pop' was convinced that I wanted to play football."

That fall, Pop Warner made Exendine a starter on the varsity football team, positioning him at right tackle, and he got some good press in *The Red*

Man and Helper for the quality of his play. The day after the Thanksgiving Day victory over Georgetown, Al and the rest of the team visited President Theodore Roosevelt, who had invited them to the White House. Also that fall, Al was elected vice-president of the Invincible Debating Society and played a Roman counsel in "The Banishment of Catiline." He was becoming a big man on campus. In the spring of 1903, he did well in track meets but, like everyone else, performed in Frank Mt. Pleasant's shadow.

During the 1903-04 school year, Exendine played left tackle without much notice in the press and improved in track, getting press coverage but again not as much as Mt. Pleasant. Several students spent their summer vacation at Hotel Beacon-by-the-Sea in Point Pleasant, New Jersey, most likely earning money working at the resort. The *Philadelphia Press* reported on a charity benefit put on by the boys, in which Al's part was a war dance. That fall was Al's first year to play football under a coach other than Warner, because Pop had returned to his alma mater. Due to convalescing from an unspecified operation in the fall of 1904, he did not play in a game until the November 5th contest against Ursinus. Al made the trip to St. Louis to play in the game against Haskell Institute on the Saturday after Thanksgiving. Not only did he get to see the World's Fair, but he also scored a touchdown. After returning to Carlisle, Al left for Medico-Chi in Philadelphia for an unspecified operation. By the end of January, he was back at school giving ex-tempore speeches for the Invincibles. His medical problems appear to have been behind him before the start of track season. In 1905, Exendine placed first many times in many meets but received mention only when he broke the school record for the shot put in a dual meet with Penn State. At season's end, he owned school records for the high jump and shot put, but Mt. Pleasant owned or shared records in four events. At the end of the school year, Al was elected to Critic for the Invincibles for the upcoming term, his senior year.

Al Exendine scoring touchdown against Chicago, 1907; *Chicago History Museum*

In the fall of 1905, Albert Exendine was active with the Invincible Debating Society and football, as usual. He played fullback in the early-season games but was shifted back to tackle for the rest of the season. As soon as football was over, Al was elected captain of the 1906 football team and, separately, captain of the Seniors' basketball team. Carlisle's graduation was generally held earlier in the spring than that of most schools, and few attended long enough to graduate. As a result, students participated in activities, such as baseball and track, after graduation but before departing for the summer. At his graduation, he spoke about blacksmithing, his specialty, as part of the ceremony. That spring, Ex again starred on the track team, although Mt. Pleasant still grabbed the headlines. After spending the summer away, he returned to Carlisle to attend school again in the fall.

Al enrolled in Conway Hall, Dickinson College's preparatory school across town, and enjoyed his breakout season in football. Prior to 1906, he had been a starter for the Carlisle varsity, generally at tackle, but this year, the year that rules revolutionizing football were implemented, he was shifted to right end. Some combination of the new rules, Warner's new formations, the legalization of the forward pass, and available talent prompted this move. The reason for the position change is much less important than the outcome as Exendine became one of the all-time greats at end. The captain's 80-yard touchdown in the victory over Penn was perhaps the highlight of his season. The referee gave ends Exendine and Gardner high marks for boxing out Penn's ends, keeping them from covering the Indians' punt returns. The two covered Carlisle's punts as well as they prevented their opponents from covering theirs. Legend has it that Ex played a significant role in a transaction that shaped football history forever, and it is likely true.

Major Mercer, who became Carlisle Superintendent in 1904 with Pratt's ouster, surely wouldn't have missed the 1906 Army-Navy game that was played in Philadelphia, given its proximity and the fact that cavalry officers were seldom stationed so close to the all-important game's location. Also, Captain Exendine could have easily traveled from Norfolk, Virginia to Philadelphia in the two days since the Indians played the University of Virginia in their last game of the season. While sitting on the sidelines, Al received a powerful slap on his back. He turned, somewhat surprised, to see Pop Warner. After exchanging pleasantries, he asked Warner why he hadn't returned to Carlisle. Warner responded, "You have coaches." To which Exendine countered, "They're not coaches," and urged Warner to talk with Mercer. The stars were aligned perfectly as Warner was having problems at Cornell with students and alumni over disciplining a star player. After the game, Warner walked up to Exendine and extended his right hand, saying, "I want you to meet the new football coach." Mercer and Warner apparently met up and struck a deal.

In the spring, Al ran track again for Carlisle but also worked as an assistant coach. Warner, as athletic director, served as head coach for track as well as football. Pop assigned him to help a new, but highly talented, team member, Jim Thorpe. Later Exendine recalled that it took Thorpe just one day to break the records he had set in track and field over his career. Al now assisted in coaching the football team along with playing right end. Fortunately for him, Thorpe was a halfback.

One of Exendine's assignments was to teach Thorpe the rudiments of football. Al was pleased with his progress. "Thorpe was a good learner. He was quick at doing things the way you showed him. He wasn't afraid and I kept at him about being mean when he had the ball or was blocking or tackling." Six decades later, Ex told reporters, "I didn't know what a football was until I went to Carlisle, but I was a mean son-of-a-gun. Those were the days of push, drag and slug football. I would get the ball and just stand there pumping my knees while other fellows pushed me into the line." But that was all changing.

Warner devised new formations to capitalize on the 1906 rule changes and continued to tinker with them. The rule changes, particularly the one that legalized the forward pass, enhanced the roles of the ends and Carlisle had a crackerjack pair in Al Exendine and Bill Gardner. Carlisle also had great passers in Frank Mt. Pleasant and Pete Hauser. Warner always considered the 1907 team as one of his best. It was definitely his best one up to that time.

Exendine gained the respect of coaches, players and pundits for his contributions to the team's 10-1-0 record that included Carlisle's first ever victory over Harvard, a thrashing of Penn, and wins over Western powers Minnesota and Chicago. Exendine's skills as a pass receiver helped establish Carlisle as one of the better practitioners of the new weapon. It was no secret in the football world how good they were.

In order to stop the Indians' passing game, Chicago had put three defenders on each end. Al later described the strategy of Chicago's legendary coach, Amos Alonzo Stagg: "They just kept knocking me down and knocking me down. In those days you didn't have to wait until the receiver touched the ball to hit him. First the end would hit me, then the linebacker, then the halfback. They were doing the same thing to our other end." Al saw an opportunity when the ball was near the sideline. With Mt. Pleasant out of the game with a broken thumb, passing duties fell to Pete Hauser. Between plays he told Pete, "Hold that ball as long as you can, then throw it to me down by the goal line." When the ball was snapped, Ex stepped out of bounds and the defenders turned their attention to Hauser. But Al didn't stop moving; he ran behind the Chicago bench, down the sideline and reemerged downfield about 50 yards from where he started. Escaping several would-be tacklers, Hauser arched the ball to his teammate who scored an easy touchdown.

Stagg was livid, Warner savored the victory more than almost any other, and the rulemakers made coming back onto the field after going out of bounds illegal.

Walter Camp, always biased heavily toward Ivy League players, only put Exendine on his All-America second team. Caspar Whitney and the *St. Louis Star-Chronicle* both named him as a first-team All-American. Years later Warner was still displeased with Camp's selections when he wrote, "… and I still maintain that they [Exendine and Gardner] have never been surpassed for sheer brilliance." Warner also related a conversation he had had with Chicago's star quarterback, Wally Steffens. When asked what he thought of Camp's selections, Steffens replied, "Well, I certainly would like to see the ends they think better than Gardner and Exendine."

The spring 1908 track season was Exendine's last as a competitive athlete in any sport unless he played some pro football under another name, but there's no record of that. He had a good run by most measures, but Carlisle still had Mt. Pleasant and some young Turks were making their marks. In football, eligibility limits were evolving and Al's had been used up. From this point forward, Ex competed as a coach – in athletic events, that is. In the courtroom, he eventually competed as an attorney.

In the fall, Albert continued his studies at Conway Hall and assisted Pop Warner in coaching the Carlisle football team. His major assignment was the second team, commonly called the "Hot Shots." The September 11 issue of *The Carlisle Arrow* reported that the "Hot Shots" had changed their name to the "Hustlers" because they "… will make every team they meet hustle pretty lively to defeat them." The school paper gave Exendine high marks for making his undersized players compete well with much heavier teams. The Hustlers won as many games as they lost but by wider margins, ending up scoring a lot more points than they surrendered. It was with the Hustlers that Ex developed the passing game that was to become his trademark when he became a head coach. In the spring Al continued to participate in the Invincible Debating Society activities and hone his public speaking skills. He also officiated at track meets. After spending the summer in Oklahoma and Mexico, he was ready to strike out on his own.

Pop Warner received a call from Otterbein College in Westerville, Ohio. They needed a new head football coach and wanted some suggestions. Warner immediately recommended "Exie" for the job. Before he left for his first head coaching assignment, Warner admonished him, "Ex, you will become a good football coach if you remember that football is football, not basketball." Warner viewed the forward pass as football's bastard child and thought that Al was a bit too fond of it. Ex made an immediate splash in the Buckeye state as reported by *The Otterbein Review*:

"The newspapers such as the [Columbus] *Dispatch*, *Cincinnati Enquirer* and other leading papers of the country, have discovered our team as one of the best in the State of Ohio. When we as students and alumni attempt to ferret out the source of this successful football season, we are confronted by this one question, 'What has made Otterbein's football team what it is to-day?' We can answer that question just as it is put by two words, "Albert Exendine," a coach respected by every man on the team, by every student and alumni of Otterbein. He is the man who has made a perfect football machine out of Otterbein's eleven, a machine which works out his marvellous [sic] plays to the letter. Coach Exendine is one of the best and cleanest coaches the Otterbein team has ever had. No man on the team can say that he has ever heard him use indecent language on the field. He is a gentleman, every inch of him. He knows every position on the team and he knows how to get the one great thing into the team-and that is 'ginger.' The newspapers of the country have recognized him as the best coach of the new game.

"In this humble way, we as members of the team, students, alumni and faculty desire to show our appreciation for what Coach Exendine has done for us. We only hope that the college will do its part in securing him for next fall."

Admittedly the words used were way over the top, but Ex had energized the school and with good reason. He led the Cardinals to a 15-7-3 record for the 1909-11 seasons. In the summer of 1911, Al did something that impacted Carlisle football as much, if not more, than had his playing. He ran into Jim Thorpe in Anadarko, Oklahoma, broke and out of a job. Ex suggested that Thorpe return to Carlisle. Warner, wanting to improve his team's lackluster 1910 record, welcomed the filled out and muscular Thorpe back to the team. Superintendent Moses Friedman wasn't exactly excited about allowing the runaway to return, but Warner prevailed and the rest, as they say, is history.

During this period, Ex also attended Dickinson School of Law, most likely in the off-seasons. Ex gained quite a reputation with his less worldly law school classmates. The *1912 Microcosm*, the school yearbook, described his view of education: "Ex. thinks there is nothing better in the world than a good Law education, unless it is free use of a million dollars, and we agree with him. We do not like to comment on this boy's character, for he once told us in class that he saw nothing unusual in stabbing a man." The Middler Class Census listed each class member's occupation, what he is, what he will be and what he knows. In their view, Exendine knew cussing, was husky, would be a leader, and knew the Theta Lambdas, his brothers in Theta Lambda Phi law fraternity. The *1913 Microcosm* listed him as a member of the Senior Class, but there is no record of his actually graduating. He may have passed the bar exam without having finished law school. Regardless, he practiced law in Oklahoma for many years. He also coached a local football team of mostly Indian players.

With only a week to practice inexperienced players, Attorney Exendine led the 1912 Anadarko, Oklahoma high school football team to a 4-2 record, which was good enough to be ranked in the top 13 in the state. The following year, he assisted Warner at Carlisle again. Not content to remain an assistant, he applied for the head coaching job at Cincinnati but didn't get it. Carlisle played Georgetown that year, and the powerhouse Indian team rolled over the Hilltoppers 34-0. "After the game Exendine remained in Washington at the request of Charley Cox, then graduate manager of athletics at the Hilltop, to help Eddie Bennis and Frank Gargan prepare the Hoyas for their final game of the year against Virginia. Exendine, the following Saturday, watched [quarterback Harry] Costello beat Virginia with three field goals in the last game played between the two old rivals," wrote Bob Considine of the *Washington Post*.

The head coaching job at Georgetown University opened up and he took it. Prior to the start of the 1914 season and several times during it, he visited Carlisle, no doubt to get advice from his mentor and former cohorts. His first game at Georgetown was a scoreless tie with Fordham. That was followed with three straight shutout losses. Ex's first victory with Georgetown was over Frank Mt. Pleasant's West Virginia Wesleyan team. The Hilltoppers finished the season at 2-4-2, not an auspicious start. After the season, newspaper reports incorrectly claimed that Ex had been signed to fill Warner's then vacant position at Carlisle. Beginning in 1915, he ran off a string of eight winning years at Georgetown, never going undefeated but never losing more than three games. A new rule was instituted at the school for the 1923 season that required coaches of athletic teams to be residents at Georgetown and members of the faculty. Exendine was neither.

The November 4, 1915 issue of *The Dickinsonian* reported that he had returned to McAlester, Oklahoma at the end of the season to practice law as a member of the law firm of Marianelli and Exendine to supplement his $2,000 income from the football season. Not known is if his law partner was Dickinson classmate Emilio Marianelli. Ex applied for the coaching job at Columbia University that was open, but that didn't materialize. He then heard the siren call of the Pacific Northwest.

With the resignation of Gus Welch in December 1922, Washington State College was in the market for a new head coach. Rumors were rampant. The day after Christmas, W. S. C. Athletic Director J. Fred "Doc" Bohler departed on an extended trip to interview candidates for the open head coaching position. He was able to interview 25 of the applicants for the job. On Valentine's Day, W. S. C. announced that Al Exendine had been selected as their next head coach. Strong references from Warner, Hugo Bezdek and Father Vincent L. McDonough may have been the deciding factor. Or familiarity in the Warner System, the one that helped them go undefeated in 1915 and 1917, not to mention their 1916 New Year's Day victory over Brown, may have been what

W. S. C. wanted. The March 16 issue of *The Evergreen* announced that the new head coach would arrive on May 15 to start spring football practice and conduct a clinic for high school coaches over the summer. Accompanying Al to Pullman were his wife, Grace, whom he had married while at Georgetown, and their year-old son, Albert Jr.

Al was welcomed to Pullman at the first spring practice by a turnout of more than 50 players from the previous year's team. That evening the student body as a whole greeted him with a pep rally. When asked about the outlook for the team, he was optimistic. Whether his optimism was misplaced or whether he was motivating the players is unknown. The Cougars went 2-4-1 in 1923. The bright spots of the season were the win and tie over the Oregon schools. Things were not heading in the right direction if the objective was to return W. S. C. to its glory days under Lone Star Dietz. Things got worse in 1924 when the team did not win a single conference game. The only non-conference win was the season opener against the College of the Pacific. The overnight emergence of Eskimo passer Joe Koenig, who could throw accurately in inclement weather using the technique his grandfather taught him for throwing a harpoon, helped but was far from all was needed to turn the season around. 1925's upset of the University of Southern California led by the brilliant play of "Butch" Meeker wasn't enough to secure Exendine's job. Three straight losing seasons were enough for W. S. C. and Exendine. After eleven years, the Carlisle-W. S. C. coaching connection was broken.

About that time, Occidental College in Los Angeles fired head football coach Sid Nichols. He had sullied himself in the school's eyes by coaching the opposition team that played against Red Grange and the Chicago Bears when their barnstorming tour came to town. Ex took the job. Coaching Occidental at that time consisted primarily of providing fodder for Pacific Coast powers such as his mentor's Stanford Cardinal. His two-year contract expired after the 1927 season, and he was not retained. The reason given was that Occidental needed to have a coach present on campus more than three months out of the year. Because Ex's law practice occupied the bulk of his time and likely provided the bulk of his income, he wasn't interested in spending more time on campus. Al took his family home to Oklahoma to stay, but he wasn't finished with football.

Back in Oklahoma in 1929, Exendine practiced law and coached football at Northeastern State Teachers College in Tahlequah in 1929, where he went 2-6. From 1930 through 1933, he assisted Lynn O. "Pappy" Waldorf coach Oklahoma State in Stillwater. In 1934, when Waldorf left for another stop on a career that landed him in the Hall of Fame, Al was elevated to head coach. It was at Stillwater that he came into close contact with his adopted brother's image and, surely, the person himself. Al's father, Jasper, had adopted an orphan by the name of Frank Eaton, Jr. some years before Al was born. Possibly because Jasper was a crack shot or because former Confederates who then called themselves "Regulators," had murdered Eaton's father in cold blood, the boy learned to handle a gun. At age 15, he earned the nickname of "Pistol Pete" by outshooting the cavalry's best marksmen in a competition at Fort Gibson. Pistol Pete then made himself a legend as a deputy for Judge Parker by tracking down his father's killers. He shot five of them but someone else beat him to the sixth. In 1923, his flambuoyant personality was captured in a charicature by Oklahoma A & M students for their new school mascot, "Pistol Pete." For 35 years, the crusty old cowboy regaled students with stories of the old west, posed for photographs, and signed autographs. He surely spent some time with his adopted brother, Al.

After two lackluster seasons at a school that had become accustomed to conference championships, his college coaching career ended. Ex's coaching record may qualify him for induction into the College Football Hall of Fame, but since he was inducted as a player, it makes little sense to promote him as the first Indian coach in the Hall. It seems unlikely that the Hall would select him when it chooses not to induct his old teammate Lone Star Dietz, who had a better coaching record.

After seemingly retiring from coaching, Albert Exendine continued practicing law and took a government position back in Anadarko as Organization Field Agent under the U. S. Indian Reorganization Act for the Bureau of Indian Affairs. While there, he coached an Indian high school team to an unbeaten season, scoring 300 points and giving up only 12. After the season, he told Bob Considine, "It took me until this late date to learn the secret of perfect seasons. I not only coached this team, but all the opponents asked me to be the referee of their games. It's a pity more coaches can't have this opportunity." After retiring from the government position in 1951, he and Grace moved to Tulsa where they remained until he died in 1973 less than a month before his 89th birthday.

Pistol Pete;
Oklahoma State University

John B. Flinchum

John Benjamin Flinchum was born on August 7, 1897, in Indian Territory near Gerty County, in present day Hughes County, Oklahoma, as the ninth child of James Samuel Washington Flinchum and Julia Turnbull Flinchum. His father, a white man, was a well-known rancher in the area and his mother was half-blood Choctaw. After attending school in Hughes County, John B. Flinchum enrolled in the Carlisle Indian School a year after Jim Thorpe achieved his great fame.

Flinchum, like most Carlisle captains, was not a one-dimensional person. He was active in the Invincible Debating Society and other school affairs. John played football but didn't make the varsity until 1916. After playing left tackle on the 1917 squad, he was elected captain of the 1918 team. Possibly because of this honor, he continued his studies at Carlisle after graduating as a member of the class of 1917. He may have had the experience of leading the team in spring practice but never in an actual game. The school was closed before football season and converted into a hospital to treat soldiers wounded in WWI.

John Flinchum, with ball;
Cumberland County Historical Society, Carlisle, PA

John Flinchum in school
uniform; *Cumberland County
Historical Society, Carlisle, PA*

Flinchum returned to Oklahoma where he married and had two children. Beginning in 1927, he was employed by the Indian Territory Illuminating Oil Company (ITIO) until his death, except for 1931 and 1932 when he was a patrolman and scout car officer for the Oklahoma City Police Department.

In February 1936, he was overcome by gas while working in a cellar in the oil fields. His brother, James M. Flinchum, believed that the gas caused pneumonia, which proved fatal. John, only 38, left behind a wife, Emily, a son, John B. Jr., and a daughter, Lorena Katherine. John's life on the oil fields was cut short as had been his football career with the closing of the Carlisle Indian School.

Name: John B. Flinchum   **Nickname:**
DOB: 8/7/1897   **Height:**
Weight: **Age:**
Tribe: Choctaw   **Home:** Gerty County, Indian Territory
Parents: James Samuel Washington Flinchum, white rancher; Julia Turnbull Flinchum, half-blood Choctaw
Early Schooling: Hughes County, OK public school
Later Schooling:
Honors:

Emil and Pete Hauser

Emil H. Hauser and Herman Peter Hauser were born at Fort Reno on the Cheyenne – Arapaho reservation in Indian Territory (present day Oklahoma) to a white army sergeant father of German extraction, Herman Hauser, and a full-blood Cheyenne mother, Amy Hauser. Herman Hauser, their father, had died and their mother married Waldo Reed in the 1895-97 timeframe. Their mother died before 1908. The boys first attended the Mennonite-operated Kriebel Farm School, an orphanage and Indian school, in Halstead, Kansas; then they went to Haskell Institute. It was at Haskell that they really started playing football. In 1904, with Pete at right end and Emil at left tackle, Haskell beat Kansas, Missouri, Texas and Nebraska. Their record and reputation made the match-up against Carlisle at the St. Louis World's Fair a natural, or so it would seem. The Carlisle Indians beat Haskell's Fightin' Indians 38-4, providing the Hauser brothers, along with six teammates, ample reason to transfer East as soon as they could.

Emil, almost 20 or 23, depending on the source, arrived at Carlisle without much ado in September of 1906 after his enrollment period at Haskell had expired. At Carlisle, he studied in the business department and didn't work in a trade shop. Soon he became the starting left tackle on the varsity football team and learned Pop Warner's new offense from Bemus Pierce and Frank Hudson. By the fifth game of the season, Emil was using his preferred name, Wauseka. He weighed 173 pounds, large by Carlisle standards, but the Harvard tackle he played opposite, although only 20 years old, weighed 193 pounds. Such weight deficits were expected for the Indians when they played the better teams. Wauseka held up his side of the line and the team had a good season.

In the spring, Wauseka caught for the baseball team and played a little summer ball for the Hagerstown, Maryland team. That summer a Hagerstown paper reported, "Admirers of baseball and particularly those in Hagerstown will learn with regret that Hauser, the big Indian catcher, who has been doing such splendid work for the local team, is going to get out of the game here.

Emil Hauser (Wauseka);
*Cumberland County
Historical Society, Carlisle, PA*

Name: Emil H. Hauser **Nickname:** Wauseka
DOB: 11/22/1886 **Height:** 5'9"
Weight: 180 **Age:** 23
Tribe: Cheyenne **Home:** Cheyenne-Arapaho reservation, OK
Parents: Herman Hauser, white army sergeant; Amy Hauser, Cheyenne
Early Schooling: Halstead School; Haskell Institute
Later Schooling: Oregon Agricultural College
Honors: American Indian Athletic Hall of Fame, 1971

He will go to Carlisle school to spend a few days and then go to Oklahoma to take possession of some valuable land he has inherited. He will devote his time to looking after his interests and expects to return to Carlisle in the fall."

After spending some time at home recruiting, he brought back with him his brother, Pete Hauser, and Mike Balenti's brother, John. Pete's reputation preceded him.

A newspaper article citing friends of Arthur Jardine, reputed to have been a star basketball player at Carlisle before Hauser's arrival, as the source, described Pete Hauser's toughness on the basketball court. When Pete was still enrolled at Haskell Institute around the turn of the last century, he played in a game played against Carlisle:

> "...[Hauser] was said to be a lad of only sixteen years, while Jardine was ten years his senior, Hauser guarded Jardine, and as the Indians played an unusually rough game many fouls were called upon them, Hauser being one of the worst offenders. Every time he fouled Jardine the latter scored the point by tossing the ball into the net. Slowly the desire to go on the warpath began to arouse itself within the dusky one.
>
> "'Throw another basket like that and I'll split you open!' hissed Pete into Jardine's ear as the crowd yelled for more gore.

Pete Hauser;
*Cumberland County
Historical Society,
Carlisle, PA*

Name:	Herman Peter Hauser	**Nickname:**	
DOB:	6/10/1887	**Height:**	5'9"
Weight:	177	**Age:**	21
Tribe:	Cheyenne	**Home:**	Cheyenne-Arapaho reservation, OK
Parents:	Herman Hauser, white army sergeant; Amy Hauser, Cheyenne		
Early Schooling:	Halstead School; Haskell Institute		
Later Schooling:			
Honors:	American Indian Athletic Hall of Fame, 1971		

"Jardine didn't see any tommyhawks hanging on Hauser, but he was the least bit scared and told Berggren about it. 'Berggy' laughed and took it as a joke. The captain decided to do the same, but he missed the first free toss after that, presumably from nervousness. Try as he would to steady himself, Jardine threw only one or two of the remaining fouls because of the hypnotic words which the Indian hissed into his ear."

The Hausers and Balentis were soon out practicing football. Carlisle's 1907 starting line-up boasted two Hausers, Emil at left tackle and Pete at fullback. This team was Carlisle's first to beat Harvard, first to have two wins over Big Four teams, and the first to have a one-loss season. Pete and Emil were significant parts of that.

The last game of the season was against what Amos Alonzo Stagg considered his finest Chicago Maroon team, and Carlisle's big ground gainer and passer, Frank Mt. Pleasant, was out with a broken thumb. So, the passing duties fell to the fullback, Pete Hauser. "Houser [sic] Was The Star," began the section of the article about the game in which Pete's play was discussed. It went on, "Houser, [sic] in fact was a whole team in himself. Backed up by impregnable interference, he carried the ball two-thirds of the time in the Indian attack and seldom failed to gain ground.... Houser's [sic] best work, however, was with his toe. Three times he negotiated goals from placement with Balenti holding the ball. As many more attempts were missed but mainly because Doseff, who was the only Chicago lineman to outplay his opponent, managed to wriggle through in time to hurry the kick."

Carlisle also scored a touchdown on a forward pass. Chicago was double and triple-teaming end Albert Exendine and William Gardner to keep them from going downfield to catch passes, so Ex came up with a plan. Between plays, he told Pete Hauser to hold onto the ball as long as he could to give him time to get downfield. When the play got underway, Ex ran out of bounds and, as expected, the defenders let him go. He ran behind the Chicago bench, downfield along the sidelines, then back onto the field and downfield as fast as he could to intercept the ball that Pete arched his way. With no defender in sight he caught the ball easily and scored a touchdown. Stagg was furious and protested to no avail. (The rules were changed during the offseason to disallow a player from returning to the field of play during a play after leaving it.) This was a victory that Pop Warner savored the rest of his life, and Pete Hauser and Exendine handed it to him on a platter. Wauseka was elected captain for 1908. Both Caspar Whitney and Walter Camp named Pete to their All America teams – to Whitney's first team and Camp's second. Not a bad fall for the Hausers.

The 1908 winter wasn't nearly as good. Pete Hauser missed a few weeks of class while he was in the hospital with a wrenched back. He most likely incurred that injury playing basketball. His classmates missed him in the classroom and on the basketball court.

Pete graduated in the spring and enrolled for graduate study in the Commercial Course. That spring, Wauseka played catcher again on the school's baseball team. After a summer away, possibly playing baseball, they returned to Carlisle in September to prepare for the upcoming season. Wauseka showed

Pete Hauser with ball against Chicago, 1907; *Chicago History Museum*

his leadership abilities while Pete demonstrated his versatility by shifting from fullback to right end. With Exendine and Gardner no longer playing, two huge voids needed to be filled at the end positions. Because there were plenty of talented backfield men at the time, Pete could serve the team better by playing at end. Both brothers got high marks for the season as players but no mention from Walter Camp. The 10-2-1 record during what some might consider a rebuilding year was evidence of Wauseka's leadership.

An incident associated with the Penn game illustrates how the football team's fame had spread. Prior to the game, students and school employees making the trip were taken to Gimbels where the school band gave a short concert before lunch. Gimbels prepared a meal specially for the Carlisle contingent. "The menu consisted of: Vegetable soup, a la Warner; Browned potatoes, touchdown fashion; fried oysters, Mt. Pleasant style; Wauseka pie with ice cream."

Apparently Wauseka had a problem with punctuality because in February *The Arrow* reported, "Emil Hauser, 'Wauseka,' has bought an alarm clock. He intends to follow Franklin's motto: 'Early to bed and early to rise,' etc." Pete became active in out-of-class (extracurricular) activities including the Invincible Debating Society. Both played on the basketball team. In the spring Wauseka appears to have sat out the baseball season. Pete pitched and played first base. As a hitter, you could say he was a good pitcher.

Ex-Captain Wauseka was at his usual position, tackle, for 1909 and Hauser was back at fullback. The team's record was only 8-3-1, but the Hauser brothers shone. So potent a weapon was Pete that, prior to the Penn game, *The Carlisle Arrow* ran a limerick about him that also made fun of the way the school's name was spelled:

Advice to Penn in Limerick Style:
Pete Hauser, full back at Carlisle.
Has the power Penn's feelings to risle.
With a stoical grunt,
He can tackle or punt,
And they'll never get next to his stysle.

The *St. Louis Republic* saw it this way: "Pete Hauser and his brother, Wauseka, and Germain, were the stonewall combination of the Indian line. Hauser was also a grizzly, on defense, He tore tremendous holes in the St. Louis line every time he hit the bull's eye. Hauser took nearly all the forward passes handled by Libby."

Wauseka, as captain of the basketball team, gave a short talk at the annual Athletic Association Awards Ceremony in early 1910. He and Fanny Keokuk later won a prize in the dance contest for the two-step. He didn't play on the school baseball team that spring because he, William Garlow and William Newashe played for the Harrisburg League Team that summer. They did, however, find time to attend the occasional Saturday night social at the school. Pete stuck closer to school that spring and participated in a variety of activities, including writing articles for the school paper, reading his essay to the YMCA meeting, holding an office with the YMCA, welcoming guests to the annual athletic banquet, co-authoring an essay on 'Practical Business Training' with Joe Libby and presenting it as part of graduation exercises and, of course, graduating upon completion of his post-graduate course in business.

Pete again pitched for the school's baseball team while Wauseka played baseball for a Harrisburg minor league team. Carlisle won the state inter-scholastic track and field meet for the third straight year with Hauser's help. According to *The Arrow*, "Hauser sprang a surprise by winning the discus throw and taking fourth place in the shot put." Wauseka got some positive press as well: "Hauser, the Carlisle Indian catcher for Harrisburg, played well in Saturday's game with Scranton. In an account it is said: 'The work of Hauser, the Carlisle Indian, was an interesting feature. His throwing was of the gilt-edge order. His part in a double play was the fastest kind of field-ing.'" While Emil played baseball for Harrisburg, Pete spent his vacation at home in Oklahoma. At summer's end he returned to Carlisle, bringing their sister, Anna, with him. It was a matter of opinion as to who were tougher, the Hauser boys or the Hauser girls, as both established reputations at Carlisle.

Warner gave Pete Hauser a prize of dubious value after being elected captain: a 15-game schedule. The Indians did not return to school in fighting form for the season ahead. The entire season was marred by injuries that often result when players are not in top condition. Another contributing factor was that the entire schedule was squeezed into a period lasting only little more than two months. All were regular season games as their schedule ended with the traditional Thanksgiving game against Brown. Players simply had too little time to heal between games. Mercifully, Western Maryland canceled, eliminating one game.

Since they were too injured to play, Warner charged former captain Antonio Lubo and Wauseka with the coaching of the third team and the Reserves, respectively. The second team, usually called the Hotshots, called themselves Wauseka's Braves that year.

Pete shone that year; against Bucknell he kicked a 45-yard field goal and electrified the crowd with a 50-yard touchdown run. He was even hurt for some games, playing either at diminished capacity or not at all. Still he was considered for some All America teams but not by Walter Camp. Pete returned home to Pawhuska, Oklahoma after the season ended.

Wauseka did not confine himself to the football field that school year. He served as President of the Bachelors' Club and entertained the membership by telling a thrilling ghost story at one meeting. He served as toastmaster for the

Commercial Department graduation dance. Over the winter, he coached the basketball team and in April assisted Warner with Carlisle's first ever spring football practice. By May, Pete was in Atlanta working with Wahoo at Spalding Brothers. He scored well on a civil service test and looked forward to getting a government job as a clerk. Emil was also in Atlanta as he and Mike Balenti had signed with the Atlanta baseball team for that summer.

The Hauser brothers' careers at Carlisle ended and their enrollments were completed. Emil's returned student report listed both his character and disposition as being very good and recommended him for positions available in government service: disciplinarian, office assistant and athletic director. Pete's work with the new football players paid off in spades the next year. That fall he assisted John Heisman with the Georgia Tech Yellowjackets in Atlanta. Wauseka wrote that he spent the summer on the Pacific Coast and hoped to visit Carlisle in the fall. That visit appears to have not taken place as he wrote in January 1912 that he was visiting his sister, Louisa, in Siletz, Oregon.

In the fall of 1912, Pete Hauser, now 25 or 28, was in Calumet, Oklahoma farming his allotment. Emil enrolled at Oregon Agricultural College (today's Oregon State University) October 1 and went out for football. The next day's *O.A.C. Barometer* had an article about the team and devoted most of a paragraph to Emil, or "Amy," as it said his friends called him. He was to play fullback, although he was 15 pounds overweight. The reporter thought Coach Sam Dolan would have no trouble trimming the fat. The team beat the alumni team and lost to Multnomah Athletic Club, an independent team from Portland. Johnny Bender, head coach of O. A. C.'s next opponent, Washington State College, challenged Emil Hauser's amateur status. A controversy ensued which culminated in a newspaper article that was circulated around the country:

"INDIAN A PROFESSIONAL

"Spokane. Wash, Nov. 8.—The question of the eligibility of Emil Hauser, the big Indian half back of the Oregon Agricultural College, which has excited wide discussion in Northwest conference circles, apparently was settled today by the receipt here of communications from Secretary Farrell of the minor association of baseball leagues, and Manager Baker of the Harrisburg, Pa., team, stating that Hauser had been under contract to and played with the Harrisburg team in 1910 at a salary of $175 a month."

Emil withdrew from college on November 21. In February 1913, he married former Carlisle student Dolly Stone in Tutuilla, Oregon. After a visit with his sister where she worked at the Siletz Reservation, the couple were to engage in farming near El Reno, Oklahoma. However, they were soon back in Oregon, if they ever left, because their children were born there. The January 7, 1916 edition of *The Carlisle Arrow* included a birth announcement in the form of a poem from the E. H. Hausers. Emil Wauseka Hauser was born on December 19, 1915. By 1920, when they were at Salem Indian School (today's Chemawa Indian School), Emil and Dolly also had a daughter, Mary Emily. Emil was employed as a night watchman and coached football at times. In 1923, son Peter Herman Hauser was born.

Pete Hauser served in the army at Fort McArthur, Texas during WWI and became active in the American Legion afterwards. He remained more active in athletics than did his brother. Pete drew $150 a month umpiring minor league baseball in Oklahoma during the 1920s. For two falls in the early 1920s, he coached the independent Hominy Indians to undefeated seasons, barnstorming across the Midwest and playing other independent football teams in the region.

In 1931, Knute Rockne wrote a syndicated column in which he recalled watching Pete Hauser play nearly a quarter century earlier:

> "…I saw this same [Wally] Steffens, who had become one of the greatest quarterbacks and field generals under Stagg of Chicago. In this game he was stopped dead by as great a pair of ends as ever played together on a football team. I refer to the Araphohoe [sic] Gardner and Exendine, who were playing for Pop Warner at Carlisle. What a delight it was to see these two men work. Their down-the-field play under Pete Hauser's punts was as fine as I've ever seen - a thing of beauty. It was so good, in fact, that in the second half Stagg changed his tactics against Pete Hauser's kicking, and put three men on each of the ends to prevent the Indian pair going down to cover the kick. The wiry Hauser was alert. The next time he kicked he stood there with the ball for at least four seconds, while in the meantime Gardner and Exendine had broken loose and streaked down the field with Chief Afraid-of-a-Bear and Lone Star, when Hauser proceeded deliberately to boot the ban his usual sixty yards.
>
> **"Deceitful Red Men**
>
> "It was in this game I saw Pete Hauser rise up behind center and mop his forehead with a sort of half yawn. The mop was just half finished and the yawn half completed when center snapped the ball and through the line went Hauser for eight yards. The Chicago line had relaxed when they saw Hauser yawning and wiping his forehead.
>
> "Bret Harte tells us about the dark ways and vain tricks of the heathen Chinee [sic], but in football laurels for cunning go to the Indians."

Peter Hauser died in a freak automobile accident in the early morning hours of July 21, 1935 on Bartlesville Road between Bartlesville and Pawhuska, Oklahoma. He was living with Chauncey Archiquette and his wife on the Osage Reservation and employed by the Indian Emergency Conservation Work at that time. He, Chauncey and George Frass were returning from a baseball game in Bartlesville when they had a flat tire. Pete was tightening the lug nuts when a car driven by a young woman struck and killed him.

Honorary pallbearers at his Catholic funeral with full American Legion rites included Pop Warner, Jim Thorpe, Albert Exendine, William LaBadie, Chauncey Archiquette, George Beaulieu, Herbert Fallis, Walter Mathews, John B. McGillis and Eddie Moore. Emil Hauser died on May 19, 1941 of a heart attack in Salem, Oregon, where he had lived for 27 years. After writing this chapter, the author learned that Mike Balenti's son heard Emil Hauser state that he had created his Wauseka name as a joke and that it wasn't his Cheyenne name as many believe.

Carlisle football players pose in 1903 Thomas Rear Entrance automobile at Union Station in St. Louis, 1908. From left to right: Little Boy, Emil Hauser (Wauseka), Mike Balenti, Fritz Hendricks, unknown; *Cecilia Balenti-Moddelmog*

Oscar Hunt

Oscar Hunt flashed through Carlisle much like a comet crosses the night sky. He appeared suddenly, made quite a splash, and disappeared abruptly. Knowledge of this enigma's ancestors is necessary to have any sense at all of who he was.

Chief Splitlog (To-oo-troon-too-ra), a Royalist, distinguished himself in battles against General "Mad" Anthony Wayne during Pontiac's Rebellion and in the War of 1812. The Wyandots he led were allied with the British. He died shortly after war but not before siring a son known to posterity as Mathias (sometimes called Matthew) Splitlog. The boy is believed to have been born around 1813, either in Canada or in New York (family and census acounts vary). He relocated to Ohio when he was three years old and lived there with his mother's people, the Cayugas. Other stories of his origins place his birth in New York, attribute his parentage to be French-Canadian, or say that he was stolen by Indians and reared by Wyandots in Ohio.

The Wyandots, called Hurons by the French, were decimated by disease and war, first with neighboring tribes who pushed them westward from the St. Lawrence River to Niagara Falls to Lake Huron. War with the Americans left fragments of the tribe in areas of Canada, Michigan and Ohio. As a young man, Mathias lived near Sandusky, Ohio among the Wyandots who settled in

Name: Oscar J. Hunt **Nickname:**
DOB: August 1881 **Height:** 5'10"
Weight: 183 **Age:** 21
Tribe: Seneca **Home:** Cayuga Springs, OK
Parents: William Hunt, Seneca; Maggie Splitlog Hunt, Wyandot
Early Schooling: St. Mary's of the Quapaws mission school, possibly; Haskell Institute
Later Schooling:
Honors:

that place. It was there that he married Eliza Barnett by tribal marriage. Chief Splitlog had converted to Catholicism but neither he nor his family practiced the religion with any regularity. However, he had little Mathias baptised as an infant.

In 1842, the Wyandots sold their Michigan and Ohio holdings to the government for about $127,000 and began the migration west to Kansas. After the 148,110 acres along the Neosho River offered by the government were rejected as being too remote, tribal leaders negotiated the purchase of 39 sections (square miles) of land from the eastern edge of the Delaware reserve for what the Wyandots considered an exhorbitant price, $48,000. This land was fortuitously located between the Kansas and Missouri Rivers adjacent to the Missouri state line opposite Kansas City. The Delawares felt a moral obligation to sell them the land because the Wyandots had sold them land in 1640.

Mathias Splitlog was a visionary. Although he was illiterate, he was able to speak seven languages and was a mechanical genius. He and Eliza selected land in the Kansas River bottoms and built a log home on a hill overlooking their lands. There, they raised their six children and begin their business empire. First, he built a grist mill and, later, a sawmill, both of which were powered by steam.

1906 Carlisle Football Team. Oscar Hunt is on the far left end of the second row. *Research Division of the Oklahoma Historical Society*

As Kansas City, Missouri expanded into Kansas in the mid-1850s, the Wyandot land became quite valuable. Aware that whites considered their land to be too valuable to allow them to keep, the Wyandots discarded their treaty and tribal rights to become citizens with all the rights and immunities that come with that status, including the right to own and sell land. White men began offering considerable sums of money for Splitlog's land. He reputedly responded, "Good for you, good for me" when rejecting one such offer. Many of his neighbors did sell and moved to Indian Territory. Needing a home, Wyandot leaders prevailed on the Senecas to give them 30,000 acres along the northern edge of their reservation in the Quapaw Agency located in the northeastern corner of Oklahoma. Long before that, the Wyandots had given the Senecas 40,000 acres of land along the Sandusky River in Ohio. Before long, Mathias's friends invited him to join them on their new land. Knowing the value of his land, he stayed put.

Mathias had the ability to figure out how a piece of machinery was constructed just by studying it in operation. In 1860, after seeing riverboats in action, he designed and built one of his own to carry freight to the settlements along the Missouri River. Reputedly, he was the only person able to operate its unique controls. Soon, the Civil War engulfed the area, pressing Mathias and his steamboat into service for the Union army, with Splitlog as its engineer. While transporting troops, the boat was captured near Lexington, Missouri. Mathias was eventually released on parole and walked home.

In 1874, Mathias sold some of his Kansas land, including his home at present-day Barnett and Tauromee Avenues and 4th and 5th Streets in Kansas City. He also sold three acres that became the site of St. Mary's Church to Father Anton Kuhle for $800. Needing a place to live, he looked at the wooded hills and clear running streams of the Seneca lands and chose a site near the Grand and Cowskin Rivers on which was a large spring. He named the spring and the town he founded in remembrance of his mother's tribe and a boat he had owned as a young man, "Cayuga Springs."

As after his previous move, Mathias's seized upon the opportunities that he saw in front of him. He first built a sawmill to process the timber on his land. Again, he built a grist mill to grind grain into such things as flour and cornmeal. He also established a general store and operated a ferry to transport his goods and machinery across the river. After building a home for his family, Splitlog built a three-story factory to build buggies, hacks and coffins, for which seasoned walnut was always on hand. Although not a participant himself, he made a room above the general store available for religious meetings. His wife, Eliza, became a devout Quaker and attended their meetings above the store. There being no public schools in the area, Mathias started a subscription school and furnished a building for its use. The teacher collected her salary from tuition payments made by the students. A former student told *The Daily Oklahoman* in 1940 that she recalled paying a nickel a day for her instruction.

Contrary to frontier building traditions, Cayuga Springs' structures were of substantial construction replete with gingerbread and cupolas in the then-current Victorian style. Family buildings were often enclosed by white board fences. The town was described as a gem in the wilderness of Indian country.

Realizing that Cayuga lacked a railroad connection to become a booming town, Splitlog was predisposed to see the possibilities when word of assays of gold and silver samples in nearby Missouri spread around the area like wildfire. He and others quickly formed a mining company and began construction of the Splitlog Line, a railroad that ran from Joplin to Neosho and, eventually, to Splitlog, Missouri. The $3,000,000 investment proved to be fool's gold because the ore samples were a fraud. Mathias lost a fortune but was not defeated.

Splitlog was adopted by the Senecas among whom he lived and employed and served as an emissary for them. That he was one of the few people who had the time and money to travel to Washington to conduct tribal business was surely a factor in his selection. Some objected, claiming that he was a white man and shouldn't have been adopted into the tribe. His adoption was likely influenced by a $500 payment he made to a chief of the Senecas.

Although baptised as a baby, he had never been a practicing Catholic. The arrival of a young priest, Father William Ketcham, changed that. He converted Eliza to Catholicism and baptised twelve Splitlogs in his five-year tenure. Priests and Bishops visited Cayuga periodically. Father Versavel was a favorite of Mathias because he could converse with him in French. Splitlog himself was confirmed after driving 40 miles through bad late-November weather. The exact sequence isn't clear but, about the time that Eliza contracted incurable cancer, Mathias started to build the Cayuga Church. The ornate limestone church that still survives wasn't completed when Eliza became gravely ill. A legend surrounds her death:

The family felt it was useless to call the priest because he was over 100 miles away and they were experiencing bad weather. Also, they knew that, because it was a Saturday, Father Ketcham would be on his way from Muskogee to Vinita to say mass the next day. However, a telegram awaited him when he arrived at Vinita on Saturday afternoon. It stated, "Come at once. My wife is dying. M. Splitlog." The priest hired a livery rig and headed for Cayuga in a pouring rain. The driver got lost in a large field causing them to arrive at the river at midnight, far too late to catch the ferry. However, the ferryman was at the river. He had been unable to sleep and, for reasons unknown to him, walked down to the ferry. His sleeplessness enabled Father Ketcham to make it to Cayuga in time to administer the last rites to Eliza before she died. No family member sent the telegram. The telegraph operator had never seen the well-dressed stranger who sent the message before or since. The mystery remains.

Mathias didn't live many years after the death of his wife and only a couple of months after the church was completed. He died in 1897 of pneumonia in Washington while on tribal business. He was buried beside his wife in the Cayuga churchyard.

Oscar J. Hunt

Mathias's daughter, Margaret "Maggie," married William Hunt, Seneca, and lived in New York with him. They had a son, Oscar, in 1881 but Maggie died soon afterward. Oscar was listed as ward or grandson of Mathias Splitlog on censuses beginning in 1885. It appears that Oscar lived with his grandparents until their deaths. He probably attended school as a youngster, either at the mission or at the subscription school. In 1886, Splitlog was certified as guardian of Oscar's share of the Seneca annuity roll. This may have been a step in establishing his grandson as an heir to his estate. Only one of his children outlived him after his death in 1897, so grandchildren were probably in line to receive substantial shares of his estate. In 1898, Oscar went to Haskell Institute in Lawrence, Kansas where he stayed for four years. In 1898, Oscar's father's name appeared on the census for the first time. It was also there in 1899. After he turned 18, Oscar was listed by himself.

While at Haskell, Oscar surely played on the athletic teams. His physical size made him a prime candidate for a line position on the football team. What he did after leaving Haskell in 1902 is not known. Perhaps, he farmed his land.

The September 1, 1905 edition of *The Arrow* reported on recent happenings around Oscar's home:

> Indians are living in "grand style" on the Seneca Reservation. During the past three weeks a hundred dollar per capita payment has been made there. Now everything is new. Gaily prancing teams are seen drawing highly polished vehicles over the settlement. The Indians are having a grand celebration over the present outcome of the long looked for Kansas Claim. But let us hope that they will soon realize the fact that it will not always be thus and that they should save a little of what they are receiving from the good government.

This makes Splitlog's certification of Oscar's share of the Seneca annuity clearer.

A small item in the September 15, 1905 edition of *The Arrow* announced, "William Gardner returned last Wednesday bringing with him Oscar Hunt from Oklahoma." A handwritten note on the reverse of Oscar's student card supports that claim: "Came with Wm Gardner from Quapaw Agency in Sept 1905." No reason was given for Gardner's trip to Oklahoma. Hunt's student card contained little more than the dates he arrived, September 20 in this case, and the dates he departed. One card did state that he enrolled in the commercial course. Participation in that course implied significant prior schooling.

The September 29 issue of *The Arrow* lists Oscar Hunt as being in the line-up for the football team's first game of the season against the Pennsylvania Railroad YMCA team from Columbia, Pennsylvania. He played center in the second half of this blowout. It was rare for a new student to make the Carlisle varsity team, let alone get into a game within days of arriving on campus. Then as now, interior linemen got little press, particularly if they didn't kick, punt or occasionally carry the ball as some did.

Oscar continued as second-string center, getting to play in the second halves of games. But against Virginia, he started and played the entire game, possibly due to another player's injury. Hunt moved back to the second team for the Dickinson College game and continued that scenario against Penn. He came in for Charles Dillon at left guard during the Harvard game. Perhaps Dillon was injured and Hunt was the best available substitute even though he was playing out of position. He didn't get into the victory over Army but started against Massillon four days later. Three days after that mud game, Oscar backed up Saunooke at center against Cincinnati. Whether he played against Canton is not known. Oscar substituted at center again in the last two games of the season against Washington & Jefferson College and Georgetown. Not bad for a first-year player. He surely played in enough games to earn his letter. Unfortunately, centers generally get mentioned in game coverage only when they foul up. Apparently, he didn't. Five days after the season ended, Hunt departed for home. The reason stated for his leaving was "Self supporting." A wire service piece that circulated around the country explained how he could be considered to be self supporting:

Millionaire Indian

Oscar Hunt, one of the Carlisle football team, is an Indian millionaire. He is from Oklahoma and has been at Carlisle for some months. When the government bought land from the Indians, the Hunt family had a great deal to sell and Oscar found himself owner of seven figures. His teammates call him "Heap Big Money Chief, Head of the Spondulix." He is studiously inclined and off the gridiron wears glasses.

It is more likely that Oscar's fortune came from Mathias Splitlog than from his father, but it is not impossible that his father was also wealthy.

Oscar returned to Carlisle on September 18, 1906 and was in the starting line-up at center in the first game of the season against Villanova. He remained there throughout the season except in the Cincinnati game, when his backup, Nikifer Schouchuk, who was often substituted for Hunt later in the games, played the entire game. He left Carlisle on December 7, 1906. The reason recorded for his departure was "Termination football season." Oscar returned home and apparently worked on his farm until tragedy struck.

Some press clippings from the Miami, Oklahoma *Record-Herald* and the *Afton Climax* from March and April of 1907 help shed light on what happened. The first one, dated March 1, 1907, in its entirety said, "Oscar Hunt is under arrest for the killing of Joe Wolfenberger in the Seneca nation last Saturday night." Two weeks later, the *Afton Climax* reported on Oscar's preliminary hearing after which he was released on $1,000 bond, which he furnished. None of the witnesses who had been with Hunt and Wolfenberger on that binge in Tiff City, could remember the details of the drunken fight on the way home that left Wolfenberger dead.

That day's *Record-Herald* provided more detail. The farmers were returning to the Seneca Nation from Tiff City, Missouri "...in inebriated condition when they stopped in a hollow to camp and complete their carousal." Oscar Hunt was bound over to the next federal grand jury and "...in the meantime Hunt will have time to look over his situation in the innermost depths of the Vinita jail."

Two weeks after that, the *Afton Climax* blared, "Oscar Hunt Gone Insane." Perhaps he had probed his innermost depths of his being, reflected upon what he may have done and couldn't handle having killed someone while drunk. So distraught was he that, "It is reported that it takes several men to hold him and it is probable that he will be taken to some asylum soon, should his condition not improve." He was released on bail to go to his home near Cayuga.

The final episode came two weeks later when the *Record-Herald* reported that Oscar Hunt had died. *The Arrow* of April 5 placed the cause of his untimely death on natural causes: "He was taken with a congestive chill and, after four days of delirium, died..."

W. G. Thompson, who had been reorganized out of a job by Major Mercer the previous summer, wrote Dr. Carlos Montezuma that Hunt had committed suicide while awaiting trial for murder. Oklahoma didn't issue death certificates at that time, so the cause of his death may never be known. From what little we know of Oscar Hunt, it is hard to tell much about his tragic end. His mother apparently died shortly after his birth and his father disappeared from his life until he was almost grown. His grandparents were very old to be raising a child and his grandfather was probably so busy with his many business and tribal responsibilities that he had little time left for the boy. Oscar may have felt adrift. And ever-present alcohol was just waiting to destroy another soul.

Victor Murat Kelley

Choc or Choctaw

"But the longest run in football history is claimed by Texas A&M. Victor M. (Choc) Kelley, who played at A&M in 1905-6-7, at Carlisle in 1908 and back at A&M in 1909, made the great run against Louisiana State. He went back and forth across the field four times, then sprinted 65 yards for a touchdown. The entire run was set at 267 yards. It would have been 277 had not Kelley gone 10 yards back of the line of scrimmage to begin his maneuver."

Harold V. Ratcliff
Southwest Conference historian

Victor Kelley was born on October 31, 1886 near Wheelock, in Indian Territory that later became part of the state of Oklahoma. It is believed that he was the son of a Scots-Irish father, J. J. Kelley, and a mother of French-Indian descent, probably Choctaw. Little is known about Kelley's early schooling, and he was accused of having played football before 1904 when he was second string quarterback at Texas A & M. The most likely place was at Presbyterian College in Durant, Oklahoma where he was reputed to have played halfback and quarterback in successive seasons. In 1905, he became a starter for the Farmers and made the most of it over the next three years.

Name: Victor Murat Kelley	**Nickname:** Choc or Choctaw
DOB: 10/31/1886	**Height:** 5'6"
Weight: 133	**Age:** 20
Tribe: Choctaw	**Home:** Wheelock, OK
Parents: J. J. Kelley, Scots-Irish; mother's name unknown, Choctaw	
Early Schooling: Presbyterian College; Texas A & M	
Later Schooling: Dickinson School of Law; Texas A & M	
Honors:	

Victor Kelley (right), head coach, and Gus Welch, assistant, 1915; *Fred Wardecker*

Choc may have also had ambitions as a newsman because the June 9, 1908 edition of *The San Antonio Light* carried a large piece under his byline on page 14. A front-page article reported that Texas A & M President Harrington had been charged with 13 offenses by the college's alumni association, and the school's board of trustees was to hear them that afternoon. Kelley's piece went into detail about the charges that covered, "… everything from using swear words to not being 'hep' to the games of the students, and one specification particularly sets forth that the president of the college permitted a quantity of the most commonly sold article that comes in bottles and barrels to be brought onto campus." Kelley went on to write, "… he denies the charges, saying that the kicks are registered by a bunch of knockers." Harrington was exonerated on June 24. It is not known if things in College Station had gotten too hot for Choc or if this tempest was unrelated to Kelley's personal situation. Regardless, Choc left town.

Victor, or Choc as he was better known, arrived in Carlisle on September 10, 1908. Quarterback was Kelley's natural position, and being so small, both in height and weight, made playing out of position on a team as talented as Carlisle's an impossibility. You see, Mike Balenti was the starting quarterback in 1908 and, after playing behind Frank Mt. Pleasant for three years, he wasn't going to allow himself to be easily unseated. Kelley got significant playing time and generated positive press for himself, but he did not log enough playing time to letter. The year wasn't a complete bust, though, because he learned the Warner System, gained a national reputation, and honed his legal skills while also attending Dickinson School of Law.

Kelley returned to College Station the next fall, bringing Mike Balenti with him. It had previously been insinuated that Carlisle and A & M were

Victor Kelley; *Texas A & M University*

not the only places Kelley had played, and upon his return someone filed a formal complaint. Ratliff recalled: "In 1909 Baylor charged that Kelley had admitted that he had performed under an assumed name, thus should be ineligible. Baylor also contended that Mike Balenti, who joined the A & M team in 1909 with Kelley, had played professional baseball in the Western Association. Baylor showed an affidavit to prove it. However, Kelley and Balenti were never ruled out."

A combination of the return of Kelley, the addition of Balenti, and the promotion of Charlie Moran to head coach improved A & M's fortunes. The Farmers went 7-0-1 and defeated arch-rival Texas for the first time since 1902. Not only did they beat the Longhorns, but the Aggies shut them out twice. It was a very good year, indeed. Choc was named All-Southwestern quarterback after A & M captured the unofficial team crown.

It's not clear what Kelley did after completing his playing career at A & M. Carlisle records indicate that he was back at home in Durant, Oklahoma. In 1913, Carlisle records had him working as a clerk for the Union Agency, established in 1875 for the Five Civilized Tribes in Muskogee, Oklahoma. By the next year, he appears to have started working for the Great Southern Life Insurance Company out of Durant, Oklahoma. Carlisle publications had him practicing law and preparing teams across the Southwest for big games. Newspaper accounts also have him back in football in Durant in 1914 as head coach of the Northeastern Oklahoma Normal School eleven. How many years he coached in Durant is not known, but it is clear that he wasn't back there in 1915.

After what he considered a disastrous season and seeing little hope of improvement, given the prevailing policies regarding the Indian school,

Pop Warner resigned his position of athletic director at Carlisle at the end of the 1914 football season. Major decisions regarding the athletic program were no longer being made at the school but, rather at the highest levels of the Department of Indian Affairs in Washington, DC. Angel DeCora, the head of the Native Art Department, was the only other person known to be hired directly by the commissioner prior to that. Several people applied for the open head coaching position, including some former players with solid coaching credentials. In April, the following appeared in newspapers across the country:

REDSKINS ARE PLEASED

"Appointment of Victor M. Kelley as football coach at Carlisle, as announced by Cato Sells, commissioner of Indian affairs, was a source of great delight to the lovers of' the game in Texas, where Kelley, familiarly called 'Choc.' matriculated in the Agricultural and Mechanical college after three years at Carlisle, and put that institution on the gridiron map.

"Glen Warner's successor holds a record as a quarterback. His work at Carlisle compares favorably with that of Thorpe, Welsh [sic], Mount Pleasant, Exendine, Calac and other stars. But Kelley thought more of his ambition to become a lawyer than a hero on the football field. Today he is said to be one of the best Indian lawyers in the state of Oklahoma and is a credit to the Cherokee [sic] tribe.

"However, he has in his spare moments devoted much of his time in the inner workings of football, and his friends are enthusiastic in the belief that he would make good at Carlisle."

The government's spin machine was apparently more interested in hyping its choice than in getting the details right. Gus Welch's contention that the choice of Kelley as coach was politically motivated was made more plausible by the government's actions.

On May 17, 1915, he wrote Carlisle asking when he should start his new job and for information about accommodations for his family, as he was then married and had a son. Superintendent Lipps responded and apologized for the delay in his response due to commencement responsibilities. Lipps informed him that, because his appointment was only for football season, he would not be required to report before September 1. Lipps also informed him that the house Warner formerly occupied was now the home of Harvey Meyer, the new director of athletics, but a room would be made available on campus for him and his family. Lipps also told him that he would be eligible to board at the Teachers' Club for a membership fee of $5 per person and a monthly fee of $13.50 to $15.00 each person. Oscar Lipps may not have been very pleased that Commissioner Sells had pulled rank in selecting the new football coach, something that would explain the cool reception Kelley received.

Victor "Choc" Kelley and Grantland Rice; *Mike Moran*

Victor Kelley wrote back on May 29 asking about the status of an assistant coach, as he had received letters from a number of people who wanted that position. Then as now, head coaches wanted to hire their own assistants, but that was not to be in this case. Lipps responded that he had hired a man named McGillis, formerly a player at Haskell Institute, who had helped out by taking care of the reserves the previous year at Carlisle. Lipps then informed Kelley that a second assistant was planned and that he would let Kelley know when a suitable man had been hired. That man would be Gus Welch.

Victor Kelley, wife, Fern, and son, Victor Jr., arrived in Carlisle in late August 1915. They were greeted by a beautiful football field made more luscious by the large amount of rain received that summer. They were most likely housed in a teacher's apartment rather than just a single room as had been implied by Oscar Lipps.

Kelley immediately went to work refamiliarizing himself with the school and the athletic department. Forty-five players turned out on the first day of practice, but the squad swelled to 75 as students dribbled in from their country outings. *The Arrow* announced that the training table would start on September 10. The school's reorganization after the 1914 congressional inquiry didn't eliminate that advantage for the athletes. Charlie Moran arrived at the end of September to serve as trainer and within 15 minutes began "… rubbing out sore muscles and stiff joints …."

The season opened optimistically enough with a 21-0 win over Albright College. However, that score pales to the 54-point margin of victory Carlisle averaged in its previous games against that foe. Things looked considerably worse in their second game, a scoreless tie with Lebanon Valley College. Prior to 1914, 26-0 was the best the Dutchman had done against the Indians in 12 encounters. Any hope for a good season was lost in the next game, a 14-0 loss to Lehigh. The heart of the season arrived and it was dismal. Harvard thrashed the Indians 29-7, and Pitt followed with a 45-0 thumping. Then came a scoreless tie with pesky Bucknell. That was followed by a 14-0 loss to William Garlow's West Virginia Wesleyan College team in a must-win game. Sources conflict about what happened and precisely when it took place. Some say that Kelley resigned rather than being fired; others blame the problems on Welch. Regardless, Kelley's resignation wasn't made public, and his family was allowed to remain on campus for the rest of the season.

Looking like the Carlisle of old, the Indians beat Holy Cross 23-21, then hung on to beat a tough Dickinson College team. The season was mercifully over after losses to Fordham and Brown. The Brown game was particularly nasty in the press. Before the game, accusations were made that Kelley, out of spite for Lone Star Dietz's comment that he wouldn't make good at Carlisle, gave Carlisle's play book to Brown's coach. Brown supporters responded that Brown was already familiar with Carlisle's offense after having played them so many times. Also, at the time, Brown thought it was playing the University of Washington, not Washington State, the team Dietz coached. *The Providence Journal* ran a particularly nasty cartoon that ridiculed the Indians. That paper also ran an article in which Welch blamed the team's problems on Kelley and accused the school of trying to shift the blame to him.

There may have been something to Welch's charge of the school's making him the scapegoat, as a "Special to the Indianapolis Star. Carlisle, Pa., Nov. 29" ran in *The Indianapolis Star* in which Kelley was defended:

> "Those on the inside, however, do not hold Kelley responsible. It is said that friction between Kelley and his assistant, Gus Welch, resulted in the disintegration of the team. The majority of players sided with Welch until they saw that his advice was treasonable and was really wrecking the machine. Superintendent G. H. Lipps has taken a hand and this week will abolish the gridiron game at Carlisle. He is said to have been contemplating the action for a long time."

Such "specials" were generally provided by Carlisle's administration. However, in this case, it may have come from the Bureau of Indian Affairs because Gus Welch maintained a cordial relationship with the Carlisle administration after this blew over.

Kelley was done with Carlisle and likely had a bad taste in his mouth. He disappeared from public view for a period. In June 1917, when he registered for the WWI draft, he was living in Globe, Arizona with his wife, son and father, John J. Kelley. He was then engaged in farming and managing oil leases, perhaps on family property near Durant, Oklahoma. He probably didn't serve in the military in WWI because he coached the Hardin Military School football team in the 1918 season. In 1920, he was living in Abilene, Texas and operating a restaurant. His household had expanded to include a daughter, Betsy Ross Kelley. He didn't stay in that business much longer because in 1921, after head coach J. Burton Rix left in midseason, he and Bill Cunningham were named co-head coaches of the Southern Methodist University Mustangs. Cunningham later recalled that Choc suited up for the second half of the Arkansas game and scored the winning touchdown. The only problem with that story was that his touchdown would have been scored for Arkansas because they beat SMU 14-0. The SMU gig didn't last long. The 1-6-1 record probably had something to do with none of the three co-head coaches returning. 1922 found him coaching the Selma American Legion football team in Fresno County, California. Kelley appears to have emerged from the football desert, metaphorically speaking, in 1924 when he began coaching high school football in the Los Angeles, California school district. He did apply for the head coaching job at Texas A & M in 1929, but Matty Bell got the nod for that position.

During a 30-year stint working for the Los Angeles School District, a good chunk of which was spent coaching future college stars at Hollywood High School, Choc had the opportunity to dabble in another local industry. Kelley was technical director for the football sequences in the 1936 film, "Pigskin Parade." He later moved to Woodrow Wilson High School, also in the Los Angeles district, where he stayed until his mandatory retirement at age 65 in 1953. Because he was a fixture in Los Angeles football for decades, 300 people attended a banquet to celebrate his career. Over the years, Choc had opportunities to return to the college coaching ranks, including some at double his salary, but he chose to remain where he was. He probably made the right decision as he turned out dozens of players that went on to play for major colleges. The players he turned out were considered to be "polished gems."

Vic looked beyond sports; he remained involved with Indian issues, even serving as president of the National Congress of American Indians for three years. His son, Victor Jr., followed in his father's footsteps becoming the sports information director for UCLA. Choc Kelley retired to Glendale, California where he lived into his late 80s, dying in August 1974.

Undefeated 1909 Texas A&M team that featured Victor Kelley and Mike Balenti; *Cecilia Balenti-Moddelmog*

12

Stacy Matlock

Lone Chief

"Stacy Matlock like most other Indians of his age knows very little about the time and place of his birth. He was born, probably in Nebraska before the removal of the tribe [Pawnee] to this reservation [Oklahoma]. When a school was started, he was a pupil under the tutelage of Mary L. Burgess. He attended school at the agency until the year 1883 when he was taken to Carlisle, Pa." *The Arrow*'s account of Stacy Matlock's life is accurate as far as it goes. Various census records place his birth in the 1866-1868 timeframe, which would most likely mean that he was born in Nebraska. He likely participated, to the extent that a small child can, in the 1873-1875 migration from what remained of Pawnee lands in Nebraska to Oklahoma. This removal was not due to war with the United States as the Pawnee never fought U. S. soldiers. In fact, they served as scouts during various Indian wars. The reasons for relocating were a depleted food supply and war with the Sioux.

Stacy's original name is lost to us because his first teacher, a white woman, found the Pawnee names difficult to pronounce and assigned English names to the students. Young Stacy was probably named in honor of a white man who had been working to build respect between the whites and Indians in Nebraska, Kansas and Oklahoma. Both men's last names were often spelled

Name:	Stacy Matlock	**Nickname:**	Young Chief
DOB:	circa 1865	**Height:**	
Weight:		**Age:**	
Tribe:	Pawnee	**Home:**	Pawnee Reservation, OK
Parents:	Stacy Matlock, white; unknown, Pawnee		
Early Schooling:	Pawnee Reservation School		
Later Schooling:	Lincoln Institute, possibly		
Honors:			

Stacy Matlock, Pawnee Chief; *Fred Wardecker*

Matlack. Stacy's father was an important man in the tribe because young Stacy was in line to be a hereditary chief. Nothing is known about his mother.

Coming to Carlisle in 1883 after his father died, Stacy Matlock was very active in school activities and a favorite of the Man-on-the-band-stand. In December 1885, he was promoted to Sergeant of Company A and by 1890 he was in charge of several class rooms. Matlock was quite active in the YMCA, both on campus and in regional events. He was active in the Standard Debating Society and was one of the students chosen to debate the merits of the Dawes Act at his commencement in 1890. His trade was harness making. He chose to go on outing after graduation and earn some money rather than to return home.

He returned to school in the fall as assistant disciplinarian but was called home in September to see his sick mother. When he returned in November, he brought a new student back with him. According to *The Indian Helper*, "Stacy reports the Pawnees as having improved since he was home last. They have better homes and better farms. He speaks well of nearly all the returned Pawnee boys and girls. There are one or two exceptions."

Later that month, he was involved in an incident that influenced the development of organized sports in the U. S. Football at Carlisle up to this time was of the intra-mural variety. Occasionally students played pick-up games with students at other local institutions, but nothing was formalized. Stacy participated in one of those games with far-ranging complications. An article in the school newspaper, likely written by the superintendent, explained what had happened:

> "One of the most serious accidents that has ever happened at our school occurred last Saturday afternoon during the foot-ball game on the Dickinson College athletic grounds between a college team and one composed of our Indian boys. The game had only begun when in the rush Stacy

Matlack [sic] fell, was trampled upon and received what the doctors call a comminuted fracture of the tibia. In plain English the large bone of the leg was broken in two places. One break is transverse and about 3 ½ inches above the ankle; the other is oblique and about the middle of the bone. He has suffered intensely at times, but everything possible is being done to make him comfortable. That Stacy is a man of strong constitution is greatly in his favor, and he will no doubt be out on crutches before long and will in time completely recover the use of his leg."

Pratt later wrote about his dislike for what he considered a brutal game and why he banned students from playing football with other schools. He considered Stacy one of his best students and did not want additional injuries. Stacy recovered and was soon involved in school activities again.

In July 1891, Stacy Matlock was one of four Carlislians who attended Moody's School for Bible Study in Northfield, Massachusetts. Stacy was selected to give a talk about missionary work in Indian Territory. He said, "In the olden times the white people did not dare to go to church without being armed for fear of being killed by Indians. Now it is reversed. The Indian does not dare to go without being armed for fear of being killed by the white men, what are called cowboys. They are trying to make the Indians quiet by shooting. Instead of the gun take the Bible to him."

That fall Stacy was appointed disciplinarian of the Fort Totten Indian School located near Devils Lake, North Dakota. This was Matlock's first position in the Indian Service. However, it didn't last long because, at about 25 years of age he was back at Carlisle as a student in March 1892. After a short period, he returned to the Pawnee Agency. In August 1893, he informed his friends at Carlisle that he and fellow Carlisle alum William Morgan had become district government farmers. Within a couple of years he married Ella, about whom little is known other than she was born in Oklahoma Territory in 1874 and was carried on the Pawnee rolls. In 1895, they had a daughter named Cecelia.

Stacy may have gotten more education, possibly at Lincoln Institute in Philadelphia, because in 1900 he worked as a bank clerk at the Arkansas Valley Bank near Tulsa. In 1901 he was appointed to the position of issue clerk at the Ute Agency in Utah by the Commissioner of Indian Affairs. However, he must have been keeping in touch with Carlisle through this time. The December 15, 1904 issue of *The Arrow* brought the news that Stacy had returned to Carlisle as Assistant Disciplinarian and brought Ellie and five new students with him. The Matlocks set up housekeeping in the cottage formerly occupied by a Mr. Weber. A month later Stacy made a trip to Washington, DC to conduct some business with the government on behalf of his tribe. He stayed in the city a couple of weeks and brought three influential Pawnee chiefs back with him to visit Carlisle. Stacy immersed himself in the busy routine that came with his position. One of his more pleasant duties was to visit the meetings of the student organizations. In December 1906, he gave a talk to the Standard Debating Society about its membership of 20 years prior when he was a student. After over two years of working at Carlisle, the Matlocks returned to Oklahoma where he worked at the Pawnee County Bank. But their comfortable life there did not last long.

Tragedy struck in October 1907 when Ellie contracted typhoid fever and died within two weeks. Stacy, now 41, and Cecelia, 13, were left without a wife and mother. Stacy was not about to remain a widower for long.

In early 1908, Eagle Chief, the principal chief of the Pawnees, passed away, leaving a leadership void. Stacy, grandson of Pipe Chief, was selected to fill that position and took the title of Young Chief. Soon after that he brought a delegation from his tribe to Washington. On that trip, he visited Carlisle. There he met or, more likely, became reacquainted with Blanche Bill, a 21-year-old Pawnee student. A handwritten note in Stacy's student file recorded the event: "Married Blanche Bill, who was next in relative line when his wife died. Married at Friedman's." Pawnee customs dictated who would replace young wives who died. This was often an unmarried sister of the deceased. They were soon married and returned to Oklahoma. No mention of their wedding was found in *The Carlisle Arrow*, possibly because of the age difference.

This union was blessed with two children: Chauncey F. in 1909 and Bessie V. four years later. During this period, Stacy made annual trips to Washington to conduct business for the tribe and visited Carlisle while in the East. He had multiple reasons for these visits because his oldest daughter, Cecelia, was enrolled at Carlisle. After a rocky start, she was soon in the middle of school activities as her father had been.

Stacy received a report that Cecelia had demonstrated poor industry in her work in the laundry, causing him to intercede on her behalf. He wrote Friedman, asking him to "go slow with her, please do not punish her right away, go slow with her, or else send her home for her punishment. She never work[ed] in her life, but she can learn as she grows older. Now Mr. Friedman take the matter up for me as a brother in Mason." Friedman responded, "I have also investigated the matter and have given instructions for those in charge of the girls to be patient with her. She is large for her age and rather slow in her movements, but the girl seems willing enough to learn how to work and I am sure that there will be a decided improvement in her report on industry if a sufficient amount of patience and tact is exercised in her behalf." Based on later reports, things worked out for Cecelia.

A 1912 *Philadelphia Record* article described Matlock as being a prime example of a new type of Indian chief:

> "This up-to-date aborigine is of massive build and in his immobile countenance one may-read the stoicism of his nature. Here his resemblance to the old-style Indian chief ends, however. Matlock dresses in

the most modern kind of clothes and does not have to be led around by an interpreter. He was graduated from the [Carlisle] school in 1890, having been one of the early students here....

"'Young Chief' is a match mentally for the most astute of Indian agents, and is fortunate in being able to deal in person with the Interior Department and the Federal Senators and Representatives with whom he has relations. He is now in Washington, arranging to have the Government compensate his tribe under an old treaty in an amount of money that will run into several millions of dollars."

Back in Oklahoma, he continued to work as a bank clerk and interpreter.

In the 1920s, Young Chief allowed ethnomusicologist Frances Denmore to observe some of the Pawnee rituals:

"The ceremony of Painting the Buffalo Skull is held every spring by the Chaui Band of Pawnee and is in [the] charge of Mr. Stacy Matlock, a prominent member of that band. The closing events of the ceremony are the Buffalo and Lance dances, which were witnessed by the writer through the courtesy of Mr. Matlock, no other white person being present. The ceremony and dances were held in a large earth lodge, several miles south of the town of Pawnee. The opening of the lodge was toward the east. At some distance was a framework, probably that of a sweat lodge. Only members of the Buffalo Society were admitted to the painting of the skull, but during the Buffalo dance the skull painted a few days previously, lay on a folded blanket in front of the 'altar' which was opposite the entrance. This occasion and the Lance dance held a few days later afforded exceptional opportunities to listen to Pawnee songs, but the semidarkness of the lodge and the solemnity of the occasion precluded the taking of notes upon either the music or the details of the ceremonial dances."

Note: Pawnees' culture differed significantly from that of their neighbors. For example, the sun dance was not an important ritual for them.

By 1925, Matlock was known as Lone Chief as he was the sole surviving Pawnee principal chieftain. In October 1925, Pawnee and Sioux chiefs smoked the peace pipe to signify the making an end to historic hostilities. According to Marie Herrin of *The Lincoln Star*, the sticking point in arranging the peace-making ceremony was that some survivors of Massacre Canon, where 156 Pawnee men, women and children were slaughtered after Sioux scouts surprised their hunting party near present-day Trenton, Nebraska, felt the 52-year-old wounds to be too fresh to be forgotten. Herrin wrote, "Of the Pawnees, Chief Ruling Hisson, who is 105 years old, John Haymond, and Chiefs Walking Son and Leading Fox were all survivors, while among the Sioux, Chiefs Spotted Weasel and Flies Above were the only ones who had actually taken part in the battle. The others of the two parties were younger men and women, sons and daughters of survivors who have now answered the call to the Happy Hunting Ground. But these younger Pawnees and Sioux had inherited their elders' hatred for each other." When the time came to actually smoke the pipe, Ruling Hisson could not do it because the memory of his wife and three children being murdered senselessly still haunted him. "'You smoke if you want to. I can't. Sioux kill my wife – my children.' And he raised his hand palm outward to the Great Spirit Terahwah, calling down once more the Pawnee curse on the Sioux." The others smoked and made peace.

Herrin's article also mentioned that, in addition to being a Carlisle graduate, Stacy Matlock was a Knight Templar and a Shriner. Other newspaper articles remarked that he had taken on all outward aspects of modern civilization.

In 1931, Lone Chief played a key role in initiating John Philip Sousa into the Pawnee tribe. Sousa was dubbed Chief Singer of the Pawnees. Stacy stood next to Sousa in a photo of the event in which the inductee wore his bandleader's uniform.

In 1934, the U. P. reported that Stacy had changed his position on drinking from one of abstinence: "'Before prohibition it was illegal to give or sell Indians whisky. Since we were denied the right to drink intoxicants, we couldn't see why the white men should, so we were for prohibition.' The ban against selling wine and beer to Indians died with [the introduction of] prohibition." It appears that his positions were based on equal rights as opposed to the merits of drinking alcoholic beverages.

Stacy Matlock lived to be about 74 years old, a ripe old age for a man of his generation, dying on July 7, 1939, after suffering a stroke some time previous to that. He was survived by his second wife, Blanche, who died in 1970.

George May

After previously announcing that they would have no football team in 1916, Carlisle fielded a team late in the season and against opponents of the caliber of their usual early season warm-up game competition. Even at that, the Indians posted only a 1-3-1 record with George May as captain.

George Henry May, full-blood Wichita, was born on December 4, 1895 near Anadarko, Indian Territory (present day Oklahoma). His mother was called Topsy and his father was likely deceased before 1900. About 1906, his mother married Stanley Punlay. George and his sisters, Katie and Margaret, were then listed as stepchildren. George started going to school and attended the Riverside School which was relatively close to his home. He transferred to Carlisle after 1910, where he was immersed in school activities and was elected captain of the 1916 football team.

Like most other Carlisle captains, May was quite active in school life as he participated in the Standard Debating Society, ran track and played football. He worked as a painter at the school. He also participated in the apprenticeship program at Ford Motor Company in Highland Park, Michigan, where he registered for the WWI draft in June 1917. It is not clear if he served in the war as so many Carlisle boys did.

He returned to the reservation in Oklahoma and married Ethel Hunter Edwards, who friends called Nora. They apparently had no children because

Name: George May	**Nickname:**
DOB: 12/4/1895	**Height:**
Weight:	**Age:**
Tribe: Wichita	**Home:** Anadarko, OK
Parents: father unknown, Wichita; Topsy, Wichita	
Early Schooling: Riverside Indian School	
Later Schooling:	
Honors:	

1916 Carlisle backfield; *U. S. Army Military History Institute*

none were listed on any census. About 1928, Nora's name dropped off the census, perhaps indicating that she had died. About 1930, George's name appeared on the Kiowa census as married to Sarah Chaheenah, Commanche. Two years later, his name reappeared on the Wichita census with no wife listed but still classified as married. Perhaps Sarah was listed on the Kiowa census. His listing remained the same through the 1937 census, the last one found for him.

George May; *Fred Wardecker*

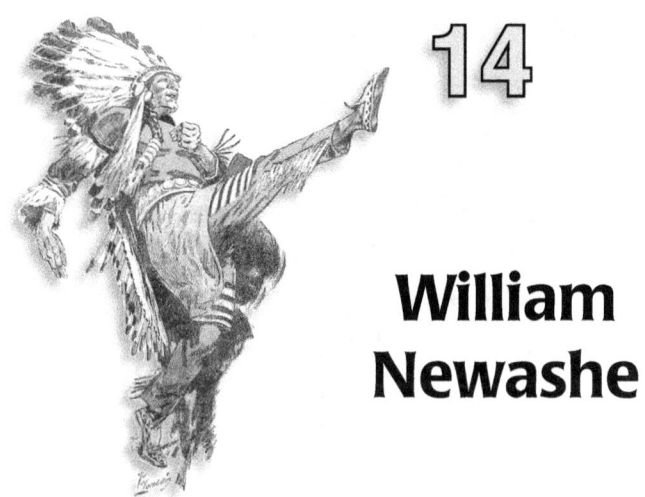

William Newashe

No sooner had Carlisle's football team become successful than it began to be criticized as being professional. Those claims were not based on the players getting paid to play football, at least initially, because there was limited opportunity to play independent or professional football for pay at that time. However, athletes could get paid for playing baseball, even if their pay just covered living expenses. Newspapers began running articles that criticized Carlisle for allowing boys who played baseball for pay to then play football. They ignored the fact that some of the college boys against whom the Indians played football also played summer ball but were more sophisticated and used fictitious names. William Newashe was one of the better baseball players to enroll at Carlisle but, ironically, his success in summer ball contributed significantly to the demise of baseball at the Indian school and gave ammunition to Carlisle's critics.

Bill and his younger sister, Emma, arrived at Carlisle in July 1905 from the Sac and Fox Reservation in Oklahoma. They were the orphaned children of a Sac and Fox father, John, and Shawnee mother, Susan, Newashe (sometimes written as Nawashe). Their father is believed to have died of tuberculosis and their mother of pneumonia. Emma soon received considerable press coverage at the school for a variety of activities, including her writing.

Name: William Newashe **Nickname:**
DOB: 10/5/1889 **Height:** 5'10"
Weight: 187 **Age:** 21
Tribe: Sac & Fox, Shawnee **Home:** Shawnee, OK
Parents: Naw-Haw-She - father, Ko-Lay-Pah-Way-Se - mother, AKA John and Susan Newashe
Early Schooling: Sac and Fox Indian Agency school
Later Schooling:
Honors:

William Newashe, 1911; *Fred Wardecker*

William got very little mention in his first years at the school and, when he did, it was almost entirely related to athletics. His first time in the limelight was a very short March 1907 piece. The reporter said he was trying to move up from the junior varsity baseball team to the varsity and wished him luck because he and Frank LeRoy were the j. v.'s best players.

Bill did make the varsity team. We know that because he was listed among the players who were off for a big road trip to Atlantic City. He reported back to his friends at Carlisle that he was having a good time on the early-season road trips. He soon broke into the starting line-up, playing first base and batting fifth or sixth. Game summaries showed that he was stealing bases, turning double plays, getting hits and scoring runs. In May, after Wauseka departed, Newashe demonstrated his versatility by shifting to Wauseka's old position, catcher.

Bill quickly found out that playing baseball for Carlisle wasn't all fun and games, especially those long road trips. *The Arrow* reported on something that happened on the team's May road trip to play Syracuse: "At the hotel in Elmira, N. Y., Wm. Newashie[sic] was barred from his room by Wm. Garlow who was his room-mate. Newashie stayed out too late and consequently Garlow locked the door and went to bed. The next morning one of the boys found him sleeping out in the hall."

Being on the diamond was no piece of cake for him either. In July, when he was away playing summer baseball in Maryland, *The Arrow* reprinted an article about a serious incident: "Newashee [sic], an Indian playing with Hagerstown, was struck in the mouth with a foul tip off his own bat on Wednesday and had to retire from the game. He was attended by two physicians who were on the grandstand." Ouch! Two weeks later, *The Arrow* had something more positive to report: "William Newashe, who is playing with the Hagerstown nine, is making good and looks forward to the time when he can sign B. L. after his name (Big League)." It was clear to him that wasn't going to happen any time soon, so after the season was over Bill returned to Carlisle. In September, he wrote about his experiences for *The Arrow*:

> "Last Spring when I went away from here I thought I would play only two or three games a week. But I soon found out that we had to play every day.
>
> "I got used to it and the first game I played seemed funny to play in a strange place, and besides it was my first time out in playing ball. I enjoyed it very much. Garlow pitched the first game against Shippensburg, and shut them out 7-0.
>
> "The first week went pretty fast for Garlow and I and we both enjoyed playing.
>
> "The team would play with Martinsburg, W. Va., Winchester, Va., Berkeley Spring, W. Va., Frederick, Md., Hanover, Pa., Carlisle, Pa., Sparrows Point, Md.
>
> "The crowds in Virginia and West Virginia were not as good as the crowds in Maryland and in Pennsylvania, and there is usually some betting done on the game nearly every day.
>
> "We played in Hanover where Mike Balenti joined us and soon some more new players came and we played ball in regular style.
>
> "There were only four members of the team that played all the season, and the rest were released, the players were Hawks, Garlow, Peaster of Baltimore, and myself, who stuck to the team from start to the finish.
>
> "I made two home runs for our team, center fielder, two home runs. Balenti one. Finnell of Baltimore one."

The Arrow also included a letter from J. Frank Ridenour praising Bill's performance both as a player and as a person. That letter was previously included in the chapter on William Garlow.

Football season had already begun when he returned to school. The 1907 team was one of Carlisle's finest, and William Newashe wasn't ready for the varsity yet, so he played on a shop team. He was so badly injured in a game between the Printers and the Tailors that he had to be replaced by little Ray Hitchcock. The same week he told an *Arrow* reporter that "…he would take us all to Philadelphia if he had his way." Bill was referring to the special train to take students, faculty and staff to the Penn game. But he didn't have the resources to get his way, and many Carlisle students couldn't afford the trainfare to the game and the tour of the art museum earlier in the day. In November, an anonymous reporter, who called himself Pigskin, reported that Newashe was coaching the junior varsity team. Apparently he was a player-coach and had healed enough to play again, because he kicked a field goal for the j. v. against the Soldiers' Orphans School team from nearby Scotland, Pennsylvania.

William Newashe tackling Possum Powell;
U. S. Army Military History Institute

William Newashe;
*Cumberland County
Historical Society,
Carlisle, PA*

A bit of sibling rivalry was reported shortly after that: "Emma Newashe, who is out in the country, expects to get ahead of her brother, William, in her studies, but William is bracing up, too." Carlisle students were sometimes able to attend public schools all day when on outing. Some students thus progressed more quickly than those at Carlisle who attended academic classes half days only.

In January of 1908, Bill organized a basketball team for the small boys and wanted to take on the freshman boys. Shortly after that he was mentioned in *The Arrow*, one of the few times for a non-athletic activity, when he visited a meeting of the Susan Longstreth Society. He then took sick and was hospitalized for a few days. However, the Susans likely played no role in his hospitalization.

In February at the Football Banquet, Bill received his letter "C" for baseball. He received nothing for football nor mention in any other sport. A month later, *The Arrow* published "Our Base Ball Team of '07," some prose found in the mail and signed J. W. T. (Joseph W. Twin who also wrote under the byline of Walter Camp) which described each player. Of Bill it said, "Newashe is our first sacker; a thrown ball can't get through 'Willie.'" The school paper again mentioned him later that month, this time for a rare vocal performance: "William Newashe favored the Dickson Society with a melodious song at the last meeting."

In the spring, William Newashe was again playing first base but was moved up to batting third in the order. Batting third probably indicated that he was becoming a better hitter, both in slugging and consistency. Bill spent the summer in Oklahoma where he most likely played baseball, as was his habit. At summer's end, he and fellow Sac and Fox football player, Jim Thorpe, returned to Carlisle. That fall he was a member of the Freshman Class.

Bill probably played football on the Second Team in 1908, but there was no mention of it in *The Arrow*. In late January 1909, it reported, "William Newashe, a member of the Freshman Class left last Monday morning for Hershey, Pa., where he will spend the rest of the winter. William, being a basketball player, will be missed immensely by his teammates as well as by all of his classmates and friends." Captain of the freshman basketball team was Bill's classmate, Jim Thorpe.

William Newashe started the 1909 baseball season behind the plate where he had finished the previous season but was now batting cleanup. The decision to shift him down one spot in the batting order was a good one because, in addition to leading the team by hitting .417, he was belting home runs. That is exactly the kind of hitter a manager wants batting clean up. Part way through the season, Bill was moved to second base and Hayes took over the catching responsibilities, likely reducing the frequency of Newashe's injuries. After a successful spring, including a win over the Hagerstown team for which he had previously played, he headed to Atlantic City to play ball that summer, probably for a hotel team that provided him room, board and tips.

That fall, in 1909, for the first time, the varsity football line up included Newashe at left end. He played well, even scoring a touchdown after catching a forward pass at his own 15 yard line. The Freshman Class chose him as captain of its basketball team. To close out his great year in December, he and Anona Crow won second prize in the twostep at the Mercers' reception.

Spring 1910 must have been an odd one for Bill; it was the first time in years that he wasn't playing baseball. That was because Carlisle dropped baseball as a sport. So Newashe joined the track team and started competing in the hammer throw. In April after commencement, he, Bill Garlow and Wauseka started playing for the Harrisburg baseball team. The proximity of Harrisburg to Carlisle made frequent visits to the school easy for the ballplayers. The *Patriot* reported Newashe's first try at a new position:

> "Newashee [sic], the Carlisle Indian, made his debut at Harrisburg Wednesday in the role of pitcher, after two of his teammates were knocked from the box, and pulled the game out of the fire. The Lancaster pitchers were found for thirteen hits. Score, Harrisburg, 10; Lancaster, 5."

The *Sentinel* told the story of his debut this way:

> "He took hold of things at a bad time and pulled through in fine style and after the third inning was over but one more run was scored off his delivery. The youngster was like both the other pitchers, wild, but he kept

his bases on balls scattered. The run in the fifth inning was secured by a single, base on balls, sacrifice and the squeeze play. While he kept things safe through his pitching he caused trouble for the visiting pitcher for he was the one that started things moving in the fifth inning with a two-bagger. Again in the sixth he was first up and singled safely to left field."

Bill returned to Carlisle in time to start practicing for the 1910 football season. For a while, he was shifted to fullback where he was an effective ballcarrier. However, Warner needed a tackle, so Newashe became the left tackle. But his talents carrying the pigskin weren't wasted. Against Penn, Pop Warner dusted off an old play – a concealed double pass – in which the back who received the snap would head toward Newashe's end of the line, he would pull out of the line, take a hidden handoff and race around the opposite end of the line for sizeable gains. He filled in at fullback for Hauser the next game and performed well. If nothing else, Bill Newashe was as versatile on the gridiron as on the diamond.

After football season was over, he went on outing to his usual location, Hershey, Pennsylvania, where something unusual happened: he and Louis Island played for the Hershey YMCA team in a basketball game against Carlisle's Varsity.

For the summer of 1911, he signed with a baseball team located in Jackson, Michigan, a town best known for the prison located there. Bill wasn't lonely that summer as Bill Garlow also played on the Jackson team. Newashe showed unusual talent: "'Chief' William Newashe, the star performer of the Carlisle Indians on the gridiron, is one of the stars of the Jackson, Mich. State League baseball team. During the past season he filled every position on the team in an acceptable manner. Michigan League sport writers predict that he will break into the big league next season."

Back at Carlisle in the fall, Newashe was again out on the football practice field. The 1911 team is considered by many to be Carlisle's best, so making the starting line up was no mean feat. He played left tackle that year and was a major ground gainer, teaming with his counterpart on the right side of the line, Lone Star Dietz, on the tackle-through-tackle play. Down with pneumonia, he missed the game with Lafayette but bounced back into his starring role when he recovered. Bill Newashe was a major cog in a legendary team, one of few that ever beat two of the Big Four in the same season.

At season's end, he apparently left the school because, in January 1912, *The Carlisle Arrow* implied that he was no longer a student: "William Newashe was in Carlisle calling on his friends last Monday afternoon." In February, Emma visited him in his home in Harrisburg which suggests that he was living and working in the area. In late February, he wrote Friedman that he was starting work at a packing company and that he intended to work there until April 25th, at which time he would start to play summer ball again. In May, a short piece in *The Arrow* confirmed that he was no longer a student but

The Bachelors Club, from left to right: Fritz Hendricks, Pete Hauser, James Garlow, Emil Hauser (Wauseka), William Newashe, William Garlow, Louis DuPuis and Harry Wheeler; *Cecilia Balenti-Moddelmog*

raised some other questions: "From the Hotel Ruhl, in Jackson, Michigan, comes a 'happy' message from Emma Newashe, Class '12, who is there with her brother William and his wife. She says: 'I am enjoying life immensely and my sincere wishes are that you and other friends at Carlisle find life as happy as I see it now.'" Who had he married? How was he supporting her? Was he still playing baseball? Why wasn't he in the majors? Later correspondence in his student file revealed that she was the daughter of J. B. and Anna Stambaugh. The Stambaughs lived in Derry Township (Hershey, Pennsylvania) in 1910 and in Carlisle by 1915. Neither censuses nor city directories list their daughter. It is quite possible that she was living on her own when she met Bill.

In November 1912, Mrs. Newashe was the luncheon guest of Angel DeCora, wife of Lone Star Dietz. Somehow, the two women had become acquainted or possibly knew each other before the Newashes married. There is just too little information to know anything with any measure of certainty. Because they were spending the off-season in Paxtang, a suburb of Harrisburg, it is reasonable to assume that Bill had a job there, possibly at the nearby Hershey chocolate plant. In March, Angel visited the Newashes in Paxtang, and later that month Bill visited Carlisle briefly. In April, Gus Welch visited them in Hershey, and they visited Carlisle during commencement week. While the school said nothing officially about Mrs. Newashe, it appears that she was known to and accepted by the Carlisle community.

Bill must have been doing well financially at this time because he bought some real estate, probably in Paxtang, that included a house and a lot with a carpenter shop on it. Emma put up some of the money and William was to repay her $50 from each of his semiannual lease payments from his allotment in Oklahoma. Things weren't going so well for him physically because his sister wrote Superintendent Friedman that, after he underwent an undisclosed operation, he would be much better. His life soon took a sharp turn downward.

In early 1914, Horace Johnson, Superintendent of the Sac and Fox Indian School wrote Oscar Lipps about Bill's situation. Johnson was concerned about Bill's financial condition: "Mr. Newashe has had something like six thousand dollars during the past two years some of which, if not much, has been spent in riotous living." He detailed some of Newashe's spending which included living several weeks in one of Oklahoma City's best hotels and mortgaging his property. In a later letter, he described Mrs. Newashe as a white woman and "somewhat of an adventuress." In February 1914, Newashe visited the Indian school, perhaps to get money. That summer he played some minor league baseball in Peru, Indiana for a time, but a major league contract was never to be.

In late 1915, Mrs. Newashe was living with her parents at 420 North Street in Carlisle and was in dire straits, both financially and physically. She wrote Superintendent Lipps at the Indian school in an attempt to get some money from her husband to replace winter clothing that he sold to buy liquor. He was in Michigan but was trying to get money from Lipps to use to come to Carlisle. Apparently the government had some of the lease money from his allotment. She supported the idea: "...which I think would be a good thing as he can't buy liquor here." She also wrote that she was preparing to go to the Mont Alto Sanitarium and that her physician, Dr. Plank, thought she should have gone six months ago. She didn't say why she needed to go to the sanitarium but it was most likely to treat tuberculosis because the Mont Alto institution had had some success in that regard. In her case, it was too late.

The remaining correspondence in Newashe's file, of which there were several, had to do with Anna Stambaugh's request for reimbursement of the $150 cost of her daughter's funeral. Some of the letters dealt with partial payments whereas others were attempts to determine where he was. He was found to have been playing for the Carlisle Indian baseball team for part of the summer of 1916. That team, or at least its booking manager, Nat C. Strong, owner of the Brooklyn Royal Giants and powerful figure in black baseball, operated out of the Pulitzer Building in New York City.

Starting around 1915, Newashe began playing professional football in the fall. That year and the part of the next, "Chief" Newashe played guard for the Detroit Heralds. He also played tackle for the Pitcairn Quakers in 1916. Shifting from team to team, even during the season, was common in those days. Some players stayed with one team an entire season but played for other teams only on Sundays on which their team had nothing scheduled.

When William Newashe registered for the WWI draft in June 1917, he was a professional baseball player, living in Oklahoma City, and single. His gravestone reflects that during WWI he served in the Military Police as a corporal.

He remarried on February 20, 1919. About all that is known about his wife is that, according to the 1920 census, her name was Myrtle Cowan, she was the niece of Louis F. Cowan, a mine operator from Miami, Oklahoma, and she had been born in Arkansas around 1897. Sac and Fox rolls listed her as a white woman, but the 1930 federal census classified her as being of mixed blood. Grandniece Donna Newashe McAllister recalls that Myrtle was a white woman who was bedridden in later years and that William, a very quiet man, cared for her.

He played baseball professionally in the Western League in 1920. He and Myrtle, spent the off-season in Miami, Oklahoma with her uncle. Around 1921, a son, William Jr., was born and his sister Susan was born three years later.

Bill's last known competitive athletic endeavor was to play for the Oorang Indians in 1923 when he was about 34 years old. He played five games at tackle for them in the latter half of the season. In 1930 he was living with Myrtle and the children in Vinita, Oklahoma and working as a machinist on an oil derrick, a pretty good job to have during the Great Depression. In 1947 William Newashe appeared as a representative of the Sac and Fox nation in a lawsuit against the Federal government. Which William Newashe, Jr. or Sr., was involved is not clear. He also raised his granddaughter, Emma Rosanne, to adolescence.

Bill's sister Emma married Fred McAllister around 1913 in Oklahoma City. They lived in a large house in Norman until 1930 when their burgeoning family moved to a farm in Luther, Oklahoma that is still owned by the family. Emma, an accomplished writer and musician, died young while giving birth to her tenth child.

About the time the Jim Thorpe biopic was playing, William was interviewed by *The Oklahoman*. When asked about Carlisle's grueling schedule, he responded, "We used to play two or three home warmup games at home then we'd travel most of the rest of the season." When asked which was the toughest opponent, he replied, "They were all tough. Our greatest rival was Pennsylvania. When we played them we'd run a special train from Carlisle and take our band along" He explained that the big eastern schools did not exactly enjoy getting beaten by small schools such as Carlisle, something that created several interesting rivalries.

When questioned about his friend, Jim Thorpe, he said, "A lot of people think Jim was all out for himself. At Carlisle he was strictly a team man. Not exactly a leader but he was always encouraging the players and was good for the morale of the team. He was a marked man at all times but he had tremendous stamina and could take it. He never did want to hog the limelight." As to their coach, Newashe said, "Warner had no pets and played no favorites. A truly fine coach."

The interview turned to then modern football. Bill opined, "We had no reserves. Every player wanted to play the full 60 minutes. There were no huddles and we wasted no time. I think the free substitution of today kills football from the spectator viewpoint but it does give more boys a chance to play."

He was a member of the Christian Church, served on the Sac and Fox Tribal Claims Council, and helped establish the service club for Sac and Fox Indians. Bill served as a pallbearer in 1953 for his former teammate and fellow Sac and Fox, Jim Thorpe. He lived until February 8, 1962 and died in Luther, Oklahoma at 72 years of age. He is buried in the Luther Cemetery Expansion.

Stancil Powell

That both Moses and his younger brother, Stancil (Stansill), Powell were enrolled at Carlisle by 1900 may indicate that their father was ill and no longer able to support the family. Although Stancil enrolled for five years in 1899, he was discharged in 1902 as "Undesirable." Something must have changed because he was allowed to re-enroll in 1906. His father was dead by that time and his guardian was Wesley Bigjim. It's not clear where the younger Powell picked up 'Possum' as a nickname, but it stuck with him at the Carlisle Indian School where he studied carriagemaking and participated in athletics. After several years at the school, Possum started getting a little press. The November 20, 1908 issue of *The Carlisle Arrow* described a game played by Carlisle's second team, The Hustlers, as a punting contest between Powell and Serber of Walbrook Athletic Club.

In January 1909, he was named as one of six players to participate in Carlisle's first ever inter-collegiate basketball game. Powell figured prominently in reports of this game against Penn: "The Indians did not have a single foul called on them during the first half, and those called on Powell in the second half were for holding, an offense to which the redman was driven by utter exhaustion."

Name: Stancil Powell
Nickname: Possum; Steamroller; Wrinklemeat
DOB: February 1890
Height: 5'10"
Weight: 176
Age: 21
Tribe: Cherokee
Home: Ocona Lufty Township, Swain County, NC
Parents: John Powell, mixed-blood Eastern Cherokee; Tooka (Dooka, Duke) Powell, full-blood Eastern Cherokee
Early Schooling: unknown
Later Schooling: Haskell Institute
Honors: American Indian Sports Hall of Fame, 1971

Stancil Powell, 1912;
Fred Wardecker

Powell playing lacrosse; *U. S. Army Military History Institute*

In May, Powell returned to the school to devote more time to his trade after working on a nearby farm for some time. Later that month at the Annual Class Meet, he placed behind Jim Thorpe and George Thomas in both the high jump and the shot put events. He placed 12th in total points for the meet. At the Fourth of July celebration, he teamed with Pierce Ute and Peter Jordan to come in 2nd in the wheelbarrow race. Soon he was involved in more serious competitions.

In the fall of 1909, Possum Powell made the varsity football team but didn't start. He was the first substitute to be put in at the end position and, as such, got some playing time, limited though it was. In the spring of 1910, he participated in track again. In that fall's football season, he got more playing time and press coverage. In the winter, he played on Wauseka's basketball team that showed "promise to become stars of the first magnitude." In the spring 1911 track season, Stancil earned his first Carlisle letter by winning the high jump and discus events in the dual meet with Dickinson College. He also placed first in the shot put against Lafayette. Powell contributed to Carlisle's winning the Pennsylvania Intercollegiate Track and Field Championship by winning the high jump and coming in second in the 16-pound shot put. After that, he left for a vacation at home in North Carolina.

The fall of 1911 was his best season at Carlisle. With Pete Hauser gone, Possum Powell was the starting fullback, and he made the most of his opportunity by being a consistent ground gainer and pretty good place kicker. He got a fair amount of press, considering that he was playing in Jim Thorpe's shadow on what many consider was Carlisle's finest team. *The North American* wrote, "Powell scattered the Penn forwards when making his plunges much in the manner that a rearing and plunging horse forces a crowd out of his way."

Chief Powell at the Wigwam; *U. S. Army Military History Institute*

After the Harvard game, the *The Boston Globe* commented, "On the direct passes from center, Powell, the fullback, in particular, found it no trouble to plough ahead for 5 and 10-yard gains." *The Boston Journal* credited the coach: "Glen Warner has molded together a wonderful team this year, and Thorpe and Powell are two of the greatest all-around football players ever seen on Soldiers Field, and that is saying a good deal." After the last game of the season against Brown, *The Providence Journal* raved, "Powell was also constantly in the limelight, the big fullback hitting Brown's line like a catapult."

Placing Jim Thorpe on his All-America First Team was all the mention Walter Camp granted the 1911 Indians. Fortunately, others saw things more clearly. *Outing Magazine*'s annual poll of coaches listed Powell at fullback in its "Football Honor List for 1911."

Back at school, Possum Powell received positive mention for cutting down all the Christmas trees used to decorate the campus that year. In February, he built a fine under-cut surrey to be used in the commencement exhibition and in March left for Mascot, Pennsylvania to work in a carriage shop. He returned from that outing in time to compete with the track team, coming in second in both the high jump and shot put in the state championship meet.

At 5'10" and 176 pounds, he played fullback for the Indians again in 1912. Although the team did well again, his performance was off from its 1911 level. The press described him as "not as effective as last year."

He spent some time at home in North Carolina and returned with a batch of new students. But he didn't stay long as he headed west to Haskell Institute in Lawrence, Kansas. Besides stating that he had no special musical ability, his Returned Student record described his character and disposition as "good, only." It deemed him suitable to work as a wagon wood worker or laborer, but "Should be under strict supervision to get good results." His instructor, Martin L. Law, saw things differently. He considered Possum's ability and conduct both to be very good and thought he "will make a first class mechanic."

The 1913 football season found Stancil Powell playing fullback once again, this time for the Fightin' Indians. Perhaps thinking his chapeau clashed with his purple and gold Haskell uniform, *The Lincoln Daily Star* commented on his attire: "Powell wore no head gear and covered his head with a red cap, recalling to the minds of the old timers, Indian [Charles] Guyon the speedy end of years ago. He is a fearless player and appeared dangerous at all times."

The fact that Powell and a teammate or two had previously played some football was not lost on *The Star*: "For the Indians, Powell an ex-Carlisle player who had the distinction of playing by the side of the famous Jim Thorpe, was head and shoulders above his teammates in both the offense and defense. In the latter part of the contest, when Nebraska was charging through the enormous gaps opened by Ross, this flashy player took the place of his opposing guard and succeeded in choking up the holes."

The former Carlisle players found themselves at the center of a controversy as opponents were objecting to their having previously played on the Carlisle varsity. Just before the Haskell-Nebraska game, *The Star* wrote, "The men were neither overconfident nor gloomy over the coming contest, preferring to retain their verdict until the Aborigines have been met. Reports continue to filter through that Coach 'Snapper' Kennedy has more than the two Carlisle players upon his squad which he has reported. In fact it is said, and from reliable sources too, that this Stover person who is evidently in the Haskell lineup is none other than the famous Ogallala, who played with the eastern redskins when they so merciless massacred the Huskers in 1908."

Carlisle did beat Nebraska 31-6 in 1908, but the records do not list anyone named Ogallala ever playing for Carlisle. Almost immediately, a reader countered the accusations:

Fort Hall, Idaho, Oct 27.—Sport Editor of *The Daily Star*.

Dear Sir:

I note in The Star of Saturday, October 25, you intimate that Stover, the center on the Haskell Indian football team, is none other than 'Ogalalla,' who helped Carlisle defeat the 'Huskers way back in 1908. As one who is in a position to know, I want to say that nothing could be further from the truth.

I lived at Haskell Institute for a number of years, though not directly connected with the school, and I know both of these Indians well. Ogalalla, whose real name is Nekifer Shoushuck, is an Alaskan; Stover is an Oklahoma Indian. Ogalalla is married and at present working in a bake shop in Lawrence. Stover entered Haskell in 1910 and I might say a 'greener' Indian never tried for the team. Kennedy, who is known for his clean sportsmanship throughout the Missouri valley, has developed Stover into one of the best centers ever at the school. Stover has never seen Carlisle, and I might add that since he is a member of what is known as the five civilized tribes, he is not eligible for enrollment at Carlisle.

The only two players on the 1913 Haskell football team who ever attended Carlisle are Powell and Charles Williams. The former entered Haskell last spring, paying his own transportation to the school. He goes to school and is learning a trade. Charles Williams is a brother of 'Bill' Williams, the captain of the Haskell team. His term of enrollment at Carlisle expired last spring and he enrolled at Haskell this fall, desiring to be with his brother. In this connection, I might say that the whole Haskell team is composed of a group of young Indian men who for manliness and cleanness can not be surpassed by any football team in the country. Most of them are active Christian workers, and have few, if any bad habits. Much of this is due to the teaching of Coach Kennedy and Captain Williams, the latter having just been elected to the presidency of the Haskell Young Men's Christian Association, an organization with about 200 members.

In closing, I, who am not an Indian, wish to say that if some of the Indian football teams of the past have had unsavory reputations, through the bringing in of 'ringers' and ineligible players, it has been because of the white men who have handled the teams and not through any desire of the Indians themselves. The newspapers ought by this time to know Coach Kennedy well enough to discredit any rumors that would in any way reflect upon his integrity or true sportsmanship. He is by long odds one of the cleanest and best sportsmen in the middle west, and The Star knows it. I left Lawrence October 1, am well acquainted with all the members of the Haskell football team, and know whereof I speak.

C. E. McBride of the *Kansas City Star* or any of the Kansas university authorities can easily certify to the truthfulness of this statement.
Very truly,
MILTON M THORNES.

The Carlisle Indian School file for Nekifer Shouchuk, to use the spelling he used himself, includes an article about the 1909 Haskell-Denver game. The Haskell lineup included O'Galla at center, Deloria at right end and Island at quarterback. Someone at Carlisle made some annotations in the right margin. "N. Shouchuk, ex-stu" alongside O'Galla, "John, ex-stu" next to Deloria and "Louis, '1908'" next to Island. The open question is why would anyone have an Aleut try to pass as Irish?

The *Salina Union* chimed in:

> A good many sport followers are greatly excited over the recrudescence of the Haskell football team. They ascribe the success of that aggregation of pigskin chasers to the 'marvelous work' of the coach. The real truth is that all Indians on the Haskell team who can play football above the high school class are graduates or former students of Carlisle, who for one reason or another are no longer eligible to play on the eastern team and have been brought to Lawrence to continue their work as professional sportsmen. The Haskell coach is a very clever imitator of other people's

good work. He has taken the veteran material secured from the east and by using the plays and tactics of Coaches Moses and Frank of the University of Kansas, has developed a fairly effective football team. There never was a successful Indian football team, either at Carlisle or Haskell, that was not rotten to the core with the worst form of professionalism.

From the editor of *The Star*:

This was written by W. C Lansdon, who was athletic manager at Kansas university while Kennedy was the coach. Evidently he has something sticking in his throat concerning the 'Snapper' which does not taste very palatable.

Stancil Powell stayed at Haskell for the 1914 season, playing fullback again and filling in when necessary at center and tackle. After leaving Haskell, he found work at an oil refinery in Tulsa, Oklahoma. When the U. S. entered WWI, Ben, as he was called in later years, enlisted in the army. He served with distinction in the 358th Infantry of the 90th Division. He was wounded once in the fighting at St. Mihiel and twice in the Argonne. After the war was over, he returned to Oklahoma where he coached the Tahlequah State Teachers College football team for a couple of years. Then he got a call from his old teammate, Jim Thorpe.

In 1923, the Oorang Indians needed help on their line, and Possum Powell was young enough and big enough – barely (5'10", 185 pounds at 32 years old) – to fill in where needed. He liked getting paid $100 a week, which was a lot of money in those days. He was dubbed "Wrinklemeat" as a more colorful name. Apparently "Steamroller" didn't sound Indian enough. Hazel Hynes, the assistant postmistress, remembered Wrinklemeat from coming in to pick up his mail: "He was a lot younger than the other Indians. He looked like a kid right out of high school, especially when he stood beside the other Indians." In a 1934 interview he said, "Football was fine in the days when I could run 10 miles without stopping for breath." Unable to do that any longer, he returned to North Carolina to farm. He married a full-blood Cherokee and in 1929 had a daughter, Dorothy. The three of them lived on the 20-acre farm until 1937 when, a few days before Christmas, his wife, Kina S. Powell, died. He continued farming until his death at age 67 on October 15, 1957 in an automobile accident.

16

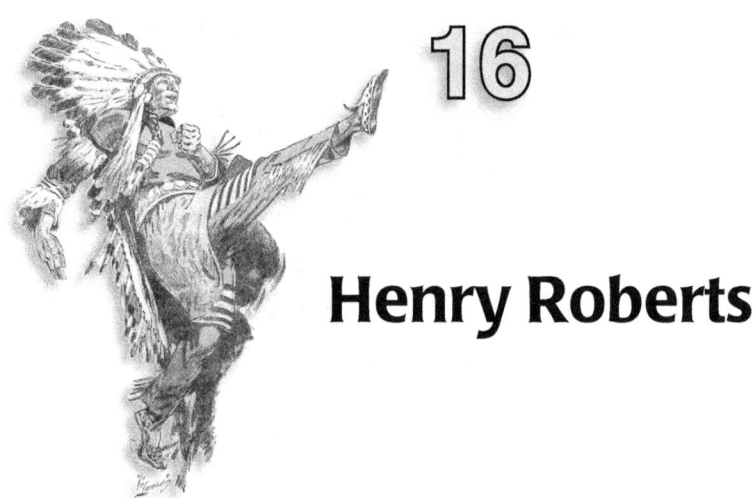

Henry Roberts

Sitting Eagle

Rush Roberts, Pawnee, was the youngest person to fight for the U. S. Cavalry under Gen. Crooks in the 1876-77 wars against his tribe's historic enemies, the Cheyenne and Sioux. Reputedly born during a buffalo hunt, Rush was just 16 or 17 when he joined Capt. North's Battalion of Pawnee scouts. As a member of Mackenzie's cavalry, he charged hostile villages with such bravery that he was awarded his father's name, "Fancy Eagle," After the war, he joined Pawnee Bill's Wild West Show. Rush attended Hampton Institute from 1885 to 1887. He eventually returned to Nebraska, married, started a large family, was removed to Pawnee, Oklahoma along with rest of his tribe, and eventually became an important Pawnee chief.

Henry Ellis Roberts, the subject of this chapter, born in 1888, was the second oldest of Rush and Lou Roberts' seven children. When he was about eight years old, he gained a step-brother his age. His parents appear to have adopted Ed Howell who was, according to Pawnee rolls, the son of his mother's late sister, Lida. In 1896 Henry's mother, Lou Howell Roberts, also died. After that, Rush Roberts married Rose Howell, his former sister-in-law. According to Pawnee customs, widowers sometimes marry sisters of their late wives.

Name: Henry Ellis Roberts **Nickname:**
DOB: 3/24/1888 or 5/24/1888 **Height:**
Weight: 185 **Age:** 23
Tribe: Pawnee **Home:** Pawnee, OK
Parents: Rush & Lou Howell Roberts
Early Schooling: Haskell Institute, Hampton Institute
Later Schooling:
Honors:

Henry Roberts;
Cumberland County Historical Society,
Carlisle, PA

Henry attended Haskell Institute as a child. In 1903 he wrote a piece for *The Indian Leader* entitled "The Indian Story." His article has been described as a "...charming conversational story written by a Pawnee fourth grade student at Haskell Institute. He touches on buffalo hunting, his father running away from Genoa Indian School in Nebraska, life in Oklahoma, and a herd of buffalo belonging to Pawnee Bill's Wild West Show." One of his classmates at Haskell was a lad by the name of Jim Thorpe. In his book on Jim Thorpe, Bill Crawford related that the assistant disciplinarian first exposed the boys to the game of football when he stuffed a sock with grass and taught the boys some of the basics. Jim was small for his age and didn't yet impress people as someone who would become a great athlete. No one could have predicted from this start that these two would one day play on one of the greatest football teams of all time.

In 1906, Henry enrolled at Hampton Institute where his older sister, Nellie, had enrolled the year before. She, however, was expelled in 1907 for "unsatisfactory conduct." After graduating from Hampton in 1908, he returned to Haskell to take their commercial course. He also played right tackle, captained, and did the kicking for the 1909 Fightin' Indians football team that beat Texas and Nebraska but lost to the great A&M team that featured Carlislians Victor Kelley and Mike Balenti. Henry also had Carlisle teammates, Nikifer Schouchuk at center and Louis Island at quarterback. At season's end, Roberts was named to the All Southwestern team as the punter. It isn't clear what Roberts did after graduating from Haskell in 1910, but his

1912 statement that he had been working for the government for two years implies that he may have taken a job of some sort with the Bureau of Indian Affairs.

How Henry Roberts came to Carlisle is unclear as all his student record states is that, at age 23, he arrived on October 8, 1911. Very little other information was recorded about him at that time. The September 29, 1911 issue of *The Carlisle Arrow* included an article entitled, "New Gymnasium Director." It announced that Henry Roberts had accepted the position left vacant by the resignation of Harry Wheeler and would be in charge of the gymnasium when the indoor season started. In the meantime, he would be assisting on the football field. It also stated that he was a graduate of Haskell and had experience in gymnasium work. Perhaps his previous government work was being in charge of the gym at Haskell. John Goslin, who had taken a physical culture course at Chautauqua, would be his assistant.

Football season was underway when Henry Roberts arrived at Carlisle, but we don't know if he was on the team for the first couple of games. The early-season drubbings of Lebanon Valley and Muhlenberg Colleges that preceded the announcement of Roberts' hiring each warranted but a scant paragraph in *The Arrow*. So, it's not clear if he played in those warm-up games or not. The October 6, 1911 edition of *The Carlisle Arrow* reported the results of the Carlisle-Dickinson College game, the first game it reported on in detail that season. Henry received mention for his play in that game. It appears that his on-field assistance was a little more strenuous than one would expect from the September 29 announcement. The October 6 issue also included a roster of the school's employees. Roberts and Goslin were not included on that list, possibly because they were not technically government employees but were paid by the athletic association. Crawford noted that Henry was paid $75 a month for doing "minor clerical work." The real mystery is how he happened to come to Carlisle.

For starters, not just anyone could step in and start on the Carlisle team, particularly on the 1911 version. Jim Thorpe and Lone Star Dietz weren't able to do that, so Henry Roberts must have been an experienced player before he arrived. He surely gained much experience at Haskell and Hampton Institutes and probably more elsewhere on independent teams. The next question is: how did Warner become aware of him? It is well known that fellow Oklahomans Jim Thorpe and Albert Exendine, then a Warner assistant, were both in Anadarko, Oklahoma in the summer of 1911. Pawnee is not all that far from Anadarko. It is not implausible that they ran into each other at a baseball game, especially considering that Roberts and Thorpe already knew each other. Roberts may have even sought out Thorpe or Exendine. Bill Newashe was playing baseball in Michigan, but Pete Hauser was probably in Pawhuska that summer before heading off to Atlanta to assist John Heisman in the fall. Although Victor Kelley appears to have been back in Durant, Oklahoma at this time, his ties to Carlisle wouldn't have been strong enough for him to have recruited Roberts. Stacy Matlock, Young Chief of the Pawnees, did have strong ties to Carlisle and would surely have wielded some influence over or for Henry Roberts. He may well have contacted Warner who would have then put him in contact with Exendine in Anadarko. This is all speculation, of course, but could well be true or at least close to what actually happened.

Athletics weren't Henry's only interest. According to later newspaper accounts, he was enrolled in the school's commercial program. Based on his later activities, it is likely that he took advantage of that educational opportunity. In Carlisle, Henry participated in extracurricular programs; on the road, he roomed with Lone Star Dietz, according to Jack Newcombe. He joined the Invincible Debating Society and was elected its president in late December. He also visited the Susan Longstreth Literary Society along with Jim Thorpe. However, his most important social contact came as the result of some unpleasant physical contact on the football field.

On November 11, 1911, the Carlisle Indian School football team achieved its greatest victory, an 18-15 defeat of mighty Harvard. A week later, they were upset by a weaker Syracuse team, due to overconfidence and listless play. Henry was injured in a desperate attempt to keep the Indians' record unblemished. So serious were his injuries that he was transported to the school's hospital. The first thing he could remember on regaining consciousness was the pretty face of Rose DeNomie, Ojibwa from the Bad River Agency near Ashland, Wisconsin. Rose worked as a nurse in the school hospital and gave this patient particular care. You see, he had been her football hero. That her loving care surely helped his quick recovery did not go unnoticed. He was determined to win her hand and studied earnestly for the civil service examination while keeping active in athletics.

Roberts also joined the varsity basketball team along with Jim Thorpe, Joel Wheelock, Bruce Goesback, Possum Powell, and Wounded Eye. However, his days of playing hoops were cut short when the civil service exam results arrived. Henry passed with high marks and soon received an appointment for a $900-a-year clerical position at the Shoshone Indian School on the Wind River Indian Reservation in Wyoming. That was enough money on which to support a young family in those days, so he was set, or so he thought. Rose wanted to marry Henry but her father, a lumberman, wanted to meet her beau before he would give his consent. They had to wait until Mr. DeNomie (Leon in a news report and Simon, Jr. on a census) eventually arrived, met with Henry, and gave his approval. On January 18, 1912, Henry Roberts and Rose DeNomie were married by Father Mark Strock of St. Patrick's Church at Superintendent Moses Friedman's home on the Indian School grounds. Rose entered as a student played the march from *Lohengrin*, (The Wedding March). After the ceremony, the football boys gave "a course dinner" in their honor. A local newspaper reporter opined, "There was a large wedding cake and some of the Indian maidens will dream over pieces of it this evening and will then anticipate similar future happiness." Afterwards, they caught the 5:40 p.m. train heading west.

It was a long train ride, actually several long train rides from Carlisle to Wind River, Wyoming. Rose entertained herself on this trip buying and sending beautiful postcards to her friends. Henry also had good people skills as his correspondence with Moses Friedman shows. He first wrote the superintendent on March 15, 1912 to thank him for sending them numerous newspaper clippings about their wedding. He also said, "Rose says she is going to make a book out of them. We received other clippings from all over the country. Even the Western papers had accounts of our marriage." Two of the clippings in his student file at the National Archives are accompanied by photos. They came from the *Chicago Record-Tribune* and the *Philadelphia North American*. Smaller papers generally didn't include the photos. The amount of coverage their wedding received reflects both the national interest in these famous football players and the ability of Warner's PR guys to write a captivating story.

Wind River, Wyoming did not turn out to be the best place to start his marriage. On June 15, 1912, Henry wrote to Moses Friedman again, this time to thank Friedman for assisting him in getting a transfer. He gushed, "And now comes this morning a letter from the Indian Office informing me of my

CARLISLE FOOTBALL STAR WINS THE HAND OF INDIAN NURSE.

ROSES DENOMIE

HENRY ROBERTS

transfer to Wisconsin, which I was pleased to get. I have accepted the transfer and want to thank you a thousand times for it, as I know it was through you that I have secured the transfer. I am sure that we can do better there than we can here, as living expenses here are so high. My wife is just tickled to go to Wisconsin." After assuring Friedman that he would work diligently at the new position, he wrote, "I can also assure you that I made a good name for ourselves and also for Carlisle, as they all know that we are Carlisle students around here and they hate to see us leave them." Earlier in the letter, he related, "I have charge of the Government Property at this agency and also render all the stenography and typewriting work in the office. I must say that when I landed here five months ago I found the property here in an awful shape, and I had to buckle right down to hard work and up to this time I am glad to say that I have the condition of the property just about right."

After arriving at his new assignment in Odanah, Wisconsin, Henry responded to a Returned Students query in which he said that he had been in the "Government Service" for about two years in "the same position that I am holding now." So, it would seem that his work at Carlisle was similar to what he did at Wind River and at Odanah and at wherever he was before coming to Carlisle. Keep in mind that he filled out this form about ten months after initially arriving at Carlisle. He had quite a year!

The form asked about his property. He claimed to, "Have 120 acres of good farming land in Oklahoma and about $1,000 in cash in the bank there in the town of Pawnee." He was, due to working away from home, renting a house in which to live. The October 25, 1912 issue of *The Carlisle Arrow* reported that he had started a football team at Odanah and expected to put up a strong fight against the other schools in the neighborhood. The January 24, 1913 *Arrow* informed readers that he was wintering in Oklahoma. His next move wasn't much of a surprise.

On February 19, he wrote Superintendent Friedman to inform him that, two weeks earlier, he had accepted a promotion and transfer to Union Agency in Muskogee, Oklahoma. He was then working as Clerk for $1,080 a year. A $180 a year raise was a lot at that time. He also requested that his address be changed so he could continue receiving copies of *The Carlisle Arrow*.

The rest of Henry's correspondence with Carlisle had to do with helping his brother, George, gain admission after being kicked out of Haskell for disobedience. Henry explained, "George is a young boy of eighteen, is one of these jolly sort of fellows who always like to make fun, being at an age when boys are inclined to be rather unruly and reckless. He doesn't mean any harm I am sure but just full of fun and perhaps takes matters a little too far sometimes. I know him to be a great tease, which I believe is partly the cause for his trouble." He went on to explain that, in normal times, his father would have paid to send George to school somewhere, but another brother, Terry, had "hip-joint disease" and treating that had been quite expensive. His father had already spent $1,000 for radium bath treatments at Claremore, Oklahoma that had been ineffective and had since enlisted a different doctor. The new one at McAlester, Oklahoma would surely cost his father additional expense.

George was eventually admitted to Carlisle in September of 1914 and immediately became active in school life. He Joined the Standard Literary Society and quickly began writing *The Blacksmith Shop* newspaper column. In December, his "Christmas Among the Pawnees" was published in *The Carlisle Arrow*. He was dropped from the student body in January 1915. Perhaps his article was found to be too similar to Lucy Little Chief's "How Pawnees Celebrate Christmas" that was published in Haskell's school paper, *The Indian Leader*, in 1907.

Henry and Rose (or Rosa or Rosie-records are inconsistent) raised their family in Oklahoma. Their first child was a daughter, Florence Mae. Next came two boys, Henry E. Jr. and Vandervort James. Following them was came Edith Muriel. Lastly came Everett E. who was born on December 15, 1927 and died on January 1, 1928.

Henry Roberts converted to Catholicism when he married. In Pawnee, he and Rose became pillars of the mostly white St. John the Evangelist Church. His younger sister, Lena, also converted when she married Tafoya, a Navajo, and also became a pillar of the church. She lived to be over 100 years old. Longevity ran in the family because Henry's father, Rush, lived to be 98 and was buried with full military honors in March 1958.

It's difficult to determine exactly where Henry and Rose lived, but the 1930 and 1931 tribal censuses listed them as living in Ponca City and Henry as working as a clerk at an oil refinery. After that, the rolls list them as living on the reservation, probably on their allotment. In 1933, he started working for the U.S. Government. After WWII, Henry took a job with the Atomic Energy Commission at Los Alamos, New Mexico, where he worked until he retired shortly after the death of his father. Co-workers purchased the typewriter he used during his 12 years of service with the AEC and gave it to him as a memento. At 70, he returned to Pawnee, Oklahoma to serve the Skidi Pawnees. He remained active and, as late as 1973, spoke at an athletic awards banquet. He died in March 1976.

Indian Blacksmiths by Lone Star Dietz

Isaac Seneca

Carlisle's First Walter Camp All-American

Isaac Seneca, Jr. was not alone at Carlisle as his brother, Victor, and sister, Nancy, attended at the same time he did. That their mother had died some years before and his father, Chief of the Senecas on the Cattaraugus Reservation, had remarried may have had something to do with the decision to send these children to the Carlisle Indian School.

Isaac spent much of his first year at Carlisle away from school on outing with a W. German in Newtown, Pennsylvania, possibly learning the blacksmith trade. He was gone from school nearly a year from mid-June 1894 to mid-May 1895. Two weeks later, he returned to his outing home and stayed there until mid-September. When actually at Carlisle and not on outing, Isaac immersed himself in the school routine and played football for his shop team, the Blacksmiths. After commencement, he returned to the country for the summer, his last summer outing.

1896 was Isaac Seneca's first year on the varsity and he got enough playing time to be included in the team photo, an honor extended to only 14 players. The *New York World* reported on a major incident in the Yale game in which he played a major role:

> "Cayou had retired in favor of Seneca, and the big chief ripped things, while the crowd howled in glee. The second half was nearing its close. There had been a tremendous scrimmage. The interference of the Indians was marvelous. Big Seneca was plunging through the line, going like a steam-engine, when he was tackled. As he fell Jamison grabbed the ball. Chauncey made a grab for him and missed. Instantly three of his mates were at Jamison's side. They galloped wildly down the field, making a touchdown.
>
> "Now, it was as fair a play as could have been. But it was not allowed. Hickok had sounded his whistle, indicating that the ball was down, that is, on the ground and not in play. The error was made by Hickok, as he himself admitted, because the ball was not dead. But inasmuch as he had

sounded the whistle there was nothing to do but to bring the ball back. The crowd howled and hissed at the decision for five minutes.

"The Indians were furious, not so much so as their teachers, however, and Hickok was so unhappy that he didn't know what to do. The professors wanted to take the Indians from the field, but they preferred to play on.

"They returned to the game. They played more determinedly than ever. You could see them standing calm, and perfectly motionless and at the word springing forward with tremendous intensity and fighting with everything in them.

"They never panted as did the Yale men; they never trembled with eagerness.

"It looked as if they must carry things before them and win another touchdown, so tremendous was their struggle. But the whistle sounded and the game was over."

The Indian Helper discussed the reaction to the Yale game: "Rarely has a contest excited such widespread attention and voluminous comment in all of the best papers of the land. Dr. Lyman Abbott in his pulpit on the following Sunday evening referred to the unfair treatment of the Indians and spoke of their noble manhood. Much of the comment was owing to what is conceded by the best football experts to be an unjust decision of the referee, which ruled out a touch-down by the Indians." A sad irony was that the referee, William O. Hickok, was also the Indians' coach. Not lost on journalists was that he was also a Yale man, having been an All-American guard in 1893 and 1894 for the Elis. He admitted that he had blown his whistle too early. Some likened him to a corrupt Indian agent.

Isaac wasn't as involved with extra-curricular activities as were many other football players, so he didn't receive much mention in the school's publications. He did receive notice in March 1897, however, for throwing a surprise party for his sister when she left for Medico-Chirurgical Hospital in Philadelphia where she had enrolled in a nursing program.

Name: Isaac Seneca **Nickname:**
DOB: 10/7/1875 **Height:** 5'9"
Weight: 155 **Age:** 23
Tribe: Seneca **Home:** Cattaraugus Reservation, NY
Parents: Isaac Seneca, Seneca; unknown, Seneca
Early Schooling: unknown
Later Schooling:
Honors:

Isaac Seneca; *U. S. Army Military History Institute*

Isaac Seneca; *Cumberland County Historical Society, Carlisle, PA*

Seneca spent the summer of 1897 at home and returned to Carlisle in time for football season. He continued to improve his skills but played in the shadows of such players as Frank Cayou, Martin Wheelock and Bemus Pierce. The most tragic accident in Carlisle Indian School history happened on November 6, 1897, when the team was returning home from the Penn game in Philadelphia. Newspapers across the country reported on the sad event. *The Indian Helper* provided more detail:

> "On the way back from Philadelphia last Saturday night, when a little way out of the city Victor Seneca put his head out of the car window and was hit by something which cut a great gash in his head causing concussion of the brain, from the effects of which he died the next day. Victor came in 1895 and had reached the third grade. He was a good, quiet, steady young man of 18 years, well esteemed by his classmates and all with whom he associated. The sad accident cast an abiding gloom over the school. On Monday night his teacher, Miss Carter, and brother Isaac Seneca, went with the remains to Versailles, N. Y., the home of the deceased. Nancy Seneca, class '97, who is at the Madico Chirurgical Institute of Philadelphia, was summoned to the death bed of her brother who she had seen and talked with but a few hours before in Philadelphia. It was a great shock to her."

The school administration often made special arrangements for the students to be able to attend the Penn game because it was a major rivalry and, of the big games, it was played closest to home. Victor had probably gone to see his brother play. One cannot imagine how this freak accident impacted Isaac, his sister and the other students.

Isaac learned the blacksmithing trade well and was soon leading the other boys. In August 1898, he took charge over summer vacation as *The Indian Helper* reported:

> "One of the most interesting places on the grounds to visit is the blacksmith shop, especially when the anvil is ringing to the tune of busy Indian boys working without an instructor, as now, when Mr. Harris is off on his vacation. Isaac Seneca is in charge and has two or three boys under him. The deftness with which they hammer bolts, braces, clevises and what-not into shape handling red hot iron with the ease that putty is manipulated in the fingers, speaks volumes for the instruction they received and would be a revelation to those who think that Indians can never learn to work skillfully."

The 1898 football season was the last one Isaac Seneca played in the shadows of more famous teammates. Perhaps it had to do with Pop Warner arriving at Carlisle in 1899; perhaps not. Regardless, Isaac Seneca came into his own that year. These year-end notes put it into perspective:

> "At a meeting of the Carlisle Indian football players, Isaac L. Seneca was elected captain of the team for the season of 1900 to succeed Martin L. Wheelock. He was the unanimous choice of the players. Seneca has played three years on the team. He belongs to the Seneca tribe of New York. He is twenty-one years old is 5 feet 10 inches in height and weighs 150 pounds. He is a fierce player and one of the best punters in the team. His position is right halfback ... he made a number of brilliant runs, twice carrying three men over the goal line. The Indians are much pleased with their successful season on the gridiron. The season was a big success in a financial way also, the Indians clearing about $10,000."

Walter Camp was so impressed with Isaac's play that he took the unprecedented step of naming an Indian to his All-America First Team. Prior to that, only six schools (Harvard, Princeton, Yale, Penn, Cornell and Chicago) had had their players named to Camp's All-America First Team. Seneca brought the total to seven, with the addition of Carlisle to this elite list. Some thought Seneca to be faster and stronger than Jim Thorpe and that is quite a comparison. A description in a 1909 edition of *The Indian Craftsman* tolled his virtues: "Seneca, Hendricks and Thorpe were great halfbacks. Seneca was a fast running back, full of fire and when not carrying the ball for good distances was always interfering for the runner. He was also a great defensive man."

Isaac graduated with his class in the spring of 1900 but, although elected captain, did not return to lead the team that fall. However, he was not done playing football. The Greensburg, Pennsylvania independent team, as part of a move to improve chances for a championship, hired Seneca for the 1900 season. On paper the team looked like a world-beater, but some losses caused it to suffer financially. PFRA Research provided an anecdote that summed up their season:

> "The Greenies' season turned on the games with Latrobe. Three had been scheduled, with the first at Greensburg on October 27. A disap-

pointing but spirited crowd of a little over 2,000 showed. When a fight broke out between Greensburg's Isaac Seneca and Latrobe's Al Kennedy, the crowd joined in to produce a general donnybrook. That was most of the excitement for Greensburg fans, as Latrobe handed their heroes a third straight loss, 6-0."

The Greenies ceased operation near the end of the season. That may also have been the end of Isaac's football career because no documentation of him playing for other teams has been found to date.

By the next summer, Isaac Seneca's name started appearing on rolls of government employees. In 1901 he was working as a blacksmith at the Cheyenne and Arapahoe Agency in Oklahoma. A November issue of *The Red Man and Helper* wrote that he was "enjoying Western life, particularly the hunting of quails and ducks." Whether he was hunting for it or not, he found something else while working there - a wife.

Rosa Frass was the orphaned daughter of a Cheyenne woman and a white man, probably from Germany. Rosa had attended Haskell Institute so she knew English. Otherwise, she and Isaac would not have had a common language.

In 1904, *The Arrow* reported on him: "Isaac Seneca class 1900, now employed at Chilocco in ordering the *Arrow* says: 'Be sure and shoot or aim one shot at Chilocco Indian School, and you'll hit me there.' Isaac was transferred from blacksmithing in the service to engineering." Some time prior to January 1907, he was married, living in Darlington, Oklahoma, and working as an instructor in blacksmithing at Chilocco Indian School. He and Bloss Jaloma, his assistant, also operated a blacksmith and wagon shop to meet the demands of the school for all repairs of iron work.

Either he, Rosa or the two of them had been investing their money because, at that time they owned a quarter section in Texas, a quarter section in Oklahoma, property of indeterminate size in old Mexico and building lots in Oklahoma City. He said that he had but $200 in savings at that time.

Their son, Russell, was born in 1906, so Isaac and Rosa were probably married some time before that date. Isaac received a $100 raise from $680 to $780 in 1910, a significant increase at that time. The timing was good because their daughter, Maurine Vivian Seneca, was born that year. In 1914, *The Arkansas City Traveler* reported, "Seneca is a cracking good mechanic and has been a very efficient blacksmith at Chilocco for some time. He is a fine specimen of the athletic Indian and is a handsome fellow to boot."

In 1930, he was still working as a blacksmith but was widowed and living in Ponca City, Oklahoma. Later in the 1930s, it appears that he and Maurine moved back to the Cattaraugus Reservation, perhaps to be near his aging father. They were living near Irving, New York in 1937.

Carlisle track team with Olympians Jim Thorpe (back row center) and Lewis Tewanima (front row left end)

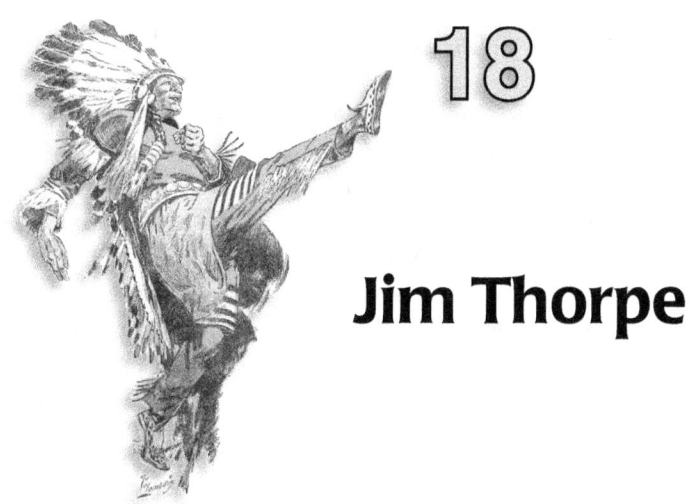

Jim Thorpe

Wa-tho-huck (Bright Path)

According to church records, James Francis (Jacobus Franciscus) and Charles Thorpe were born on May 22, 1887 near Konawa in Pottawatomie County, Oklahoma. Jim later claimed to have been born on May 28, 1888 south of Bellemont, Pottawatomie County, Oklahoma. As with many others in this book, the details of his birth are unclear; unlike anyone else, he became the world's greatest athlete. The purpose of this chapter is not to chronicle Thorpe's life – excellent biographies have already been written by Robert W. Wheeler (1975) and Bill Crawford (2005) – but to provide an overview for those unfamiliar with him and, hopefully, to provide a new tidbit or two of information to those who are familiar with Big Jim.

If there were a theme to Jim Thorpe's life, it was loss. The twin boys were born to an Irish-Sac and Fox father, Hiram P. Thorpe, and a Potawatomie-

Name: James Francis Thorpe	**Nickname:** Big Jim; Libbling
DOB: 5/22/1887 or 5/28/1888	**Height:** 6'0"
Weight: 178	**Age:** 22
Tribe: Sac and Fox	**Home:** Pottawatomie County, OK
Parents: Hiram P. Thorpe, Irish & Sac and Fox; Charlotte Vieux Thorpe, Potawatomie-Menominee-Kickapoo & French	
Early Schooling: Sac and Fox Reservation Boarding School; Haskell Institute	
Later Schooling:	
Honors: Citizens Savings Athletic Foundation, 1950; College Football Hall of Fame, Charter Member, 1951; Professional Football Hall of Fame, Charter Member, 1963; American Indian Athletic Hall of Fame, Charter Member, 1971; Oklahoma Sports Hall of Fame, Charter Member, 1986; Athlete of the Century, 1999	

Menominee-Kickapoo-French mother, Charlotte Vieux Thorpe. He once told a reporter that his family background made him an "American Airedale." His mother was a devout Catholic. According to his daughter, Grace, "Grandpa was a horse breeder, a wife-beater and the strongest guy in the county. He was a polygamist and had two wives. My understanding was he kicked them out when he met Charlotte, my grandmother." Hiram loved horses and raised them, leaving the farm work to Charlotte. He enjoyed horse trading, racing, wrestling, betting and drinking. "He was a big, ornery guy. He liked to drink and fight. When Grandpa would come along in his wagon along Moccasin Trail, folks would turn off their lights, 'cause he liked to shoot them out as he came down the road." Such was the environment in which the boys grew up.

When away from their father, the twins had a great time – from a boy's point-of-view – hunting, fishing, trapping, berry-picking, swimming and wrestling on the family's 1,200-acre allotment. That all ended in early 1897 when a typhoid epidemic took Charlie before his tenth birthday. Jim was devastated and became a loner, taking up the habit of hunting raccoons all night with only a dog for a companion.

Hiram and Charlotte were both literate, a rarity in that time and place, and sent their children to be schooled at the government boarding school on the Sac and Fox Reservation. There has been some speculation that family strife, rather than the desire to see their children educated, prompted the Thorpes' decision. Jim hated it and ran away. A teacher considered him incorrigible. After a series of runaways and beatings from his father, young Jim was sent, "… so far you will never find your way back home." That would have worked with most boys, but not Jim. Haskell Institute in Lawrence, Kansas was not too far away for him to find his way home. He then spent some time in Texas breaking horses, a task that helped develop his strength and coordination. This was something he enjoyed.

Charlotte Thorpe died in November 1901, and Hiram quickly remarried. Jim lived at home and attended Garden School for awhile. He didn't run away from that school because, outside of school hours, he was free to hunt and fish – and he found it more bearable than being at home. Through a chain of events that will likely never be unraveled, Jim, now 17, enrolled at Carlisle on February 6, 1904, for a five-year enrollment. Hiram Thorpe died later that year of an infection that developed from a hunting accident. Jim was then an orphan.

Although a natural athlete, he was small at 5'5 ½ " tall and weighing 115 pounds, so he didn't immediately become involved in varsity sports but did play on shop teams. Also, he might not have felt comfortable competing for a position on the school team due to having had little previous exposure to organized athletics, especially those played with proper equipment and according to standardized rules. James, as did the other students, attended

Jim Thorpe making a mighty punt; *U. S. Army Military History Institute*

academic classes half day and worked in a trade the other half. He worked as a painter. Periodically, he went on outings to work on farms.

The story of the beginning of Jim Thorpe's involvement in Carlisle athletics is well known and can be found in Mike Bynum's autobiography of Pop Warner as well as in Thorpe biographies; that part of the story will be presented as briefly as possible here. In April 1907, wearing overalls and borrowed gym shoes, he broke the school record in the high jump. A track team member, believed to be Al Exendine, informed Warner of his feat. The coach then assigned Exendine the task of working with Thorpe. The result was that the lad soon broke all of Ex's records and some others. Jim was a rising star on the track team, but he wasn't satisfied; he wanted to play football, too. According to others' reports, he didn't see much point to running track because there was no money to be made in it. Warner did not want to risk his then skinny, up-and-coming track star to a career-ending injury in football; however, Thorpe insisted on a tryout. Pop accommodated him by having him give the varsity some tackling practice. That would surely change his mind, or so thought Warner. That plan blew up in the Old Fox's face when the upstart ran through the entire team. "Nobody going to tackle Jim."

The 1907 football season was a frustrating one for Jim because he spent most of the time on the bench learning from the first team. Being new to the game, he knew neither the rules nor the halfback position. Something else he didn't like was the training table at which, as a member of the varsity, he took his meals. Joe Guyon later related, "Jim hated the training table, because it never had enough on it to eat. He loved steaks. Pop Warner, our coach at Carlisle, would ration off steaks to us, and Jim would buy them off the other players. He could do that. Oklahoma Indians had money."

1908 was a better year football-wise for Jim. He became a starter at left halfback, which was the tailback in Warner's single-wingback formation. That position was ideally suited for a triple-threat player like Thorpe who could run, pass and kick with the best of them. Walter Camp rewarded the young back's efforts by placing Jim on his All-America Third Team. Not bad for a second year player.

In the winter, Jim Thorpe captained the Freshman Class basketball team and played on the varsity squad. He was also elected captain of the 1909 varsity track team. Open dates in a great track season gave Jim opportunities to pitch a couple of shutouts for the school's baseball team. That summer he joined some other Carlisle students to play summer baseball for the Rocky Mount Railroaders in the Eastern Carolina League. Thorpe had completed his five-year term, but school records listed him as a deserter. Superintendent Friedman may have been angry that he left to play baseball.

Thorpe, apparently feeling that he wasn't a deserter, spent Christmas at the school visiting old friends. He also brought some new students with him. However, he didn't stay or return for track season as *The Arrow* suggested he would. Carlisle heard little more from its prodigal son until Al Exendine encountered him, broke, on an Anadarko, Oklahoma street in the summer of 1911. Ex called Warner to inform him, among other things, that Thorpe was no longer a skinny kid but, at 24 years old, had grown to 5'11" tall and weighed 185 pounds. Warner wanted him back; Friedman didn't. Warner won out and Thorpe made history.

Pop Warner and Moses Friedman did not distinguish themselves in their handling of this situation. They surely were aware that Thorpe had played minor league baseball for pay, something that was clearly against the rules for college and Olympic athletes of that time. However, they were also surely aware that it was a widespread practice for college athletes to play summer baseball. The difference was that college boys were more sophisticated than Indian youths, who were in the difficult process of assimilating into white man's society, and, being better informed about such things as maintaining one's amateur status, played under assumed names. Discussing Thorpe's return to Carlisle presents an ethical challenge for the author because his conclusion is that Thorpe should have broken the rules. Had Thorpe not been allowed to play football and run track at Carlisle, he might not have been allowed on the Olympic team. Had he not played college sports or been an Olympic champion, he may lived a life of quiet obscurity or one very similar to that of his father. Playing at Carlisle created numerous opportunities for him that he would most likely have never had.

The football team of 1911 was arguably Carlisle's finest team, losing but a single game and beating two of the Big Four, Penn and Harvard. Jim was named to Walter Camp's All-America First Team. In a 1944 interview with John M. Flynn, Jim said his fondest memories of 23 years of playing football were from the November 11, 1911 game with Harvard in Cambridge. In spite of an injured right leg, Thorpe kicked four field goals to defeat the Crimson for only the second time in Carlisle history. He considered it the most fiercely played game in which he ever participated. Sportswriters of the day dubbed it "the most spectacular football battle ever seen in the East."

Jim was definitely the big man on campus at this time and against strong competition, except in the eyes of one fair maiden. Mamie Mt. Pleasant, younger sister of Frank Mt. Pleasant, told her grandchildren of the time he asked her out on a date. She said she turned him down because he was too ugly. Ugly to her may have extended beyond physical beauty because she was a refined young lady who may not have found Jim's less sophisticated ways attractive. Fortunately for Jim, there were plenty of other pretty girls on campus.

Thorpe's triumphs during the 1911-12 school year weren't limited to the gridiron. Jim was also spectacular in track in 1912 while he prepared for the Stockholm Olympic Games. Thorpe's performance in the 1912 Olympic Summer Games is legendary. He won gold medals in two grueling events, the pentathlon and decathlon, which are composed of five and ten separate events, respectively. He also competed in two other events but did not medal in either. Additionally, he participated in an exhibition baseball game. At the awards ceremony on the closing night of the game, King Gustav V of Sweden famously said, "You sir are the greatest athlete in the world." And Thorpe, just as famously, responded, "Thanks, King." Afterwards he had fun in other forms of competition while in Europe.

A reporter who covered the Olympics wrote about how Jim entertained himself in his free time:

> "We were in Paris and a lot of athletes and scribes were lolling in the hotel when Thorpe came in, and asked us to go with him. Said he had found a place where we could have more fun than any other place he ever saw. So we trotted along, and Thorpe led us to a joint under the shadow of Montmartre, a regular batcave, full of hard looking Apaches.
>
> "'Where's the fun here, Jim?' I queried. Thorpe grinned a foot wide. 'Big lots fun,' said he. 'Here last night. Had to lick seven Frenchmen.

Maybe so we get fine fight tonight. All we need do, just go in, act noisy, have elegant fight. Come along!'"

He was his father's son.

Thorpe was accompanied to the Olympics by Coach Warner and Louis Tewanima, the silver medalist in the 10,000 meters, a Hopi Indian and member of the Carlisle track team. Gus Welch qualified for the 1912 Olympics but did not compete due to injury. Upon their return, the Olympic team was treated to a New York City ticker tape parade which an estimated 1,000,000 people attended. Thorpe was the toast of the world.

Football season started soon after that, and Thorpe again showed that he was the best player by scoring 25 touchdowns. The team piled up a total of 504 points in this one-loss season. Their defeat of an Army team led by Dwight David Eisenhower is the topic of a recent book by Lars Anderson. Walter Camp again named Thorpe to his All-America First Team. In 1912, Jim had had the greatest year an athlete has ever had, but 1913 was different.

In mid-January, a story usually attributed to Roy Johnson of the *Worcester* [Massachusetts] *Telegram* broke saying that Thorpe had been paid for playing for the Winston-Salem minor league baseball team for two summers. Charles Clancy, manager of the team, was quoted making racial and personal attacks against Thorpe. Thorpe huddled with Warner to decide what to do. Although a lawyer, Warner failed to look at the rules regarding challenges, perhaps because he was preoccupied with saving his own skin. Thorpe was convinced that he had to admit playing for pay. There were even photographs of him in the team's uniform. It is unclear if he composed the letter in which he, a simple Indian boy ignorant of all the rules in the white man's world, admitted to having played for the Rocky Mount and Fayetteville teams, but he wrote it out and signed it. He also followed Warner's advice about returning the medals, and he regretted doing so the rest of his life. Now that Jim was no longer an amateur, he could not play on Carlisle teams, nor could he tour with the AAU. Put another way, the days of his being exploited because he was an amateur were over. He was now a professional and would be paid to play – and paid very well at that.

There were plenty of teams – major league baseball teams, that is – ready to sign him up to big contracts. They knew he would be a big box office draw. Outside of New York, the press was rather supportive of Thorpe and critical of the AAU. Even the Brits favored Thorpe. The Fayetteville team claimed it had Thorpe under contract in an attempt to extort money from the major league team that would sign him, but that failed.

Possibly feeling a bit guilty over how Jim was treated, Warner stepped in as his agent to negotiate a contract for him. About the time Thorpe was ready to sign with Cincinnati, Warner's old fried John McGraw, manager of the New York Giants, called and doubled the highest offer. Being a lawyer, Warner was able to draw up a contract and he did – a very good one at that.

The Giants were to pay Thorpe $6,000 a year for five years. That was more money than many people earned in their lifetimes, even professional players.

Shortly after the beginning of spring training, criticisms of Thorpe's baseball abilities started to surface. From Washington, DC came, "Jim Thorpe, the Indian, who was recently declared a professional by the A. A. U., is an inferior ball player, and if the New York Giants have signed him at a fancy salary somebody has been badly stung, in the opinion of five Washington boys who played in the Eastern Carolina League in 1909 and batted against Thorpe. They all state that the Indian was only a fair minor league pitcher, a poor hitter and a worse fielder, and that his only asset was speed on the bases, which availed him little, as he seldom got on the bags." Apparently John McGraw agreed with them.

On March 28, a report came out of New York that indicated Thorpe wasn't going to make the team:

> "Jim Thorpe will be released by the Giants after the first trip west has been finished, according to a private tip that comes indirectly from Manager McGraw. Thorpe, it is said, is a failure as a ball player and McGraw has not the time to develop him this season. The Indian signed a regular National League contract, in which the usual ten-day notice of release is included. His salary is said to have been set at $6,000 for the season, or $1,000 a month, beginning on April 10, 1913."

However, when the season started, Big Jim was in the Giants' dugout and McGraw was singing his praises. Could the critics have been wrong? A later article clears up the mystery:

> "He put his signature to a contract that couldn't be broken with one of the kaiser's forty-two centimeter guns. The parchment called for five years of service at a big salary, with the ten-day clause deleted, as the censors say. Under the terms of the parchment Thorpe can't be farmed out or even slapped on the wrist for violating any of McGraw's rules. The only power reserved by the Giants is to pay him his salary; otherwise they haven't a word to say.
>
> ...
>
> "The little Napoleon strove hard to pass this red elephant to another manager, including Pat Moran, but hasn't been able. Everybody is wise to the contract."

Warner apparently took care of Thorpe by leaving some standard clauses out of his contract. Jim would remain with the Giants. Not only would he stay in the big leagues through the season but, because the Giants finished in first place, he was with the team at the World Series. (Prior to expansion in the 1960s, the World Series was played between the winners of the National and American Leagues, each of which had eight teams, as God intended.)

While sitting in the dugout, watching his teammates flail at fellow Carlisle alum Albert "Chief" Bender's pitches along the way to a 4 game to 1 game loss to the Philadelphia Athletics, Jim had plenty of time to plan his upcoming wedding. Tight planning was needed because the Giants and the White Sox were starting an around-the-world exhibition tour right after the World Series.

Iva Margaret Miller lost her mother to tuberculosis when she was five and not long after that her father died or left. Having only a trace of Indian blood, Iva did not qualify for admission to Carlisle, so her sister, knowing the requirements, filled out the enrollment forms in such a way as to make it appear that Iva was at least ¼ blood, and thus allowed to enter the government Indian school. Iva, Jim and Gus Welch were classmates. Thought by many to be the prettiest girl in school, she attracted the attentions of both of the young warriors. Iva picked Jim in spite of, or perhaps because of, disapproval by relatives and faculty members. Even Pop Warner counseled Ivy, as her friends called her, against the marriage but she was very strong-willed.

One of the things Jim did while watching the Giants get eliminated from the World Series was to negotiate the sale of movie rights for his wedding. To show how far ahead of the time that Hollywood types would sell the film rights to their wedding festivities, consider that a feature film had yet to be shot in Tinseltown. The World Series in which his team, the Giants, played was filmed that year. Perhaps he and the movie moguls (they were still in Fort Lee, New Jersey) thought Thorpe's marriage would make a perfect segue between the coverage of the World Series and the world tour. It might also attract more female patrons. The wedding, held at St. Patrick's in Carlisle, was quite an extravaganza with uncounted bridesmaids and other assorted attendants. Jim had plenty of money to spend on the wedding because a player's share on the losing team in that year's World Series was $2,361.16. Moses Friedman, the Jewish superintendent of the Indian School, gave away the bride at the high mass officiated by Father Mark Stock in what is called today the Shrine Church. After a reception at the superintendent's house attended by 200 of their closest friends, the couple dashed off to New York to join the Giants on their globe-trotting tour. Six to eight newlywed

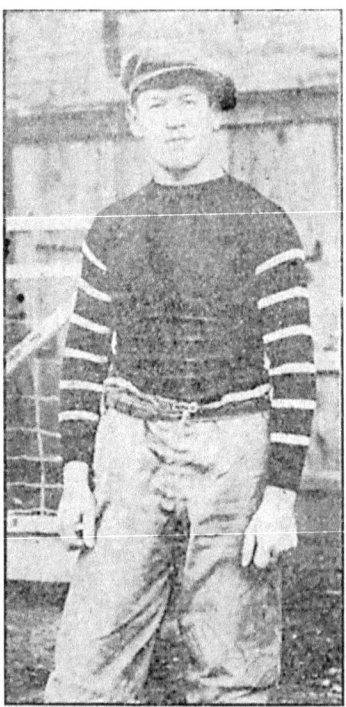

Assistant Coach Thorpe,
Indiana Daily Student

couples were on the tour. It wasn't possible to determine the exact number because some of the ballplayers were having difficulty convincing their brides to be to tie the knot on such short notice.

Whether John McGraw added players to his roster for the tour to rest injured ones or to take a look at some others is unclear. But the result was that he gave Jim much more playing time than he had during the season. McGraw, being no fool, may have played Thorpe to increase the box office. Jim responded with some powerful hitting. The team worked its way west across the U. S. playing 35 games in 31 cities before setting sail from Seattle on November 19. They stopped to play games in Vancouver, British Columbia, baseball-mad Tokyo, Shanghai, indifferent Hong Kong, Manila, Brisbane, Sydney, Melbourne, Ceylon, Cairo, Rome, Monte-Carlo, Paris and London before returning home on the *Lusitania*. Jim and Iva Thorpe were the biggest celebrities in foreign countries with their photos often appearing on front pages of newspapers. She was as sought after as he was.

The tour ended in time for spring training - a little late actually, but these guys had played all winter. Jim didn't spend the season with the big league club as he was sent down to the minors to play in Toronto in April. 1915 wasn't much better baseball-wise but his first son, James Jr., was born that year.

That fall Jim took a job as assistant coach of the Indiana University football team. He, Iva and Jim Jr. arrived in Bloomington in October, after the end of baseball season. The *Indiana Daily Student* (*IDS*) gave their newly-arrived celebrities much coverage, but not all of the usual type. "The Fair Sex Forum," edited by Betty Carothers, '17, interviewed Iva whose responses probably weren't what the reporter expected: "It's just too bad I can't tell you more about Indians, as they draw pictures of them in books, with all the wildness there. I can't understand, you know, how some of my Indian friends can go back to the Indian reservation and wrap themselves in the same old blanket, and never make any use of the education they received at school. I have asked some of them how in the world they do it, and they tell me there is the only place their friends and relatives are and that they would be ostracized if they didn't." As the reporter started to leave, Iva said, "My! You are fortunate here in Indiana, to have gentlemen call on you so much – how many times a week is it? Four! Why, at Carlisle, Mr. Thorpe got to see me but once a week!"

Then Jim changed history - again. Up to this time, professional football had been a marginal enterprise at best. Clubs were frequently insolvent and players had to have day jobs to survive. Jack Cusack, manager of the Canton, Ohio Bulldogs, heard that arch-rival Massillon was loading up on former All-Americans for their upcoming games and felt that he needed to strengthen his team. So, he dispatched Thorpe's former teammate at Carlisle and Canton stalwart, William Gardner, to Bloomington to recruit Thorpe. Cusack, a pioneer of professional football, directed Gardner to offer Thorpe

$250 per game to play for the Bulldogs – not just for a single game, but for every game. This was unheard of. Star players were sometimes paid large amounts to play as ringers in key games, but no one had ever been paid this much to play all the time. The best players were only getting $100 a game and the rest a lot less than that. Some thought Jack was going to bankrupt the team. Thorpe, no fool, accepted the offer.

Jim Thorpe's first known game as a professional football player was played on the second Sunday of November in Massillon. However, he didn't do much playing as Canton's then coach, Harry Hazlett, for reasons of his own, kept Thorpe on the bench for much of the game; when Jim got on the field, quarterback Don Hamilton seldom called his number. Canton lost the game, but Jack Cusack turned a tidy profit because 6,000 people paid to see the game. Hazlett was fired, Hamilton quit, and Thorpe was named captain. Also, a few more stars were signed. After all, Canton needed quality players to compete with the likes of Notre Dame and Massillon stars, Rockne and Dorais.

Cusack left the schedule for Thanksgiving week open to allow his players to rest and recuperate before the rematch with Massillon to be played in Canton on the fourth Sunday of November. This gave Thorpe the opportunity to pick up a $250 pay check from the Pine Village Indians. Pine Village, Indiana, a town of 300 people referred to by one resident as "a half-horse town," was the home of an independent football team that hadn't lost a game to another town or college team in a decade. However, they did not play teams of the caliber of Canton and Massillon. Pine Village arranged a big Thanksgiving Day game to be played in Lafayette against a team of college stars and needed some help. Big Jim, conveniently located in Bloomington, was the right man for the job.

To prepare for the contest, Jim scrimmaged against the Indiana University starting eleven. That's right: Thorpe, by himself, took on the entire starting line-up. But they played according to special rules he developed especially for the contest: the ball was kicked off from the 40-yard line and, if a player caught it, he could run five steps unmolested and punt the ball as far as he could or attempt a field goal. The *IDS* reported the outcome of the scrimmage: "Despite the efforts of the big eleven to kick the ball to all sides of the field, Thorpe's legs were able to get him under the ball and thereby gain a run of five steps. Of course he could punt the ball easily twice as far as his opponents and when he crossed the 40-yard line, the hearts of the eleven began to falter, because he was 'Dead-eye Dick' on a drop-kick anywhere within this distance. Thorpe won several games even with the wind against him, and all the sting was taken out of the minds of the men opposing him whenever one of those high balls went sailing over the goal posts, by that laugh which could be heard from one end of the field to the other."

Big Jim didn't collect splinters on Pine Village's bench; he was the star of the game and helped preserve the Indians' 108 game winning streak. His 81-yard punt wowed fans and sportswriters alike. He also played in the second Canton-Massillon game at which 8,000 fans turned out to see the big Indian in action. The game was a defensive struggle in which few first downs were made by either team. In spite of this, Jim had drop-kicked a field goal from the 18-yard line and place kicked another from the 45 to give his team a 6-0 lead into the fourth quarter. Jack Cusack recalled, "At this juncture I saw that something was wrong with [Earl] Abel, our new tackle. Our opponents were making far too much yardage through his position, and when Captain Thorpe made no move to replace him I took it upon myself to do so – in keeping with an agreement I had with Thorpe that it would be my right to substitute from the bench if I felt it necessary. (I might mention, too, that Jim was sometimes hesitant to substitute, especially as to replacing a player with All-American qualifications.) I found that Abel was ill with a heavy cold, and I replaced him with Charlie Smith, the Negro from the Michigan Aggies."

Canton eventually won the game and claimed the championship after a strongly disputed ending. As time ran out, a Massillon player, Maury "Windy" Briggs, caught a Gus Dorais pass at the two-yard line in the midst of a crowd of spectators who had flowed onto the field, but the ball bounded out of the crowd and Charlie Smith pounced on it to preserve the victory. Briggs was livid, stating that a policeman had knocked the ball out of his hands. However, it was common knowledge that Canton had no police force at that time and Canton prevailed. A decade later the man in the blue uniform with brass buttons, a streetcar conductor, acknowledged that he had done the deed because he had bet heavily on the game. Thorpe's appearance in a Canton uniform lifted professional football to a higher level, one of economic viability. Had Jim not played pro football, the game may have languished until Red Grange's arrival in 1925.

Thorpe and Canton were a perfect match and Jim was soon joined by some old friends. But before he could put on the moleskins again, Jim had another baseball season in front of him – after some time off for hunting, of course. After spring training, John McGraw sent him down to Milwaukee of the American Association to spend the 1916 season honing his skills. Jim definitely improved by leading the league in steals and hitting the longest ball hit in the Louisville Colonels' park to that time. In the fall, he was back in the majors again to play football, but he did take a little time off to help Pop Warner prepare his Pitt team for a big game with Syracuse.

The 1916 Canton Bulldogs were very likely the best pro team assembled to that time. Jim's old buddies Pete Calac, William Gardner, William Garlow and Gus Welch on the Canton roster were part of the reason the Bulldogs had an undefeated season. Some sports writers considered Jim to be playing the best football of his life at that time. He must have thought so, too when he said, "I am better than I ever was. A few more years hasn't hurt me in the least. Of course I have taken care of myself." Others might disagree with his last statement because of his reputation for drinking and carousing. Canton management might agree with Jim because 10,000 people bought tickets for each of the Canton-Massillon games.

In the 1917 baseball season, McGraw loaned Thorpe to Cincinnati after he played in 26 games. At Cincinnati, he played in 77 games, more big league games than he had played in the National League in 1913-15 combined. He also had 251 at bats, more than twice as many in those years combined. Pop Warner believed that Jim Thorpe would have had a much better baseball career, had he been sent directly to the minors for some proper coaching prior to playing in the majors. Also, he and McGraw had a personality clash, and Little Napoleon either didn't know how to deal with Thorpe or wouldn't allow himself to get Thorpe the coaching he needed. Perhaps he never got past Pop Warner putting one over on him with the missing clauses in Jim's contract.

Tragedy struck Thorpe again that year. James Jr. contracted infantile paralysis and died. Jim took it very hard and John McGraw showed him no sympathy. Joe Guyon remembered it well many years later: "Jim took some tough blows in his lifetime. Like the time they took away his Olympic medals because they found he had played some professional baseball. Oh, gosh, he took that hard. He said, 'Well, they can have the damn things but they can't take back the honor.' And then he lost his boy, just a youngster, and that really knocked him down."

Jim Thorpe with Giants, 1913; *Library of Congress*

At least 1917 was good football-wise for Thorpe and the Bulldogs as they went 9-1 again. Joe Guyon joined Jim and Pete Calac on the Bulldogs. The three would play together for many years more. The U. S. had entered WWI earlier that year, and teams were quickly becoming depleted of quality players. Jim played baseball for the Giants in 1918, riding the bench mostly, even though McGraw had many players go to war. Pro football was suspended for the duration and armistice came too late to get a season started that year. Jack Cusack left Canton and took a job in the oil fields of Oklahoma, leaving the management of the Bulldogs in the capable hands of Ralph Hay, a local automobile dealer.

Jim played his last, and best, year of major league baseball in 1919 when, in August, after having had but three at bats in two games for the Giants that season, he was sold to the Boston Braves. He hit .327 in his 60 games with the Braves. Not bad at all and he must have hit a few curve balls to accomplish that. Throughout his baseball career, he had the rap of not being able to hit a curve, but it appears that he had overcome that obstacle. All he did in the fall was to lead the Bulldogs to yet another football championship.

1920 marked Thorpe's permanent demotion into minor league baseball, where he stayed the rest of his career. However, he got a major promotion in football. In August, owners and managers of a few professional football teams met in Ralph Hay's Hupmobile dealership and, while seated on running boards and sipping beers, formed the American Professional Football Association (APFA) and named Jim Thorpe as the league's president. Thorpe was not picked because of his administrative skills, of which there were few, but because his name gave the league stature. Also, he was allowed to continue playing on one of the league's teams. After a so-so year with Canton, Jim's attention strayed.

He signed with the Cleveland Indians Football Team which was unfortunately owned by a large mercantile firm. During the season, Jack Cusack returned to Ohio to recuperate from malaria that he had contracted while building a refinery in Arkansas. Jim asked Jack to look after his interests because his contract included both a guaranteed amount per game plus a percentage of the gate. Jim was concerned that he was not receiving what was due him under the contract. After the last regular season game, the team's management got the players to play a game in New York for free but agreed to cover their travel expenses from the guarantee to be paid to the team. While in New York, the team's management reneged on the travel expenses. After enlisting the police and some burly football players, Cusack convinced Cleveland's management that it was not in their best interest to skip town without paying the players what had been agreed upon. Jack then took over the team and scheduled two more games. He and the players divvied up the proceeds from these games and the team disbanded, ending his involvement with professional football. Jack had much to say about his experience with Jim:

> "Many of the stories written about the great Jim Thorpe were pure fabrication. One such tale that went the rounds was that Jim's shoulder pads were made of sheet metal or cast iron. Maybe they felt like that to the men the big Indian tackled or knocked aside on his terrific plunges through the line, but the only metal involved was just enough interior ribbing to hold the layers of felt padding in place.
>
> "I had those pads made at Jim's suggestion. They were constructed of hard sole leather, riveted together, and their legality was never questioned while Thorpe played for me. The Indian and I planned to put them on the market and advertise them as 'The Jim Thorpe Shoulder Pad,' but the manufacturer we approached feared they might be classed as illegal, and we abandoned the project.
>
> "Another story current in those days was that Thorpe bet $2,200 on one of our games with Massillon. This was pure fiction, because to my certain knowledge Jim never carried more than $200 during an entire season. At his own request, I kept all of his earnings until the end of the season and then gave him a check for the full amount, which he banked when he went back to Oklahoma. There was not one iota of truth, either, in that preposterous story that Thorpe made a standing offer to pay $1,000 to any team that could keep him from gaining 10 yards in four downs. He simply wasn't the type to do a foolish thing like that."

Jim and his friend Walt Lingo hit on an idea: they would buy an NFL (the league name had already changed) franchise (heck, they only cost $100) and field an all-Indian team to promote Lingo's Oorang Airedales. He coached and played on the Oorang Indians for two years: 1922 and 1923. More about this team can be found in the chapter on all-Indian teams. Thorpe played for a few other NFL teams until he retired in 1928 when he was at least 40 years old.

Shortly before his tragic death in 1931, Knute Rockne, in his "Rockne Recalls" syndicated newspaper column, recalled,

> "In review of my playing career, one hard day stands out above all others – the day I tried to stop the greatest football player of all, the Indian Jim Thorpe.
>
> "My job was to tackle Thorpe, which I did. successfully and with much suffering, three times. After the third time Thorpe smiled genially at me.
>
> "'Be good boy,' he said. 'Let Jim run.'
>
> "He took the ball again and I went at him. Never before have I received such a shock. It was as if a locomotive had hit me and been followed by a ten-ton truck rambling ever the remains. I lay on the field of battle while Thorpe pounded out a forty-yard run for a touchdown.

"He came back, helped me to my feet, patted me fraternally on the back and, smiling broadly, said:

"'That's a good boy, Knute. You let Jim run.'"

That story was borrowed by a number of after-dinner speakers who replaced Rockne with themselves. They apparently considered it an honor to be run over by Jim Thorpe.

In a 1932 interview by *The Saturday Evening Post*, Red Grange reminisced: "I played against Thorpe only once – in a pro game in Florida in 1926. By then, Jim was old, fat and slow, yet he could still hit hard. He smacked me once and I still remember it!"

When Myron Cope interviewed Joe Guyon, he responded, "You've asked me, is it true that Jim Thorpe drank too much? Well, he participated pretty much after he got back from the Olympic games and everybody wanted to entertain him. But I can't tell you a lot about Jim's drinking because we didn't enjoy the same things. I never touched the stuff. Nightclubs didn't appeal to me. But I'll say this – if it was a big game coming up, Jim knew he had to take care of himself. Pop Warner put the theory of conditioning into him, and he knew the importance of it. But if it wasn't a big game coming up, then, yes, he'd go out and fill up."

After his playing career was over, he worked at a variety of jobs that included movie work, lecturing and physical labor. He even served in the Merchant Marines in WWII. He had children, divorces and remarriages but managed to weather them all. In 1949, Warner Brothers decided to produce his biopic, "Jim Thorpe – All-American." Although he no longer owned the rights to his life story, having sold them some time earlier, he was hired as a technical advisor for the film. The film, starring Burt Lancaster, was released in August 1951 and had two premieres: one in Oklahoma City, the other in Carlisle.

On March 28, 1953, Jim, then about 65, suffered his third heart attack, a massive one, and died in Lomita, California where he was living at the time. The good-hearted, easy-going Indian was gone but not forgotten.

For decades people attempted unsuccessfully to have his Olympic medals restored. Many blamed Avery Brundage, then head of the American Olympic Committee, who had finished well behind Thorpe in both the pentathlon and decathlon at Stockholm. In 1982, largely through the efforts of Florence Ridlon and her husband, Thorpe biographer Robert W. Wheeler, the International Olympic Committee reinstated Thorpe's medals and records.

Warner home (on right just inside gate)

Superintendent Pratt's office

Captains

In the earliest days of American football, team captains were more akin to modern day head coaches than to current-day captains. Even after head coaches, often called trainers at that time, were introduced to the game, captains still played major roles in running the teams. Many functions associated with modern football coaches were the responsibility of captains around the turn of the last century. Captains played a major role both in running a team and conditioning the players and in field management. Lists of team captains' names were published nationally after elections were held and ownership of a team, in a literary sense, was often attributed to the captain. For example, in the 1880s Harvard played Captain Camp's team [Yale]. Team members played both offense and defense; most stayed on the field the entire game unless they were too seriously injured to continue. Coaches were not allowed to send in plays, not even via substitute players. Instead, a designated player, often the quarterback, called the plays. Pop Warner was sometimes accused of breaking this rule.

Players generally elected their captains, typically at the end of one season for the next. Captains were selected at this time because the outgoing captain was often a graduating senior, and it made more sense to have the same man captaining the team in both the fall and spring practice. Most often it was a single person. Co-captains were not the norm, nor were captains elected for different platoons. The multiple-captain concept came much later.

Captains were not just good players; they were team leaders. Some of the best players, such as Joe Guyon and Frank Mount Pleasant, for instance, were never elected captain. Generally a captain served for just a year, but in the early days of the Carlisle program Bemus Pierce served for three years running. The only others to repeat after that were Martin Wheelock in 1899 and 1901 and Pete Calac, who completed an unfinished term in 1914 before being elected for a full season of his own.

Captains of Carlisle Indian School Football Team

1894 Benjamin Caswell	1895 Bemus Pierce	1896 Bemus Pierce
1897 Bemus Pierce	1898 Frank Hudson	1899 Martin Wheelock
1900 Edward Rogers	1901 Martin Wheelock	1902 Charles Williams
1903 James Johnson	1904 Arthur Sheldon	1905 Nicholas Bowen
1906 Albert Exendine	1907 Antonio Lubo	1908 Emil Hauser
1909 Joseph Libby	1910 Peter Hauser	1911 Sampson Bird
1912 James Thorpe	1913 Gustavus Welch	1914 Elmer Busch
1915 Peter Calac†	1916 George May	1917 George Tibbetts
1918 John B. Flinchum		

†Also served as Captain last half of 1914 season.

Captain Leadership

In 1924 J. P. Glass and George Byrnes interviewed Pop Warner for a syndicated column that was distributed nationally by the North American Newspaper Alliance (NANA). In this interview, Warner told of the heroic efforts in 1902 of several past, present and future Carlisle captains: Martin Wheelock, Antonio Lubo, Charles Williams, James Johnson and Albert Exendine, in a big game with Warner's alma mater. This is the story in Warner's own words:

"Two men who were dallying with death and should have been in hospital; a third who would have looked well in an invalid's chair; two pieces of leather, which, joined together, closely resembled a puttee; and, finally, a brace of aluminum plate that resembled nothing so much as the rubbing portion of a washboard — these were the chief factors in making possible a strategy that decided one of the most sensational football battles I ever saw.

"It was way back in 1902, during my first term of coaching the famous Carlisle Indian team. In those days our annual game with Cornell was one of the biggest events of the season, notwithstanding that during the course of the hectic schedule which the Indians always played we were apt to engage almost every important team in the country. We set a lot of store on winning from the Ithacans, but this year, as the game approached, it looked as if victory was going to be impossible. In earlier games hard luck gave us a kick that sent us reeling, and Saturday, October 18, the day set for our engagement with Cornell, didn't promise to be an occasion for jubilation.

..."To begin with, my brother Bill had been a big help. Bill was guard at Cornell and one of the best in the game. This year he was captain of the team and mighty anxious to have it make a good showing. Cornell didn't start its training season until September 15 while the Indians got into action on September 1....

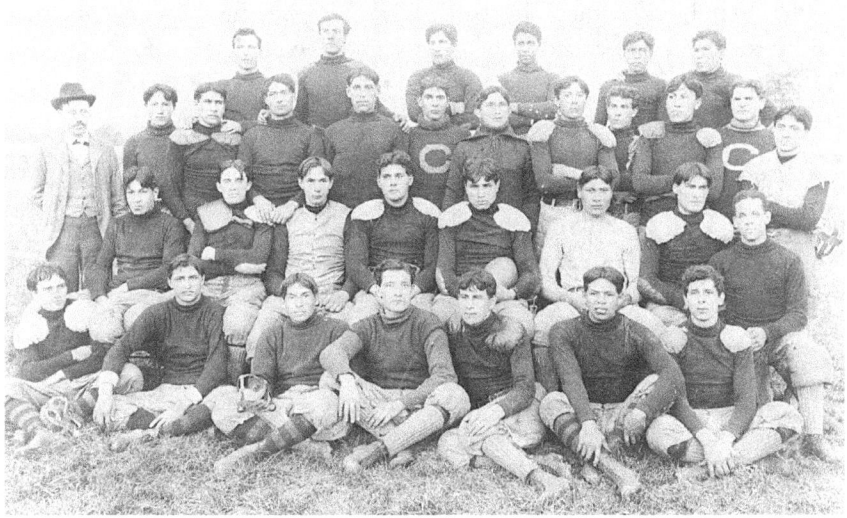
1899 team featured several captains, past, present and future; *Library of Congress*

"I could picture the rest of my brother's thoughts. He stood over six-feet-one himself and weighed 220 pounds. The Cornell center, Davitt, and the left guard, Hunt, were built in the same proportions. Nobody ever had punctured the Ithacans' lines while those lads were holding forth, but they had done a lot of damage to the other fellows' defense.

"So I knew Bill was going back to Cornell to tell his comrades just what he was thinking then: namely, that the Ithacans must keep possession of the ball when they met us a month later and batter our line to pieces. And I had a hunch that the formation he would have in mind for accomplishing this purpose would be their famous guards-back play. In that, you know, one guard got back of the other to carry the ball, with the whole backfield in tandem formation helping them to plow through the enemy's line....

"Just then everything went wrong. First, after the initial game of the season, Wheelock, our star left tackle, probably the best man in the position that year and the leading drop and place kicker who did all our booting, was taken sick and sent to the school infirmary. He was thought to have pneumonia, but that was averted and then he had a recurrence of pleurisy from which he had suffered the previous year. His pain was so great that he couldn't bear even to have the bedclothes touch him, and the hospital attendants had to rig up a special apparatus that suspended his sheet above him an inch away that they protected him without coming in contact with his body.

"Second, Exendine, our great right end, wrenched his ankle so badly in a succeeding game he could scarcely run.

"Third, Schouchuk, who played at center and was as good as there was in the country, was so badly hurt the week before the Cornell game he had to be placed in the hospital.

"There I was, with the big battle less than a week away, with a line that my brother Bill had called only "pretty good" completely shot to pieces. What could I do? Exendine partly solved my troubles. He insisted he would play despite his bad ankle. It was out of the question for him to take his end assignment. We bound his crippled limb with tape so tightly that he couldn't move his foot and shifted him to right tackle, sending Whitely, who played the position regularly, to fill the left tackle place vacated by Wheelock's illness.

"But I still had no center and no right end. I could throw in a center that might fill Schouchuk's shoes acceptably, but I could not replace Wheelock, whose kicking would be sadly missed. He was my best offensive weapon, having made at least one field goal in every game he played.

"It was at this time that I was given two demonstrations of the red man's courage which fully upheld all the legends of their stoical indifference to suffering ever told. In 1901, when he played the Navy at Annapolis, Lubo, our left tackle, a thin, wiry fellow, who made up in bravery and football brains what he lacked in size—he only weighed 160 pounds — had his left wrist smashed and cut open. The injury was slow to heal. We didn't tell him at the time, but the school physician thought he had a tubercular infection. The superintendent of the academy positively refused to let him play any more football. His arm was placed in a sling and he was instructed to indulge in no exercise except walking, and even then he must conserve his strength.

"Lubo couldn't play, but there was nothing to prevent his watching his team-mates during practice. Throughout my brother Bill's sojourn, he trudged up and down the field, observing everything that was done, listening to everything that was said. He was a true Indian, talking little but retaining every scrap of information that came his way, although in this case it could be of no value to him.

"He was really a pathetic figure. In form, he would have been a tower of strength for us, for despite his size he could hold his own against the huskiest of opponents. But he had been carrying his arm in the sling for a year now and it was shriveled away almost to mere bone.

"All the time, though, he was hoping against hope that luck would turn his way. At the start of the season, he applied for permission to play, but the superintendent's only reply was an order to me.

"'Don't even give him a uniform,' he said. "His health means more to the school than winning a couple of football games."

"Nevertheless he continued his appeals. And when the injury to Schouchuk capped the climax of our troubles he decided to make one more try.

"Four nights preceding the Cornell game a knock brought me to my door. There stood Lubo.

"'Coach,' he said without any preliminary, 'I'd give anything if I could play against Cornell. I know how Schouchuk and Wheelock can't play. I'd like to go up there for you and for Carlisle.'

"I brought him inside and explained as gently as I could that it wasn't possible.

"'Not with that arm,' I said.

"'But that wouldn't make any difference,' he protested.

"'I've been exercising and have kept in good shape in every other way. Besides, coach, I think I can do as much with my right arm as with two arms. I can protect my left so it won't get hurt.'

"I asked where he thought he could play.

"'Tackle, in Wheelock's place.'

"'No. that's out of the question. A tackle must have both arms.'

"'Well, then, center.'

"'No, a center must use both hands to pass the ball.'

"'Well,' he declared. 'I know I could play somewhere on the team.'

"I had to tell him it was impossible, although I appreciated his spirit. But when he left, after two hours of argument, he insisted. 'Somehow, I'm going to play.'

"As to when he saw the superintendent I don't know, for it was half past ten o'clock when he left my house. But the next morning the chief telephoned me to come to his office. Lubo had been to see him again, he said, and had asked to be allowed to face Cornell.

"'I told him, no,' he added, 'but the boy said he must play - he owed it to Carlisle. He's so fine I'm inclined to be lenient, if you and the doctor think it is possible.'

"I didn't because I believed Lubo would be performing merely on his ambition. But when the physician told me that, except for his left arm, the Indian was in fine condition, I began to change my mind. We could at least let him practice a bit. I told him so the next day, which was the Wednesday preceding the date at Ithaca on Saturday.

"He was on hand promptly. It didn't take him long to convince me that, handicapped though he was, he was better than any substitute I could use. If only he hadn't had that withered arm.

"That night he came around to see me again.

"'Coach,' he said, 'there must be some way to fix my arm.'

"I thought hard. I've always been handy at repairing injured players and finally hit on a scheme. I dug up two strips of leather. These I sewed around his bad wrist, extending from the tips of his finger to his elbow. We stuffed the inside with cotton and bound the whole in tape. It seemed to offer adequate protection.

"'Lubo, it looks like you were going to get into that game,' I said.
He just stood there smiling and saying over and over, 'Thank you, Coach, thank you.'

"I don't mind telling you I felt pretty weepy.

"Of course Lubo couldn't play end or tackle. I decided to switch Beaver, the right guard, who had done some playing at end, to Exendine's old position and use Lubo in his place.

"News of this decision soon got me into trouble. All the cripples around the place asked for harness that would enable them to play. But the biggest shock I got came when [Martin] Wheelock showed up at my house. He had been in the infirmary three weeks but in the last few days had been allowed out in the air a bit. Still he was in such pain he couldn't bear to have any one lay a hand on him.

"'Now look here, Coach,' he said, 'if you can fix Lubo you can fix me. There's nothing wrong with my arms or legs; all I've got is pleurisy.'

"I didn't argue with him. Arguments didn't seem to count much with those Indians. We went up to the engineering school and asked for help. Someone dug up two wide sheets of aluminum, resembling, as I said before, the metal portion of a washboard.

"'That's the stuff!' said Wheelock. 'First I'll put on a heavy shirt. Then you can fix these on me, one in front and one in back. Bind them with tape, so they won't slip. Put my jersey on over all and I'll be absolutely all right.'

"There was left but one vacancy on the team. That was center. Fortunately this would be the one position where Wheelock would suffer a minimum of pain, although he was bound to have plenty of it no matter where he was placed. I assigned him to it.

[Warner then discussed some strategy and the events of the game's first half that put Cornell ahead, 6-5.]

"The second half got under way with Cornell rushing us off our feet. And yet, just when it seemed that she was about to score, an Indian would appear from nowhere and throw the man carrying the ball for a loss on third down. Mostly it was Lubo and Wheelock. How Lubo did it with his lame arm I don t know. And time after time Wheelock winced in pain as he came in contact with his opponents. But always they are on the job diving over or under interference and bringing down the man with the ball. Williams backed up both. Johnson was wonderful in running back punts. The lame Exendine, at tackle, more than held his own. Well into the second half we got a break which repaid our cripples for their devotion to the team. Williams, standing on Carlisle's 30-yard line, delivered the best punt of the day. It was a wonderful kick that carried the ball a full 50 yards before it touched on Cornell's 30-yard line.

"Brewster, the Cornell quarter [back], apparently figured that the ball would roll clear to the line. He decided to let it pass, so that it could he brought out again on the 20-yard line. But after one high bound, the ball took a backward instead of forward leap, and struck the leg of Tydeman, right end, who had run back to give Brewster interference. This made a free ball of it and Bradley, Carlisle right end, who had charged down the field, grabbed it.

"It was Carlisle's ball on Cornell's 13-yard line, and Quarterback Johnson immediately proceeded to the most brilliant strategy of the game. This consisted in using the same formation, with variations, four times in succession.

[Warner described an early incarnation of his single-wingback formation which was designed to protect his crippled players. Johnson's brilliant strategy used fakes, deception and speed to confuse the defense as to where the ball was going and who was carrying it. On the fourth play of the series, Willliams dove over the middle of the line for the go ahead touchdown.]

"Lubo was able to continue after this play, but Wheelock's outraged body could endure no more. He fell in an agony of pain and had to be taken from the field. This necessitated the only substitution of the game. We missed the goal after touchdown and the score was Carlisle 10; Cornell, 6.

"But the game was won. Williams played center on defense and we held the Ithacans until the whistle blew.

"Was Lubo happy? Was he! And that reminds me. After the game that night I talked again with Bill, my brother.

"'How did Lubo impress you, Bill?' I asked.

"'Say, Glenn, was that fellow in uniform when I was down at Carlisle?'

"'No, he's the one who followed you around with his arm in a sling watching you at practice.'

"'Well, if that fellow can play like that when he's crippled,' replied Bill, 'I'd hate to tackle him when he was in good condition.'

"In view of the fact that Bill was placed on the All-American that year by Walter Camp and all the other critics, his performance in the Carlisle game being praised particularly, I consider he paid Lubo a fine tribute. But the boy deserved everything good that could be said about him.

"And Wheelock, too. The strategy by which Johnson won the game was fine; but never so wonderful as the splendid feat of these two boys in playing that day. When you get down to facts, it was their devotion to their school and their team that beat Cornell. There's a lesson in it for every lad that aspires to play the game."

Fact or Fiction

A review of the record shows that Warner's memory of a set of extraordinary events that took place over two decades earlier appears to have been fairly accurate, although he incorrectly remembered the winning touchdown as being made in the second half. *The Redman and Helper* announced Lubo's return from a summer vacation at home in California on September 19 and stated that he wouldn't be playing football. The reason was not given. Carlisle played Cornell on Saturday, October 18, 1902 at Ithaca, New York and won 10-6. Game accounts list Exendine, Lubo and Wheelock in the lineup at tackle, guard and center, respectively. Steckbeck, probably unaware of the situation, noted that this was Wheelock's first game at center. The *Syracuse Post-Standard* had the Indians at full strength and Cornell crippled. Two days later that paper described Cornell's claims of being crippled as a "lame excuse." The game account discussed Bradley's recovery of the punt that hit Tydeman's leg. On the Wednesday preceding the Cornell game, Carlisle played Bloomsburg Normal (today's Bloomsburg University) at Carlisle. Warner would very likely have viewed the mid-week 50-0 thrashing of a normal school as little more than a scrimmage. Newspaper reports of the game indicate that both Lubo and Wheelock played some of that game. It is probable that Warner tested the protective gear for Lubo and Wheelock in this fortuitously timed scrimmage. He wouldn't have needed his star players to beat a weak opponent, but they provided an opportunity to test and improve the gear if necessary.

A diagram of the special formation Warner used to protect Lubo and Wheelock and which James Johnson used brilliantly to score the winning touchdown accompanied the article. This may have been the earliest use of a wingback in football, but the development of the single-wing is a story for another time and place.

Appendices

Carlisle Indians Inducted into the College Football Hall of Fame

Player*	Position	Year Inducted
Albert Exendine	End	1970
Joe Guyon	Halfback/Tackle	1971
James Johnson	Quarterback	1969
Ed Rogers	End	1968
Jim Thorpe	Halfback	1951†
Gus Welch	Quarterback	1975
Glenn S. "Pop" Warner	Coach	1951†

Carlisle Indians Inducted into the Professional Football Hall of Fame

Player	Position	Year Inducted
Joe Guyon	Halfback	1966
Jim Thorpe	Halfback	1963†

Citizens Savings (originally Helms) Athletic Foundation

Player	Position	Year Inducted
Lone Star Dietz	Coach	1976
Jim Thorpe	Halfback	1950
Glenn S. "Pop" Warner	Coach	1951

*Lone Star Dietz on 2010 ballot as coach.
†Charter member.

Selected Bibliography

Carlisle Indian Industrial School publications

The Indian Helper, weekly newspaper, 1885-1900.
The Red Man, weekly magazine, 1888-1900.
The Red Man and Helper, weekly combined newspaper and magazine, 1900-1904.
The Arrow, weekly newspaper, 1904-1908.
The Carlisle Arrow, weekly newspaper, 1908-1917.
The Indian Craftsman, monthly literary journal, 1909-1910.
The Red Man, monthly literary journal, 1910-1917.
The Carlisle Arrow and Red Man, monthly combined newspaper and magazine, 1917-1918.

Other School Publications

Alumni Record. Dickinson College, Carlisle, Pa.
Anadarko Yearbook. Anadarko High School, Anadarko, Ok.
Aucola. American University, Washington, D. C.
The Badger. University of Wisconsin, Madison, Wi.
Bizarre. Lebanon Valley College, Annville, Pa.
The Calendar. Hutchinson Central High School, Buffalo, NY.
Catalog. Dickinson College, Carlisle, Pa.
College News. Lebanon Valley College, Annville, Pa.
The Dickinsonian. Dickinson College, Carlisle, Pa.
The Evergreen. Washington State University, Pullman, Wa.
The Franklin and Marshall Weekly. Franklin and Marshall College, Lancaster, Pa.
Georgetown College Journal. Georgetown University, Washington, D. C.
The Hatchet. Washington University, St. Louis, Mo.
HailToPurple.com. Northwestern University, Evanston, Il.
The Hoya. Georgetown University, Washington, D. C.
The Indiana Daily Student. Indiana University, Bloomington, In.
Instano. Indiana University of Pennsylvania.
The Microcosm. Dickinson College, Carlisle, Pa.
Murmurmonte. West Virginia Wesleyan College, Buckhannon, WV.
O. A. C. Barometer. Oregon Agricultural College, Corvallis, Or.
Oriflamme. Franklin and Marshall College, Lancaster, Pa.
The Pharos. West Virginia Wesleyan College, Buckhannon, WV.
The Pow Wow. Washington State University, Pullman, Wa.
The Quittapahilla. Lebanon Valley College, Annville, Pa.
The Rotunda. Southern Methodist University, Dallas, Tx.
The Sophist. Indiana University of Pennsylvania, Indiana, Pa.
The Tiger. Clemson University, Clemson, SC.
Taps. Clemson University, Clemson, SC.
Ye Doomesday Booke. Georgetown University, Washington, D. C.

Books

Alft, E. C. *Elgin: an American history*. Elgin, Il.: Crossword Communications, 1984.

Boren, Lyle H., and Boren, Dale. *Who Is Who In Oklahoma (a biographical history of men and women in Oklahoma life today.)* Guthrie: The Co-Operative Publishing Company, 1935.

Braunwart, Bob, and Carroll, Bob. *The Journey to Camp: the origins of American football*. Huntingdon, Pa.: P. F. R. A., 1997.

Bynum, Mike, ed. *Pop Warner Football's Greatest Teacher: the epic autobiography of major college football's winningest coach, Glenn S. (Pop) Warner*. Football Gridiron Properties Corp., 1993.

Carroll, Bob. *The Tigers Roar: professional football in Ohio: 1903-1909*. Huntingdon, Pa.: P. F. R. A., 1990.

Carroll, Bob, and Braunwart, Bob. *Pro Football: From AAA to '03: the origin and development of professional football in Western Pennsylvania, 1890-1903*. Huntingdon, Pa.: P. F. R. A., 1991.

Carroll, Bob, and Gill, Bob. *Bulldogs on Sunday 1919: twilight of the Ohio League*. Huntingdon, Pa.: P. F. R. A., 1991.

Carroll, Bob, and PFRA Research. *The Ohio League: 1910-1919*. Huntingdon, Pa.: P. F. R. A., 1997.

Cope, Myron. *The Game That Was: the early days of pro football*. Cleveland: The World Publishing Company, 1970.

Crawford, Bill. *All American: the rise and fall of Jim Thorpe*. Hoboken: John Wiley & Sons, Inc., 2005.

Curran, Bob. *Pro Football's Rag Days*. New York: Bonanza Books, 1964.

Danzig, Allison. *Oh, How They Played the Game: the early days of football and the heroes who made it great*. New York: The Macmillan Company, 1971.

Finoli, David, and Aikens, Tom. *The Birthplace of Professional Football: Southwestern Pennsylvania*. Charleston, SC: Arcadia Publishing, 2004.

Fry, Richard B. *The Crimson and the Gray: 100 years with the WSU Cougars*. Pullman: Washington State University Press, 1989.

Gridley, Marion E. *Indians of Today*. Crawfordsville, In.: Lakeside Press, 1936.

Gridley, Marion E. *Indians of Today*. Chicago: Millar Publishing Company, 1947.

Gridley, Marion E. *Indians of Today*. 3rd ed. Chicago: Towertown Press, 1960.

Groshans, Lorraine. *The Complete Borzoi*. New York: Howell Book House, 1981.

Hart, Charles. *Memories of a Forty-Niner (1896-1945)*. Philadelphia: Dunlap Printing Company, 1946.

Heimel, Paul W. *Eliot Ness: the real story*. Nashville: Cumberland House, 2000.

King, C. Richard, ed. *Native Americans in Sports*. Armonk, NY: Sharpe Reference, 2004.

Lester, Robin. *Stagg's University: the rise, decline, and fall of big-time football at Chicago*. Urbana and Chicago: University of Illinois Press, 1995.

Marsh, Scott; Hope Stout, and Debbie Moore, comps. *Here's to the High School on the Hill: a scrapbook of 105 years of Mechanicsburg Indian football*. Mechanicsburg, Oh., 2004.

McCallum, John D., and Pearson, Charles H. *College Football U. S. A. 1869-1971: official book of the National Football Foundation*. Greenwich, Conn.: Hall of Fame Publishing, Inc., 1971.

McClellan, Keith. *The Sunday Game: at the dawn of professional football*. Akron: The University of Akron Press, 1998.

McDaniel, Mike. *Stand Up and Cheer: the official history of du Pont Manual High School, Louisville, Kentucky*. Louisville: Butler Books, 2005.

Newcomb, Jack. *The Best of the Athletic Boys: the white man's impact on Jim Thorpe*. Garden City: Doubleday & Company, 1975.

O'Conner, Candace. *Beginning a Great Work: Washington University in St. Louis*. St. Louis: Washington University in St. Louis, 2003.

Ohio, State of. *The Official Roster of Ohio Soldiers, Sailors and Marines in the World War 1917-1918*. Columbus: The F. J. Herr Printing Co., 1926.

Oriard, Michael. *King Football: sport & spectacle in the golden age of radio & newsreels, movies & magazines, the weekly & the daily press*. Chapel Hill, The University of North Carolina Press, 2001.

Pratt, Richard H. *Battlefield and Classroom: four decades with the American Indian, 1867-1904*. New Haven and London: Yale University Press, 1964.

Ratliff, Harold V. *The Power and the Glory: the story of Southwest Conference football*. Lubbock: Texas Tech Press, 1957.

Roster of the men and women who served in the army or naval service (including the Marine Corps) of the United States or its allies from the state of North Dakota in the World war, 1917-1918. Bismarck: The Bismarck Tribune Company, 1931.

Samuelsen, Rube. *The Rose Bowl Game*. Garden City: Doubleday & Company, 1951.

Smith, Ronald A. *Sports & Freedom: the rise of big-time college athletics*. New York: Oxford Press, 1988.

Steckbeck, John S. *Fabulous Redmen: the Carlisle Indians and their famous football teams*. Harrisburg, Pa.: J. Horace McFarland Company, 1951.

Thisted, Moses N. *Pershing's Pioneer Infantry of World War I*. Hemet, Ca.: Alphabet Printers, 1982.

U. S. Army, Special Staff. *Order of Battle of the United States Land Forces in the World War (1917-19): Zone of the Interior*. Washington: U. S. Government Printing Office, 1931.

Warner, Glenn Scobey. *A Course in Football for Players and Coaches*. Carlisle, Pa.: Warner, 1912.

Warner, Glenn Scobey. *Football for Coaches and Players*. Stanford University: Warner, 1927.

Weyand, Alexander M. *The Saga of American Football*. New York: The Macmillan Company, 1955.

Wheeler, Robert W. *Jim Thorpe: world's greatest athlete*. Norman: University of Oklahoma Press, 1975.

Whitman, Robert L. *Jim Thorpe and the Oorang Indians: N. F. L.'s most colorful franchise*. Defiance, Oh.: The Marion County Historical Society, 1984.

Whittingham, Richard. *Sunday Mayhem: a celebration of pro football in America*. Dallas: Taylor Publishing Company, 1987.

Williams, E. I. F. *Heidelberg, democratic Christian college 1850-1950*. Menasha, Wi.: The George Banta Publishing Company, 1952.

Williams, Eustace. *That Old Rivalry: Manual vs. High School 1893-1940*. Louisville: John P. Morton & Co., 1940.

Winchester, Shirley Phillips, Jones, Saundra Phillips, and Hall, Helen Phillips. *The Heritage of Caldwell County North Carolina Volume I*. Winston-Salem: Hunter Publishing Company, 1983.

Witmer, Linda F. *The Indian Industrial School: Carlisle, Pennsylvania 1879-1918*. Carlisle, Pa.: Cumberland County Historical Society, 1993.

Periodicals

Baine, William. "Key to Shorthand Notes," *The Stenographer*, 8 no. 7 (1898: 186).

Becker, Carl M. "Jim Thorpe and the Oorang Tribe," *Timeline*, 20, no. 5 (2003): 2-17.

Braunwart, Bob; Bob Carrol and Joe Harrigan. "Going to the Dogs," *The Coffin Corner*, 3 (1981).

Grange, Red. "The College Game is Easier," *The Coffin Corner*, 25 no. 6 (2003): 3-8.

Kish, Bernie. "Sideline Chatter," *Journal of the College Football Historical Society*, 21 no. 2 (2008).

Phelon, William A. "On the Home Stretch of the Great 1912 Pennant Races," *Baseball Magazine*, 9 no. 6 (1912): 15-24.

Prescott, Archie. "Time Tunnel," *College Football Historical Society Newsletter*, 3 no. 3 (1990): 11-12.

Plummer, Maggie. "Long Time Sleep: the stuff legends are made of," *Char-Koosta News*, October 25, 2007.

Santorum, Rick. Senate resolution 91, *Congressional Record – Senate,* S4607, 1999.

Scott, Hugh. "The Oklahoma Athletic Hall of Fame," *Oklahoma Today*, 22 no. 2 (1972): 13-17.

Shoemaker, Arthur. "Hominy Indians," *Oklahoma Today*, 17 no. 4 (1967): 7-9.

Tanner, Virginia ed. "B&O's Indian Engineers," *B&O Magazine*, 38 no. 10 (1952): 1-3, 46.

Wells, Fred. "Foot Ball Season Brings Memories of Mt. Pleasant," *The Arrow*, 3 no. 11 (1920): 12.

Ephemera

Minnesota, University of. *Souvenir Program, Minnesota vs. Wisconsin*, November 15, 1902.

Minnesota, University of. *Souvenir Program, Dedication of Northrop Field*, September 19, 1903.

Minnesota, University of. *Souvenir Program, Michigan vs. Minnesota*, October 31, 1903.

Southern Methodist University. *Texas Aggies -6 vs. S. M. U. -17 Official Program*, November 11, 1922.

Index

Alabama, University of, 20, 67
Albright College, 22, 24, 115
Arcasa, Alex, 16, 35
Armstrong, Samuel Chapman, 5, 58
Bailey, Mary, 10
Balenti, Mike, 33, 53, 57, 59-67, 96, 98, 101, 103, 112, 113, 129, 144
Baronovitch, Cecilia, 63-65
Beaver, Frank, 177
Bergie, Joseph, 35
Bill, Blanche, 122, 124
Bird, Sampson, 174
Bloomsburg Normal, 180
Blumenthal, Mose, 12
Boutwell, Leon A., 44
Bowen, Nicholas, 174
Broker, Joseph Henry, 44
Brown University, 9
Buffalo Soldiers, 5
Buffalo, University of, 21
Busch, Elmer, 174
Calac, Pete (Pedro), 4, 19, 36, 40, 42, 45, 167, 169, 173
California, University of, 11
Camp, Walter, 8, 10, 12, 15, 16, 27, 28, 49, 50, 52, 62, 63, 88, 98-100, 130, 139, 151, 154, 160-162, 179
Carleton College, 78
Carlisle Barracks, 5, 17, 25, 51
Caswell, Benjamin, 174
Cayou, Francis M., 4, 9, 19, 21, 33, 69-82, 151, 153
Cayuga, 104-107, 110
Charles, Wilson, 19
Cherokee, 83, 114, 142
Cheyenne, 5, 54, 57-59, 61, 95, 103, 143, 155
Cheyenne Belle, 57-59
Chicago, University of, 21, 27
Chippewa, 51
Choctaw, 22, 93, 111
Cincinnati, University of, 10, 13, 14, 35, 60, 65, 72, 89, 90, 162, 168
Columbia University, 71, 90
Conway Hall, 22, 23, 33, 86, 88

Cornell University, 10, 12, 19, 48, 49, 52, 55, 86, 154, 174, 175-180
Crawford, Bill, 144, 145, 157
Cusack, Jack, 34-36, 40, 165, 166, 167, 169
DeCora, Angel, 18, 19, 114, 133
Delaware, 6, 83
DeMille, William C., 71, 76, 77
Denny, Wallace, 18
DeNomie, Rose, 146
Dickinson College, 20, 22, 33, 70-73, 76, 86, 116, 120, 138, 145
Dickinson School of Law, 33, 89, 112
Dietz, William H. Lone Star, 1, 16, 19, 21, 22, 25, 40, 56, 91, 92, 116, 132, 133, 145, 146
Dillon, Charles, 12, 109
Duquesne Athletic Club, 30
Eaton, Frank Jr. (Pistol Pete), 91, 92
Eckersall, Walter, 77, 78, 81
Exendine, Albert A., 4, 21, 22, 83-92, 159, 160, 174-176, 178
Flinchum, John B., 93, 174
Francis, John, 24
Franklin and Marshall College, 24
Friedman, Moses, 17-19, 25, 55, 134, 148, 160
Gardner, William J., 98, 165, 167
Garlow, William, 19, 36, 63, 99, 116, 129, 167
George Washington University, 6
Georgetown University, 21, 30, 85, 90, 91
Georgia Tech, 24, 33, 101
Georgia, University of, 20, 49
Goddard, Ives, 50
Grange, Harold Red, 39, 40, 91, 167, 171
Great Lakes U. S. Navy Base, 29, 81
Guyon, Charles Wahoo, 19-21, 26
Hampton Institute (Hampton University), 5, 143-145
Harvard University, 8-17, 20, 22, 27, 41, 50-54, 63, 79, 87, 95, 97, 116, 139, 146, 154, 161, 173

Haskell Institute, 13, 24, 25, 33, 43-46, 85, 95, 96, 115, 139, 140-142, 144, 145, 148, 149, 155, 158
Hauser, Emil (Wauseka), 19, 95-103, 174
Hauser, Peter, 19, 45, 54, 56, 61, 87, 95-103, 138, 145
Hudson, Frank, 13-15, 21, 50, 52, 65, 95, 174
Hunt, Oscar, 104-110
Illinois Athletic Association, 81
Illinois, University of, 38, 39, 73-77
Indiana University, 35, 74-80, 134, 165, 166
Iowa Agricultural College, 49, 79
Island, Louis, 60, 61, 132, 144
Jamison, Jake, 9, 151
Johnson, James, 12, 33, 56, 174, 178-180
Jordan, Peter, 138
Kelley, Victor M., 22, 23, 63, 64, 111-118, 144, 145
Lassaw, Nicholas, 44
Lebanon Valley College, 7, 22, 23, 116, 145
Lehigh University, 19, 22, 33, 116
Libby, Archie, 60
Libby, Joseph, 100
Lipps, Oscar H., 18, 20, 23, 28, 81, 114, 115, 134
Longstreth, Susan, 6, 130, 146
Lubo, Antonio, 19, 100, 174-180
Matlock, Blanche Bill, 122, 124
Matlock, Cecilia, 63-68
Matlock, Stacy, 119-124, 146
May, George, 125, 126, 174
McClellan, Keith, 30, 35
Mercer, William A., 6, 16, 52, 86, 110
Michigan Agricultural College, 77
Michigan, University of, 39
Mission, tribe, 83
Montezuma, Carlos, 110
Moody, Dwight Lyman, 72, 121
Moran, Charlie, 65, 113, 115
Mt. Pleasant, Franklin P., 4, 15, 19, 21, 30, 33, 53, 60-63, 87, 97, 112, 161
Mt. Pleasant, Mamie, 161
Neale, Alfred Earle Greasy, 40
Newashe, Emma, 127, 130, 133
Newashe, William, 61, 99, 127-136

Northeastern State Teachers College, 91, 142
Northwestern University, 33, 76
Notre Dame, University of, 19, 20, 30, 35, 38, 43, 75, 76, 79, 166
Oberlin College, 34
Occidental College, 91
Ohio State University Medical College, 72
Oklahoma State University, 67, 91
Omaha, 69, 82
Oregon Agricultural College, 91, 101, 103
Otterbein College, 88, 89
Pacific, College of, 90, 91, 101
Pawnee, 119-124, 143-145, 148, 149
Pennsylvania, University of, 8, 11-16, 19, 24, 28, 50-52, 54, 63, 71, 73, 85-87, 99, 129, 132, 137, 138, 153, 154, 161
Pierce, Bemus, 13-15, 19, 21, 30, 52, 56, 95, 153, 173, 174
Pierce, Hawley, 31, 51, 56
Pistol Pete, 92
Pittsburgh, University of, 21, 22
Powell, Stancil, 137, 140, 142
Pratt, Richard H., 1, 5, 8, 12, 49-52, 70
Presbyterian College, 111
Princeton University, 8, 11, 12, 15, 16, 50, 52, 53, 154
Purdue University, 74-77
Pyle, C. C., 39
Ridlon, Florence, 171
Roberts, Henry, 33, 143-150
Roberts, Rush, 143
Rockne, Knute, 35, 38, 102, 170
Rogers, Edward L., 26, 33, 56
Rose Bowl, 28, 56
Rubenstein, Nancy F., 71
Sac and Fox, 47, 127, 131, 134-136, 157, 158
Schouchuk, Nikifer, 110, 144, 175, 176
Seger, John H., 57-59
Seneca, 56, 106, 107, 151, 153-155
Seneca, Isaac, 12, 31, 50, 151-156
Sheldon, Arthur, 174
Sheridan, Philip, 5
Sherman Institute, 44
Sickles, Caleb, 26
Sioux, 54, 119, 123, 124, 143

South, The University of the, 14, 65, 67, 117
Southwestern University, 65, 113, 144
Splitlog, Mathias, 104
St. Germain, Thomas, 19
Staunton, Illinois, 78, 79
Steckbeck, John S., 1, 14, 17, 72, 180
Stone, Dolly, 101
Strongheart, 69, 76, 77
Susquehanna University, 23
Taylorville, Illinois, 38, 74
Temple University, 25
Texas A & M, 22, 33, 111-114, 117, 118
Texas, University of, 22, 113
Thompson, W. G., 110
Thorpe, James Francis (Jim), 1, 2, 15, 16, 25, 28, 33, 35-37, 40, 42-45, 53-55, 63, 65, 80, 87, 89, 93, 103, 131, 135, 136, 138-140, 142, 144-146, 154, 156-172
Tulane University, 78
Tulsa, University of, 92, 121, 142
Vanderbilt University, 14, 78, 79
Villanova University, 61
Virginia, University of, 86
Wabash College, 75-79
Wardecker, Fred, 12, 18
Warner, Glenn S. Pop, 1, 2, 10-12, 14-23, 25, 28, 30, 32, 33, 47-56, 63, 79, 81, 82, 84-90, 95, 98-103, 112, 114, 132, 136, 139, 145-147, 154, 159, 160, 162-164, 167, 168, 171, 173-180
Warner, William, 55, 174-176, 179
Washington and Jefferson College, 16, 29
Washington State College, 21, 23, 28, 90, 101, 116
Washington State University, 21, 23, 28, 90, 101, 116
Washington University of St. Louis, 78
Washington, University of, 23, 116
Welch, Gustavus, 4, 16, 18-24, 30, 36, 56, 90, 114-116, 133, 162, 164, 167
West Virginia Wesleyan College, 22, 90, 116
Western Maryland College, 16, 100
Wheeler, Robert W., 145, 157, 171
Wheelock, Dennison, 10, 74
Wheelock, Hugh, 35
Wheelock, Joel, 23, 35, 146
Wheelock, Martin, 11, 50, 56, 153, 173-180
Wichita, 48, 125, 126
Williams College, 72
Williams, Charles, 141, 174, 178-179
Wisconsin, University of, 9, 71
Wyoming, University of, 146, 147
Yale University, 8, 9, 27-29, 43, 71, 72, 151, 152, 154, 173
Zuppke, Robert, 39

Keep A-goin': the life of Lone Star Dietz
by Tom Benjey
Lone Star Dietz was the most colorful coach football has known and continues to be controversial over 40 years after his death. So interesting was the man that even his critics are fascinated by him. Dietz was a Forrest-Gump-like character in that he rubbed shoulders with many famous people and brought him to several historic events. Tom Benjey's award-winning biography tells the story of a Renaissance man who was a capable artist, singer, movie actor, athlete, educator, championship dog breeder and Hall-of-Fame-worthy coach. 356 pages, hardback and softcover.

Doctors, Lawyers, Indian Chiefs
by Tom Benjey
Jim Thorpe & Pop Warner's Carlisle Indian School football immortals tackle socialites, bootleggers, students, moguls, prejudice, the government, the government, ghouls, tooth decay and rum. Follow more than 50 stars through their lives on and off the reservation. 352 pages, softcover.

A Course in Football for Players and Coaches: Offense
by Glenn S. "Pop" Warner
Reprints of the 1908 Offense pamphlet, 1909 supplement and 1910 revision from Warner's ground-breaking correspondence course on the rudiments of football. Also includes Tom Benjey's interpretation of the birth and early evolution of the single-wing offense. 80 pages, softcover.

A Course in Football for Players and Coaches
by Glenn S. "Pop" Warner
Reprint of Warner's 1912 hardbound version of his correspondence course on the rudiments of football. Includes an early incarnation of the single-wing offense. Concepts explained with the aid of photos of Carlisle Indian School stars such as Frank Mt. Pleasant and Jim Thorpe. Cover art by Lone Star Dietz. 152 pages, softcover.

Football for Coaches and Players
by Glenn S. "Pop" Warner
Reprint of Warner's 1927 classic on the rudiments of football. Includes fully evolved unbalanced-line single-wing and double-wing formations. Illustrated by Lone Star Dietz. 220 pages, softcover.

Tuxedo-Press.com

www.ingramcontent.com/pod-product-compliance
Lightning Source LLC
Chambersburg PA
CBHW052028070526
44584CB00016B/1955